ILTS
Science: Biology (239)

SECRETS

Study Guide
Your Key to Exam Success

TEST PREPARATION

Dear Future Exam Success Story:

First of all, **THANK YOU** for purchasing Mometrix study materials!

Second, congratulations! You are one of the few determined test-takers who are committed to doing whatever it takes to excel on your exam. **You have come to the right place.** We developed these study materials with one goal in mind: to deliver you the information you need in a format that's concise and easy to use.

In addition to optimizing your guide for the content of the test, we've outlined our recommended steps for breaking down the preparation process into small, attainable goals so you can make sure you stay on track.

We've also analyzed the entire test-taking process, identifying the most common pitfalls and showing how you can overcome them and be ready for any curveball the test throws you.

Standardized testing is one of the biggest obstacles on your road to success, which only increases the importance of doing well in the high-pressure, high-stakes environment of test day. Your results on this test could have a significant impact on your future, and this guide provides the information and practical advice to help you achieve your full potential on test day.

Your success is our success

We would love to hear from you! If you would like to share the story of your exam success or if you have any questions or comments in regard to our products, please contact us at **800-673-8175** or **support@mometrix.com**.

Thanks again for your business and we wish you continued success!

Sincerely,
The Mometrix Test Preparation Team

Need more help? Check out our flashcards at: http://MometrixFlashcards.com/ILTS

Copyright © 2020 by Mometrix Media LLC. All rights reserved.
Written and edited by the Mometrix Exam Secrets Test Prep Team
Printed in the United States of America

TABLE OF CONTENTS

Introduction

Thank you for purchasing this resource! You have made the choice to prepare yourself for a test that could have a huge impact on your future, and this guide is designed to help you be fully ready for test day. Obviously, it's important to have a solid understanding of the test material, but you also need to be prepared for the unique environment and stressors of the test, so that you can perform to the best of your abilities.

For this purpose, the first section that appears in this guide is the **Secret Keys**. We've devoted countless hours to meticulously researching what works and what doesn't, and we've boiled down our findings to the five most impactful steps you can take to improve your performance on the test. We start at the beginning with study planning and move through the preparation process, all the way to the testing strategies that will help you get the most out of what you know when you're finally sitting in front of the test.

We recommend that you start preparing for your test as far in advance as possible. However, if you've bought this guide as a last-minute study resource and only have a few days before your test, we recommend that you skip over the first two Secret Keys since they address a long-term study plan.

If you struggle with **test anxiety**, we strongly encourage you to check out our recommendations for how you can overcome it. Test anxiety is a formidable foe, but it can be beaten, and we want to make sure you have the tools you need to defeat it.

Copyright © Mometrix Media. You have been licensed one copy of this document for personal use only. Any other reproduction or redistribution is strictly prohibited. All rights reserved.

Secret Key #1 – Plan Big, Study Small

There's a lot riding on your performance. If you want to ace this test, you're going to need to keep your skills sharp and the material fresh in your mind. You need a plan that lets you review everything you need to know while still fitting in your schedule. We'll break this strategy down into three categories.

Information Organization

Start with the information you already have: the official test outline. From this, you can make a complete list of all the concepts you need to cover before the test. Organize these concepts into groups that can be studied together, and create a list of any related vocabulary you need to learn so you can brush up on any difficult terms. You'll want to keep this vocabulary list handy once you actually start studying since you may need to add to it along the way.

Time Management

Once you have your set of study concepts, decide how to spread them out over the time you have left before the test. Break your study plan into small, clear goals so you have a manageable task for each day and know exactly what you're doing. Then just focus on one small step at a time. When you manage your time this way, you don't need to spend hours at a time studying. Studying a small block of content for a short period each day helps you retain information better and avoid stressing over how much you have left to do. You can relax knowing that you have a plan to cover everything in time. In order for this strategy to be effective though, you have to start studying early and stick to your schedule. Avoid the exhaustion and futility that comes from last-minute cramming!

Study Environment

The environment you study in has a big impact on your learning. Studying in a coffee shop, while probably more enjoyable, is not likely to be as fruitful as studying in a quiet room. It's important to keep distractions to a minimum. You're only planning to study for a short block of time, so make the most of it. Don't pause to check your phone or get up to find a snack. It's also important to **avoid multitasking**. Research has consistently shown that multitasking will make your studying dramatically less effective. Your study area should also be comfortable and well-lit so you don't have the distraction of straining your eyes or sitting on an uncomfortable chair.

The time of day you study is also important. You want to be rested and alert. Don't wait until just before bedtime. Study when you'll be most likely to comprehend and remember. Even better, if you know what time of day your test will be, set that time aside for study. That way your brain will be used to working on that subject at that specific time and you'll have a better chance of recalling information.

Finally, it can be helpful to team up with others who are studying for the same test. Your actual studying should be done in as isolated an environment as possible, but the work of organizing the information and setting up the study plan can be divided up. In between study sessions, you can discuss with your teammates the concepts that you're all studying and quiz each other on the details. Just be sure that your teammates are as serious about the test as you are. If you find that your study time is being replaced with social time, you might need to find a new team.

Copyright © Mometrix Media. You have been licensed one copy of this document for personal use only. Any other reproduction or redistribution is strictly prohibited. All rights reserved.

Secret Key #2 – Make Your Studying Count

You're devoting a lot of time and effort to preparing for this test, so you want to be absolutely certain it will pay off. This means doing more than just reading the content and hoping you can remember it on test day. It's important to make every minute of study count. There are two main areas you can focus on to make your studying count:

Retention

It doesn't matter how much time you study if you can't remember the material. You need to make sure you are retaining the concepts. To check your retention of the information you're learning, try recalling it at later times with minimal prompting. Try carrying around flashcards and glance at one or two from time to time or ask a friend who's also studying for the test to quiz you.

To enhance your retention, look for ways to put the information into practice so that you can apply it rather than simply recalling it. If you're using the information in practical ways, it will be much easier to remember. Similarly, it helps to solidify a concept in your mind if you're not only reading it to yourself but also explaining it to someone else. Ask a friend to let you teach them about a concept you're a little shaky on (or speak aloud to an imaginary audience if necessary). As you try to summarize, define, give examples, and answer your friend's questions, you'll understand the concepts better and they will stay with you longer. Finally, step back for a big picture view and ask yourself how each piece of information fits with the whole subject. When you link the different concepts together and see them working together as a whole, it's easier to remember the individual components.

Finally, practice showing your work on any multi-step problems, even if you're just studying. Writing out each step you take to solve a problem will help solidify the process in your mind, and you'll be more likely to remember it during the test.

Modality

Modality simply refers to the means or method by which you study. Choosing a study modality that fits your own individual learning style is crucial. No two people learn best in exactly the same way, so it's important to know your strengths and use them to your advantage.

For example, if you learn best by visualization, focus on visualizing a concept in your mind and draw an image or a diagram. Try color-coding your notes, illustrating them, or creating symbols that will trigger your mind to recall a learned concept. If you learn best by hearing or discussing information, find a study partner who learns the same way or read aloud to yourself. Think about how to put the information in your own words. Imagine that you are giving a lecture on the topic and record yourself so you can listen to it later.

For any learning style, flashcards can be helpful. Organize the information so you can take advantage of spare moments to review. Underline key words or phrases. Use different colors for different categories. Mnemonic devices (such as creating a short list in which every item starts with the same letter) can also help with retention. Find what works best for you and use it to store the information in your mind most effectively and easily.

Copyright © Mometrix Media. You have been licensed one copy of this document for personal use only. Any other reproduction or redistribution is strictly prohibited. All rights reserved.

Secret Key #3 – Practice the Right Way

Your success on test day depends not only on how many hours you put into preparing, but also on whether you prepared the right way. It's good to check along the way to see if your studying is paying off. One of the most effective ways to do this is by taking practice tests to evaluate your progress. Practice tests are useful because they show exactly where you need to improve. Every time you take a practice test, pay special attention to these three groups of questions:

- The questions you got wrong
- The questions you had to guess on, even if you guessed right
- The questions you found difficult or slow to work through

This will show you exactly what your weak areas are, and where you need to devote more study time. Ask yourself why each of these questions gave you trouble. Was it because you didn't understand the material? Was it because you didn't remember the vocabulary? Do you need more repetitions on this type of question to build speed and confidence? Dig into those questions and figure out how you can strengthen your weak areas as you go back to review the material.

Additionally, many practice tests have a section explaining the answer choices. It can be tempting to read the explanation and think that you now have a good understanding of the concept. However, an explanation likely only covers part of the question's broader context. Even if the explanation makes sense, **go back and investigate** every concept related to the question until you're positive you have a thorough understanding.

As you go along, keep in mind that the practice test is just that: practice. Memorizing these questions and answers will not be very helpful on the actual test because it is unlikely to have any of the same exact questions. If you only know the right answers to the sample questions, you won't be prepared for the real thing. **Study the concepts** until you understand them fully, and then you'll be able to answer any question that shows up on the test.

It's important to wait on the practice tests until you're ready. If you take a test on your first day of study, you may be overwhelmed by the amount of material covered and how much you need to learn. Work up to it gradually.

On test day, you'll need to be prepared for answering questions, managing your time, and using the test-taking strategies you've learned. It's a lot to balance, like a mental marathon that will have a big impact on your future. Like training for a marathon, you'll need to start slowly and work your way up. When test day arrives, you'll be ready.

Start with the strategies you've read in the first two Secret Keys—plan your course and study in the way that works best for you. If you have time, consider using multiple study resources to get different approaches to the same concepts. It can be helpful to see difficult concepts from more than one angle. Then find a good source for practice tests. Many times, the test website will suggest potential study resources or provide sample tests.

Practice Test Strategy

When you're ready to start taking practice tests, follow this strategy:

Untimed and Open-Book Practice

Take the first test with no time constraints and with your notes and study guide handy. Take your time and focus on applying the strategies you've learned.

4

Copyright © Mometrix Media. You have been licensed one copy of this document for personal use only. Any other reproduction or redistribution is strictly prohibited. All rights reserved.

Timed and Open-Book Practice

Take the second practice test open-book as well, but set a timer and practice pacing yourself to finish in time.

Timed and Closed-Book Practice

Take any other practice tests as if it were test day. Set a timer and put away your study materials. Sit at a table or desk in a quiet room, imagine yourself at the testing center, and answer questions as quickly and accurately as possible.

Keep repeating timed and closed-book tests on a regular basis until you run out of practice tests or it's time for the actual test. Your mind will be ready for the schedule and stress of test day, and you'll be able to focus on recalling the material you've learned.

5

Copyright © Mometrix Media. You have been licensed one copy of this document for personal use only. Any other reproduction or redistribution is strictly prohibited. All rights reserved.

Secret Key #4 – Pace Yourself

Once you're fully prepared for the material on the test, your biggest challenge on test day will be managing your time. Just knowing that the clock is ticking can make you panic even if you have plenty of time left. Work on pacing yourself so you can build confidence against the time constraints of the exam. Pacing is a difficult skill to master, especially in a high-pressure environment, so **practice is vital**.

Set time expectations for your pace based on how much time is available. For example, if a section has 60 questions and the time limit is 30 minutes, you know you have to average 30 seconds or less per question in order to answer them all. Although 30 seconds is the hard limit, set 25 seconds per question as your goal, so you reserve extra time to spend on harder questions. When you budget extra time for the harder questions, you no longer have any reason to stress when those questions take longer to answer.

Don't let this time expectation distract you from working through the test at a calm, steady pace, but keep it in mind so you don't spend too much time on any one question. Recognize that taking extra time on one question you don't understand may keep you from answering two that you do understand later in the test. If your time limit for a question is up and you're still not sure of the answer, mark it and move on, and come back to it later if the time and the test format allow. If the testing format doesn't allow you to return to earlier questions, just make an educated guess; then put it out of your mind and move on.

On the easier questions, be careful not to rush. It may seem wise to hurry through them so you have more time for the challenging ones, but it's not worth missing one if you know the concept and just didn't take the time to read the question fully. Work efficiently but make sure you understand the question and have looked at all of the answer choices, since more than one may seem right at first.

Even if you're paying attention to the time, you may find yourself a little behind at some point. You should speed up to get back on track, but do so wisely. Don't panic; just take a few seconds less on each question until you're caught up. Don't guess without thinking, but do look through the answer choices and eliminate any you know are wrong. If you can get down to two choices, it is often worthwhile to guess from those. Once you've chosen an answer, move on and don't dwell on any that you skipped or had to hurry through. If a question was taking too long, chances are it was one of the harder ones, so you weren't as likely to get it right anyway.

On the other hand, if you find yourself getting ahead of schedule, it may be beneficial to slow down a little. The more quickly you work, the more likely you are to make a careless mistake that will affect your score. You've budgeted time for each question, so don't be afraid to spend that time. Practice an efficient but careful pace to get the most out of the time you have.

6

Copyright © Mometrix Media. You have been licensed one copy of this document for personal use only. Any other reproduction or redistribution is strictly prohibited. All rights reserved.

Secret Key #5 – Have a Plan for Guessing

When you're taking the test, you may find yourself stuck on a question. Some of the answer choices seem better than others, but you don't see the one answer choice that is obviously correct. What do you do?

The scenario described above is very common, yet most test takers have not effectively prepared for it. Developing and practicing a plan for guessing may be one of the single most effective uses of your time as you get ready for the exam.

In developing your plan for guessing, there are three questions to address:

- When should you start the guessing process?
- How should you narrow down the choices?
- Which answer should you choose?

When to Start the Guessing Process

Unless your plan for guessing is to select C every time (which, despite its merits, is not what we recommend), you need to leave yourself enough time to apply your answer elimination strategies. Since you have a limited amount of time for each question, that means that if you're going to give yourself the best shot at guessing correctly, you have to decide quickly whether or not you will guess.

Of course, the best-case scenario is that you don't have to guess at all, so first, see if you can answer the question based on your knowledge of the subject and basic reasoning skills. Focus on the key words in the question and try to jog your memory of related topics. Give yourself a chance to bring the knowledge to mind, but once you realize that you don't have (or you can't access) the knowledge you need to answer the question, it's time to start the guessing process.

It's almost always better to start the guessing process too early than too late. It only takes a few seconds to remember something and answer the question from knowledge. Carefully eliminating wrong answer choices takes longer. Plus, going through the process of eliminating answer choices can actually help jog your memory.

Summary: Start the guessing process as soon as you decide that you can't answer the question based on your knowledge.

Copyright © Mometrix Media. You have been licensed one copy of this document for personal use only. Any other reproduction or redistribution is strictly prohibited. All rights reserved.

How to Narrow Down the Choices

The next chapter in this book (**Test-Taking Strategies**) includes a wide range of strategies for how to approach questions and how to look for answer choices to eliminate. You will definitely want to read those carefully, practice them, and figure out which ones work best for you. Here though, we're going to address a mindset rather than a particular strategy.

Your chances of guessing an answer correctly depend on how many options you are choosing from.

How many choices you have	How likely you are to guess correctly
5	20%
4	25%
3	33%
2	50%
1	100%

You can see from this chart just how valuable it is to be able to eliminate incorrect answers and make an educated guess, but there are two things that many test takers do that cause them to miss out on the benefits of guessing:

- Accidentally eliminating the correct answer
- Selecting an answer based on an impression

We'll look at the first one here, and the second one in the next section.

To avoid accidentally eliminating the correct answer, we recommend a thought exercise called **the $5 challenge**. In this challenge, you only eliminate an answer choice from contention if you are willing to bet $5 on it being wrong. Why $5? Five dollars is a small but not insignificant amount of money. It's an amount you could afford to lose but wouldn't want to throw away. And while losing $5 once might not hurt too much, doing it twenty times will set you back $100. In the same way, each small decision you make—eliminating a choice here, guessing on a question there—won't by itself impact your score very much, but when you put them all together, they can make a big difference. By holding each answer choice elimination decision to a higher standard, you can reduce the risk of accidentally eliminating the correct answer.

The $5 challenge can also be applied in a positive sense: If you are willing to bet $5 that an answer choice *is* correct, go ahead and mark it as correct.

Summary: Only eliminate an answer choice if you are willing to bet $5 that it is wrong.

8

Copyright © Mometrix Media. You have been licensed one copy of this document for personal use only. Any other reproduction or redistribution is strictly prohibited. All rights reserved.

Which Answer to Choose

You're taking the test. You've run into a hard question and decided you'll have to guess. You've eliminated all the answer choices you're willing to bet $5 on. Now you have to pick an answer. Why do we even need to talk about this? Why can't you just pick whichever one you feel like when the time comes?

The answer to these questions is that if you don't come into the test with a plan, you'll rely on your impression to select an answer choice, and if you do that, you risk falling into a trap. The test writers know that everyone who takes their test will be guessing on some of the questions, so they intentionally write wrong answer choices to seem plausible. You still have to pick an answer though, and if the wrong answer choices are designed to look right, how can you ever be sure that you're not falling for their trap? The best solution we've found to this dilemma is to take the decision out of your hands entirely. Here is the process we recommend:

Once you've eliminated any choices that you are confident (willing to bet $5) are wrong, select the first remaining choice as your answer.

Whether you choose to select the first remaining choice, the second, or the last, the important thing is that you use some preselected standard. Using this approach guarantees that you will not be enticed into selecting an answer choice that looks right, because you are not basing your decision on how the answer choices look.

This is not meant to make you question your knowledge. Instead, it is to help you recognize the difference between your knowledge and your impressions. There's a huge difference between thinking an answer is right because of what you know, and thinking an answer is right because it looks or sounds like it should be right.

Summary: To ensure that your selection is appropriately random, make a predetermined selection from among all answer choices you have not eliminated.

Copyright © Mometrix Media. You have been licensed one copy of this document for personal use only. Any other reproduction or redistribution is strictly prohibited. All rights reserved.

Test-Taking Strategies

This section contains a list of test-taking strategies that you may find helpful as you work through the test. By taking what you know and applying logical thought, you can maximize your chances of answering any question correctly!

It is very important to realize that every question is different and every person is different: no single strategy will work on every question, and no single strategy will work for every person. That's why we've included all of them here, so you can try them out and determine which ones work best for different types of questions and which ones work best for you.

Question Strategies

Read Carefully

Read the question and answer choices carefully. Don't miss the question because you misread the terms. You have plenty of time to read each question thoroughly and make sure you understand what is being asked. Yet a happy medium must be attained, so don't waste too much time. You must read carefully, but efficiently.

Contextual Clues

Look for contextual clues. If the question includes a word you are not familiar with, look at the immediate context for some indication of what the word might mean. Contextual clues can often give you all the information you need to decipher the meaning of an unfamiliar word. Even if you can't determine the meaning, you may be able to narrow down the possibilities enough to make a solid guess at the answer to the question.

Prefixes

If you're having trouble with a word in the question or answer choices, try dissecting it. Take advantage of every clue that the word might include. Prefixes and suffixes can be a huge help. Usually they allow you to determine a basic meaning. Pre- means before, post- means after, pro - is positive, de- is negative. From prefixes and suffixes, you can get an idea of the general meaning of the word and try to put it into context.

Hedge Words

Watch out for critical hedge words, such as *likely, may, can, sometimes, often, almost, mostly, usually, generally, rarely*, and *sometimes*. Question writers insert these hedge phrases to cover every possibility. Often an answer choice will be wrong simply because it leaves no room for exception. Be on guard for answer choices that have definitive words such as *exactly* and *always*.

Switchback Words

Stay alert for *switchbacks*. These are the words and phrases frequently used to alert you to shifts in thought. The most common switchback words are *but, although*, and *however*. Others include *nevertheless, on the other hand, even though, while, in spite of, despite, regardless of*. Switchback words are important to catch because they can change the direction of the question or an answer choice.

10

Copyright © Mometrix Media. You have been licensed one copy of this document for personal use only. Any other reproduction or redistribution is strictly prohibited. All rights reserved.

Face Value

When in doubt, use common sense. Accept the situation in the problem at face value. Don't read too much into it. These problems will not require you to make wild assumptions. If you have to go beyond creativity and warp time or space in order to have an answer choice fit the question, then you should move on and consider the other answer choices. These are normal problems rooted in reality. The applicable relationship or explanation may not be readily apparent, but it is there for you to figure out. Use your common sense to interpret anything that isn't clear.

Answer Choice Strategies

Answer Selection

The most thorough way to pick an answer choice is to identify and eliminate wrong answers until only one is left, then confirm it is the correct answer. Sometimes an answer choice may immediately seem right, but be careful. The test writers will usually put more than one reasonable answer choice on each question, so take a second to read all of them and make sure that the other choices are not equally obvious. As long as you have time left, it is better to read every answer choice than to pick the first one that looks right without checking the others.

Answer Choice Families

An answer choice family consists of two (in rare cases, three) answer choices that are very similar in construction and cannot all be true at the same time. If you see two answer choices that are direct opposites or parallels, one of them is usually the correct answer. For instance, if one answer choice says that quantity x increases and another either says that quantity x decreases (opposite) or says that quantity y increases (parallel), then those answer choices would fall into the same family. An answer choice that doesn't match the construction of the answer choice family is more likely to be incorrect. Most questions will not have answer choice families, but when they do appear, you should be prepared to recognize them.

Eliminate Answers

Eliminate answer choices as soon as you realize they are wrong, but make sure you consider all possibilities. If you are eliminating answer choices and realize that the last one you are left with is also wrong, don't panic. Start over and consider each choice again. There may be something you missed the first time that you will realize on the second pass.

Avoid Fact Traps

Don't be distracted by an answer choice that is factually true but doesn't answer the question. You are looking for the choice that answers the question. Stay focused on what the question is asking for so you don't accidentally pick an answer that is true but incorrect. Always go back to the question and make sure the answer choice you've selected actually answers the question and is not merely a true statement.

Extreme Statements

In general, you should avoid answers that put forth extreme actions as standard practice or proclaim controversial ideas as established fact. An answer choice that states the "process should be used in certain situations, if…" is much more likely to be correct than one that states the "process should be discontinued completely." The first is a calm rational statement and doesn't even make a definitive, uncompromising stance, using a hedge word *if* to provide wiggle room, whereas the second choice is a radical idea and far more extreme.

Copyright © Mometrix Media. You have been licensed one copy of this document for personal use only. Any other reproduction or redistribution is strictly prohibited. All rights reserved.

Benchmark

As you read through the answer choices and you come across one that seems to answer the question well, mentally select that answer choice. This is not your final answer, but it's the one that will help you evaluate the other answer choices. The one that you selected is your benchmark or standard for judging each of the other answer choices. Every other answer choice must be compared to your benchmark. That choice is correct until proven otherwise by another answer choice beating it. If you find a better answer, then that one becomes your new benchmark. Once you've decided that no other choice answers the question as well as your benchmark, you have your final answer.

Predict the Answer

Before you even start looking at the answer choices, it is often best to try to predict the answer. When you come up with the answer on your own, it is easier to avoid distractions and traps because you will know exactly what to look for. The right answer choice is unlikely to be word-for-word what you came up with, but it should be a close match. Even if you are confident that you have the right answer, you should still take the time to read each option before moving on.

General Strategies

Tough Questions

If you are stumped on a problem or it appears too hard or too difficult, don't waste time. Move on! Remember though, if you can quickly check for obviously incorrect answer choices, your chances of guessing correctly are greatly improved. Before you completely give up, at least try to knock out a couple of possible answers. Eliminate what you can and then guess at the remaining answer choices before moving on.

Check Your Work

Since you will probably not know every term listed and the answer to every question, it is important that you get credit for the ones that you do know. Don't miss any questions through careless mistakes. If at all possible, try to take a second to look back over your answer selection and make sure you've selected the correct answer choice and haven't made a costly careless mistake (such as marking an answer choice that you didn't mean to mark). This quick double check should more than pay for itself in caught mistakes for the time it costs.

Pace Yourself

It's easy to be overwhelmed when you're looking at a page full of questions; your mind is confused and full of random thoughts, and the clock is ticking down faster than you would like. Calm down and maintain the pace that you have set for yourself. Especially as you get down to the last few minutes of the test, don't let the small numbers on the clock make you panic. As long as you are on track by monitoring your pace, you are guaranteed to have time for each question.

Don't Rush

It is very easy to make errors when you are in a hurry. Maintaining a fast pace in answering questions is pointless if it makes you miss questions that you would have gotten right otherwise. Test writers like to include distracting information and wrong answers that seem right. Taking a little extra time to avoid careless mistakes can make all the difference in your test score. Find a pace that allows you to be confident in the answers that you select.

12

Copyright © Mometrix Media. You have been licensed one copy of this document for personal use only. Any other reproduction or redistribution is strictly prohibited. All rights reserved.

Keep Moving

Panicking will not help you pass the test, so do your best to stay calm and keep moving. Taking deep breaths and going through the answer elimination steps you practiced can help to break through a stress barrier and keep your pace.

Final Notes

The combination of a solid foundation of content knowledge and the confidence that comes from practicing your plan for applying that knowledge is the key to maximizing your performance on test day. As your foundation of content knowledge is built up and strengthened, you'll find that the strategies included in this chapter become more and more effective in helping you quickly sift through the distractions and traps of the test to isolate the correct answer.

Now it's time to move on to the test content chapters of this book, but be sure to keep your goal in mind. As you read, think about how you will be able to apply this information on the test. If you've already seen sample questions for the test and you have an idea of the question format and style, try to come up with questions of your own that you can answer based on what you're reading. This will give you valuable practice applying your knowledge in the same ways you can expect to on test day.

Good luck and good studying!

Copyright © Mometrix Media. You have been licensed one copy of this document for personal use only. Any other reproduction or redistribution is strictly prohibited. All rights reserved.

Copyright © Mometrix Media. You have been licensed one copy of this document for personal use only. Any other reproduction or redistribution is strictly prohibited. All rights reserved.

Science Process Skills

Chemical Nature of Biology

All organisms are made up of matter and display the typical physical and chemical properties of matter. Every cell of an organism is composed of molecules, atoms, and ions. Chemistry is needed to explain the structure and function of all cellular processes at the molecular level. Organic chemistry involves many large and complex molecules including the biochemical compounds carbohydrates, lipids, proteins, and nucleic acids. Chemical reactions occur in the daily function of organisms even at the cellular level. Chemical reactions that are important for life include oxidation-reduction, dehydration synthesis, hydrolysis, phosphorylation, and acid-base reactions.

Use of Mathematics in Biology

Mathematics in becoming increasingly prevalent in modern biology especially with the use of computers for statistical programs. Mathematics is used in the studies of populations. For example, biologists study human population growth, bacteria growth, and virus growth. Populations of organisms in feeding relationships such as predator and prey are studied. Mathematics is used in classical genetics. For example, biologists use probability theory to predict offspring in genetic crosses. Mathematics is used extensively in bioinformatics. For example, biological data are extracted and analyzed using sophisticated computer programing. Mathematics is used in studies of epidemics. For example, studies concerning the spread of the flu and acquired immune deficiency syndrome (AIDS) have been performed.

Physical Laws and Principles Governing Biological Systems

Biological systems are governed by the same physical laws and principles that govern the rest of the universe. For example, biological systems must obey the laws of thermodynamics. These laws govern energy and the transformations of energy. The first law of thermodynamics is the law of conservation of energy, which states that energy is neither created nor destroyed but can change forms. The energy needed for life on Earth comes from the Sun. Sunlight reaches the Earth and is transformed by green plants and cyanobacteria during photosynthesis into the chemical bonds of ATP molecules, which can be used by these organisms for energy. Consumers eat the producers or other consumers in order to obtain energy. The second law of thermodynamics states that systems tend toward more disorder or entropy and less energy. This is evident in the fact that organisms must continually acquire energy to sustain life. Energy is continuously entering the biosphere from the sun, and that energy is continuously being dissipated as stated in the second law of thermodynamics.

Observations

The two main categories of observation are quantitative and qualitative. Quantitative observations should be objective rather than subjective. Quantitative observations involve numbers and measurements. Quantitative observations can be made with instruments. Results are based on statistics and numerical analyses. Quantitative observations are used in most scientific research. Qualitative observations are typically more subjective than quantitative observations. Observing human behavior is one type of qualitative observations. Qualitative observations use the senses: sight, hearing, smell, touch, and taste. Qualitative observations are often used in the social sciences.

Hypothesis

After scientists choose a problem and make observations, they need to form a hypothesis. After studying the observations, scientists make a sensible prediction or educated guess that answers the question introduced in the problem. Hypotheses are often stated in the form an if/then statement. A good

15

Copyright © Mometrix Media. You have been licensed one copy of this document for personal use only. Any other reproduction or redistribution is strictly prohibited. All rights reserved.

hypothesis is testable, which means that it should enable the scientist to make predictions that can then be tested. Next, the scientist designs an experiment that tests the hypothesis and predictions. A valid experiment will have several controls, one independent variable, and one dependent variable. When performing the experiment, meticulous data collection must be undertaken. Scientists should conduct as many trials as are reasonably possible.

> **Review Video: Scientific Hypothesis and Theories**
> Visit mometrix.com/academy and enter code: 918083

Variables and Controls in Scientific Experiments

Scientific experiments involve many factors, which can be classified as either variables or controls. Variables are usually described as independent or dependent. An independent variable is the factor that is manipulated or varied during the experiment. A dependent variable is the factor that is influenced by the independent variable. This is the factor that is being measured. Controls are factors that remain unchanged or are held constant during an experiment. These factors are held constant to keep them from affecting the dependent variable when the independent variable is being varied. Therefore, controls are factors that are not being tested. Controls are used for comparison.

> **Review Video: Experimental Science**
> Visit mometrix.com/academy and enter code: 283092

Drawing Scientific Conclusions

After performing an experiment, scientists need to examine the data to form conclusions. Conclusions should summarize the results and state the relationship between the dependent and independent variables. Then, the scientist compares these results with the initial hypothesis. Either the experiment supports the hypothesis, or the data refute or do not support the hypothesis. Although a hypothesis can be rejected, a hypothesis is never proven true. The data cannot prove the hypothesis is true 100% of the time. They can only support the hypothesis.

> **Review Video: Fact, Conclusion, Cause and Effect, Model, and Scientific Law**
> Visit mometrix.com/academy and enter code: 534217

Testable Nature of Hypotheses

A valid hypothesis must be testable. A testable hypothesis should generate predictions of outcomes and tests or experiments that can be formed from those predictions. A testable hypothesis should limit variables. From a testable hypothesis, it should be clear which variable is the independent variable and which one is the dependent variable. From a testable hypothesis, an experiment that varies the independent variable while monitoring or measuring the dependent variable should be able to be constructed. If the variables cannot be measured, then a valid experiment is not possible, and the hypothesis is not valid. If the other factors associated with the experiments cannot be controlled, then the hypothesis is not valid.

> **Review Video: The Scientific Method**
> Visit mometrix.com/academy and enter code: 191386

Formulation of Theories Based on Accumulated Data

Scientific theories can be formulated based on the accumulated data from the testing of valid hypotheses. Whereas hypotheses are narrow, theories are much broader. A scientific theory can

16

Copyright © Mometrix Media. You have been licensed one copy of this document for personal use only. Any other reproduction or redistribution is strictly prohibited. All rights reserved.

summarize several related hypotheses that have been supported by repeated tests as shown in the accumulated data. As data accumulate in support of these hypotheses, a theory is developed to summarize them. The theory is then accepted as a valid explanation or model of the phenomenon examined by the testing. Theories remain valid unless they are disproved. Theories may be modified as more information and newer technologies become available. Occasionally, theories become scientific laws.

Durability of Scientific Laws

The very nature of scientific laws makes them durable. Scientific laws are based on observations from repeated experiments. Scientific laws are concise statements that describe some phenomenon or relationship in the world. Unlike scientific theories, scientific laws do not explain the phenomenon or relationship they describe. A scientific law is always valid under the same conditions and should imply a causal relationship between elements. Many scientific laws are written as mathematical equations. For example, Isaac Newton's second law of motion can simply be stated as $F = ma$, in which F is the force applied to an object, m is the mass of the object, and a is the object's acceleration. Scientific laws are rarely refuted.

Cell Theory

The cell theory states that all living things are composed of cells and that cells come from preexisting cells. Cells were first observed in 1655 by Robert Hooke when he was studying thin slices of a piece of cork under his primitive microscope. Because the cork cells were dead, Hooke actually only observed the cell walls of the cork cells. Hooke was the first to use the word "cell," which comes from the Latin word *cellula*, which means small compartment. Hooke documented his observations with sketches and published his work in his book commonly called *Micrographia*.

Germ Theory of Disease

The germ theory of disease states that most infectious diseases are caused by germs or disease-causing microbes or pathogens. The germ theory is the foundation of microbiology and modern medicine. Pasteur studied the fermentation of wine and the spoiling of milk. He discovered that yeast caused the fermentation of wine and bacteria caused the spoiling of milk. He developed the process of pasteurization of milk that killed the harmful microbes without ruining the taste of the milk. Then he studied diseases in silkworms and was able to determine that the causes of those diseases are protozoa and bacteria. Pasteur also thought that microbes in hospitals came from preexisting microbes instead of spontaneous generation. He disproved spontaneous generation with his work with bacteria and broth. He discovered that weakened microbes could be used in vaccines or immunizations to prevent or protect against the diseases caused by those microbes. Pasteur discovered viruses in his work, developing the rabies vaccine and treatments for those already infected with the rabies virus.

Mendel's Contributions to Genetics

Johann Gregor Mendel is known as the father of genetics. Mendel was an Austrian monk who performed thousands of experiments involving the breeding of the common pea plant in the monastery garden. Mendel kept detailed records including seed color, pod color, seed type, flower color, and plant height for eight years and published his work in 1865. Unfortunately, his work was largely ignored until the early 1900s. Mendel's work showed that genes come in pairs and that dominant and recessive traits are inherited independently of each other. His work established the law of segregation, the law of independent assortment, and the law of dominance.

Copyright © Mometrix Media. You have been licensed one copy of this document for personal use only. Any other reproduction or redistribution is strictly prohibited. All rights reserved.

Darwin's Contributions to Theory of Evolution

Charles Darwin's theory of evolution is the unifying concept in biology today. From 1831 to 1836, Darwin traveled as a naturalist on a five-year voyage on the *H.M.S. Beagle* around the tip of South America and to the Galápagos Islands. He studied finches, took copious amounts of meticulous notes, and collected thousands of plant and animal specimens. He collected 13 species of finches each with a unique bill for a distinct food source, which led him to believe that due to similarities between the finches, that the finches shared a common ancestor. The similarities and differences of fossils of extinct rodents and modern mammal fossils led him to believe that the mammals had changed over time. Darwin believed that these changes were the result of random genetic changes called mutations. He believed that mutations could be beneficial and eventually result in a different organism over time. In 1859, in his first book, *On the Origin of Species*, Darwin proposed that natural selection was the means by which adaptations would arise over time. He coined the term "natural selection" and said that natural selection is the mechanism of evolution. Because variety exists among individuals of a species, he stated that those individuals must compete for the same limited resources. Some would die, and others would survive. According to Darwin, evolution is a slow, gradual process. In 1871, Darwin published his second book, *Descent of Man, and Selection in Relation to Sex*, in which he discussed the evolution of man.

> **Review Video: Darwin's Contributions to Theory of Evolution**
> Visit mometrix.com/academy and enter code: 898980

Contribution to Genetics by Alfred Hershey and Martha Chase

Alfred Hershey and Martha Chase did a series of experiments in 1952 known as the Hershey-Chase experiments. These experiments showed that deoxyribonucleic acid (DNA), not protein, is the genetic material that transfers information for inheritance. The Hershey-Chase experiments used a bacteriophage, a virus that infects bacteria, to infect the bacteria *Escherichia coli.* The bacteriophage T2 is basically a small piece of DNA enclosed in a protein coating. The DNA contains phosphorus, and the protein coating contains sulfur. In the first set of experiments, the T2 was marked with radioactive phosphorus-32. In the second set of experiments, the T2 was marked with radioactive sulfur-35. For both sets of experiments, after the *E. coli* was infected by the T2, the *E. coli* was isolated using a centrifuge. In the first set of experiments, the radioactive isotope (P-32) was found in the *E. coli*, showing that the genetic information was transferred by the DNA. In the second set of experiments, the radioactive isotope (S-35) was not found in the *E. coli*, showing that the genetic information was not transferred by the protein as was previously thought. Hershey and Chase conducted further experiments allowing the bacteria from the first set of experiments to reproduce, and the offspring was also found to contain the radioactive isotope (P-32) further confirming that the DNA transferred the genetic material.

Contributions to the Knowledge of DNA

The three-dimensional double-helix structure of the DNA molecule was formulated by James Watson and Francis Crick in 1953. But the actual discovery of DNA took place in 1869 when Friedrich Miescher discovered DNA, which he called "nuclein" in the nuclei of human white blood cells while attempting to isolate proteins. Years later in 1919, Phoebus Levene identified the components of a nucleotide. Then in 1950, Erwin Chargaff published his discovery that DNA varies among species and states what is now known as Chargaff's rule: Adenine always combines with thymine, and cytosine always combines with guanine. In 1951, Rosalind Franklin studied the molecular structure of DNA using x-rays. Her work laid the foundation for the work that Watson and Crick did in 1953, in which they discovered the three-dimensional double-helix structure of DNA. Watson and Crick showed that the complementary bases are joined by hydrogen bonds. Franklin also studied the structure of RNA and discovered that RNA is a single-strand helix structure, not a double strand like DNA.

Copyright © Mometrix Media. You have been licensed one copy of this document for personal use only. Any other reproduction or redistribution is strictly prohibited. All rights reserved.

Historical and Current Kingdom Systems

In 1735 Carolus Linnaeus devised a two-kingdom classification system. He placed all living things into either the *Animalia* kingdom or the *Plantae* kingdom. Fungi and algae were classified as plants. Also, Linnaeus developed the binomial nomenclature system that is still used today. In 1866, Ernst Haeckel introduced a three-kingdom classification system, adding the *Protista* kingdom to Linnaeus's animal and plant kingdoms. Bacteria were classified as protists. Cyanobacteria were still classified as plants. In 1938, Herbert Copeland introduced a four-kingdom classification system in which bacteria and cyanobacteria were moved to the *Monera* kingdom. In 1969, Robert Whittaker introduced a five-kingdom system that moved fungi from the plant kingdom to the *Fungi* kingdom. Some algae were still classified as plants. In 1977, Carl Woese introduced a six-kingdom system in which in the *Monera* kingdom was replaced with the *Eubacteria* kingdom and the *Archaebacteria* kingdom.

Domain Classification System

In 1990, Carl Woese introduced his domain classification system. Domains are broader groupings above the kingdom level. This system consists of three domains- *Archaea*, *Bacteria*, and *Eukarya*. All eukaryotes such as plants, animals, fungi, and protists are classified in the *Eukarya* domain. The *Bacteria* and *Archaea* domains consist of prokaryotes. Organisms previously classified in the *Monera* kingdom are now classified into either the *Bacteria* or *Archaea* domain based on their ribosomal RNA structure. Members of the *Archaea* domain often live in extremely harsh environments.

Accuracy and Precision

Accuracy is the exactness of a measurement. It expresses how close a measurement is to the actual or true value. Precision is the repeatability or the consistency of a measurement. It expresses how close measurements are to each other. For example, a sample weighs 10.0 grams, and the measured values of this sample are 8.8, 8.7, 8.8, 8.9, and 8.8 grams. These measurements are precise because they are all close to each other. However, although these measurements are precise, they are not accurate because they are not close enough to the actual value. For example, a sample weighs 200.0 grams, and the measured values of this sample are 200.1, 200.2, 199.9, 200.0, and 200.1 grams. These measurements are precise because they are close to each other, and these measurements are accurate because they are close to the actual value.

Scientific Notation and Significant Figures

Significant figures indicate the precision of a measured value. All measurements are approximations and have uncertainty. The uncertainty in measurements is due to the accuracy of the measuring devices and the skill of the scientist performing that measurement. Measurements are usually recorded to the first uncertain digit. The last digit is uncertain. The rules for using significant figures determine where to round the answers when doing calculations. Scientific notation is an easy way to write numbers that are extremely large or small. It is also a convenient way to correctly convey the correct number of significant figures in a measurement or calculations. The format for scientific notation is $M \times 10^n$, in which M is a number between 1 and 10 and n is a positive or negative integer. The first number (M) is the coefficient, and the second number (10^n) is the base. For numbers greater than 1, n is positive. For numbers less than 1, n is negative. When converting from scientific notation, the decimal point is moved the same number of places as the exponent. The decimal is moved to the right if the exponent is positive, and the decimal is moved to the left if the exponent is negative.

Metric Units and Notations for Scientific Measurements

Quantity	Unit Name	Symbol
Volume	Liter	L

19

Copyright © Mometrix Media. You have been licensed one copy of this document for personal use only. Any other reproduction or redistribution is strictly prohibited. All rights reserved.

Length	Meter	m
Time	Second	s
Amount of a substance	Mole	mol
Mass	Kilogram	kg
Absolute temperature	Kelvin	K
Force	Newton	N
Energy	Joule	J
Pressure	Pascal	Pa
Electric current	Ampere	A
Frequency	Hertz	Hz

Unit Conversions

A convenient way to perform unit conversions is dimensional analysis. In this method, conversion unit factors are used to obtain the needed unit. For example, because 1 kilogram is equal to 1,000 grams, and 1 gram equals 1,000 milligrams, the possible conversion factors are $\left(\frac{1\text{ kg}}{1,000\text{ g}}\right)$ and $\left(\frac{1\text{ g}}{1,000\text{ mg}}\right)$. The reciprocals of these factors may also be used. To convert 2,800 mg to kg, multiply (2,800 mg)$\left(\frac{1\text{ g}}{1,000\text{ mg}}\right)\left(\frac{1\text{kg}}{1,000\text{ g}}\right)$ = 2.8 x 10^{-3} kg. To convert 3,900 kg to mg, multiply (3,900 kg)$\left(\frac{1,000\text{ g}}{\text{kg}}\right)\left(\frac{1,000\text{ mg}}{\text{g}}\right)$ = 3.9 x 10^9 mg.

Linear and Logarithmic Scales

On a linear scale, when moving from one data point to the next, the change in output is based on the difference between the two values or addition. On a logarithmic scale, the change in output is based on the ratio between the two values or multiplication. With a logarithmic scale, the value of the logarithm of a quantity is used instead of the quantity itself. Logarithmic scales cover a much broader range of values than for linear scales. For example, on a linear scale, a change from 1 to 2 could be the same as the increase from 10 to 20. But on a logarithmic scale, a change from 1 to 2 could be the same as the increase from 10 to 100. In this example, 10 was added for each increment of the linear scale, but 10 was multiplied for each increment of the logarithmic scale. One example of a logarithmic scale is the pH scale. For each increase in 1 in the value of pH, the concentration of hydronium ions increases by a factor of 10.

Identifying Patterns and Trends in Data

Trends and patterns in data can be often be seen when reading tables, graphs, and charts by recognizing correlations between the data for the independent and dependent variables. If both sets of data increase or decrease together, then the correlation is positive. If one set of data increases and the other set of data decreases, then the correlation is negative. Often, data are represented in scatter plots, in which correlations are more readily seen. Correlations can be linear or curvilinear. Lines of best fit can be drawn for linear correlation and used to make predictions.

Graphs and Charts

Pie charts are best used when comparing parts to the whole. For example, a pie chart could be used to show the components of blood and their respective percentages. Line graphs are best used when showing small or large changes over time. For example, a line chart could be used to record the weekly rainfall of a region. Bar graphs can be used to compare groups or track large changes over time. For example, a bar graph could be used to compare the average plant height of three groups of plants used in an experiment. Scatter plots are used to determine if there is a correlation between two sets of data. For

Copyright © Mometrix Media. You have been licensed one copy of this document for personal use only. Any other reproduction or redistribution is strictly prohibited. All rights reserved.

example, hours of sleep could be plotted against waking blood pressure to determine a possible correlation.

Types of Errors

Random errors, systematic errors, and personal errors are three types of error. Random errors are unpredictable because they are from unknown causes and cannot be eliminated. Systematic errors arise from faulty equipment or faulty procedures. Although they are difficult to detect, they may be eliminated. Personal errors are human error such as the improper use of equipment or incorrectly following a procedure. Personal errors can be eliminated or at least minimized by proper training. To calculate percent error, subtract the theoretical value from the experimental value and then divide by the theoretical value. Finally, multiply by 100 and add the percent sign.

$$\text{Percent error} = \frac{\text{experimental value} - \text{theoretical value}}{\text{theoretical value}} \times 100\%.$$

Review Video: Identification of Experimental Problem and Design
Visit mometrix.com/academy and enter code: 653245

Review Video: Identifying Controls in a Research Summary
Visit mometrix.com/academy and enter code: 911077

Use of Graphs to Identify Correlations and Make Predictions

In order to more easily draw conclusions and make predictions, data can first be graphed. Next, the scientist looks for patterns and trends in the data to identify correlations between the independent variable and the dependent variable. Then, the scientist checks to determine if the trends and correlations observed from experimentation support or reject the hypothesis. The conclusion should state whether or not the trends in the data support the hypothesis. Predictions can often be made if the data support the hypothesis. If the data have a linear correlation, a line of best fit enables the scientist to make predictions.

Models

Models are visual representations or replicas of natural phenomena such as objects or processes that are based on scientific evidence. Models can be used to make predictions. Models help scientists explain natural phenomena that are difficult to understand. Models usually have specific limits. Models usually make approximations when describing natural phenomena. Models should be as simple as possible while still maintaining their accuracy. Many models cannot incorporate all the details of the phenomena being studied due to the complexity of the phenomena. Models have to be simple enough to use to make predictions. Models should make visualizing a process easier, not more difficult, but simplicity may be sacrificed at the expense of accuracy.

Population Models

Ecologists use population models to study the populations in an ecosystem and their interactions of populations with the environment. Population models are mathematical models that are designed to study population dynamics. Ecologists can model the growth of a population. For example, models can be designed to describe increases, decreases, or fluctuations in the size of populations due to births, deaths, and migrations. Ecologists can model the interactions of populations with other populations. For example, models of the interactions between predator and prey describe the fluctuating cycles associated with these relationships. Models can also include other factors such as diseases and limiting resources.

Copyright © Mometrix Media. You have been licensed one copy of this document for personal use only. Any other reproduction or redistribution is strictly prohibited. All rights reserved.

Gel Electrophoresis

Gel electrophoresis is a technique used to separate macromolecules such as nucleic acids and proteins. Fragments of DNA and RNA are separated according to length. Proteins are separated according to length and charge. The technique is relatively simple. For example, to separate DNA strands, a solution containing the DNA strand is placed in a gel. When an electric current is passed through the gel, the DNA strands migrate from the negative end of the container to the positive end due to their negative charge because of their phosphate ions. Shorter DNA strands migrate faster than the longer DNA strands. This results in a series of bands. Each band contains DNA strands of a specific length. A DNA standard is placed in the gel to provide a reference to determine the strand length. Lengths are measured in base pairs (bps).

Microscopy

Microscopy is used in microbiology. Bacteria, viruses, cell components, and molecules are too small to be seen by the naked eye. Several types of microscopes are available to examine these samples. There are light microscopes, which use visible light to study samples, and electron microscopes, which use beams of electrons. The light microscope (also called the compound microscope) uses two types of lenses (ocular and objective) to magnify objects. These are typically used when studying samples at the cellular level. Basic compound light microscopes are typically used in high school biology classes. Other compound light microscopes such as the dark-field microscope, phase-contrast microscope, and the fluorescent microscope are available for more specific uses. For tiny samples, such as viruses, cell components, or individual molecules, electron microscopes can be used. Electron microscopes use beams of electrons instead of light. Because beams of electrons have shorter wavelengths, electron microscopes have greater resolution than light microscopes. Resolution is the ability of a lens to reveal two points as being distinct. The two types of electron microscopy are transmission electron microscopy (TEM) and scanning electron microscopy (SEM). SEM is a newer technology than TEM and produces three-dimensional images.

Safety and Emergency Procedures for Science Classrooms and Laboratories

Laboratory safety rules should include the following. Never perform unauthorized experiments. Read all Safety Data Sheets (SDSs) before each lab. Always pour acids into water. Avoid skin contact with chemicals. If chemicals come in contact with skin or eyes, immediately flush the contacted area with water. Never use a carbon dioxide fire extinguisher on a person—use a fire blanket. Wear appropriate apparel in the laboratory including safety goggles, aprons, and gloves when necessary. Rules for behavior include the following. No horseplay. No eating, drinking, or chewing gum. Always wash your hands when done in the laboratory. In addition to the above rules, these standard emergency procedures should be followed. Notify the instructor in case of an emergency. Be aware of fire evacuation routes and the locations of fire blankets and fire extinguishers. In the event of a fire, pull the fire alarm. In cases of ingestion of chemicals, call a poison control center.

Ethical Concerns of Embryonic Stem Cells for Research

Research involving the use of embryonic stem cells offers hope for genetically related health issues. However, ethical issues are seriously debated. New therapies could be developed using embryonic stem cells that would greatly alleviate suffering for many people. However, that benefit comes at the cost of human embryos. Proponents of embryonic stem cell research argue that an early embryo is not yet a person because the embryo cannot survive without being implanted in the uterus. Some believe that the embryo should have no moral status and that fertilized eggs should be treated as the property of the parents who should have the right to donate that property to research. Opponents of embryonic stem cell research argue that the embryo is a human life at fertilization and should have full moral status at fertilization, and that a human embryo is a human being. Opponents argue that judgments determining

Copyright © Mometrix Media. You have been licensed one copy of this document for personal use only. Any other reproduction or redistribution is strictly prohibited. All rights reserved.

when an embryo is viable or when an embryo is fully human cannot be made. Some opponents of stem cell research do not believe that the fertilized egg is a human being, but they still argue that by removing the stem cells from the early embryo, the embryo is prevented from becoming a human being. They argue that embryonic stem cell research destroys potential life.

Ethical and Societal Concerns Regarding Genetically Modified Food

Genetically modified (GM) foods are transgenic crops that have had their genes altered by technology. For example, herbicide-tolerant soybeans and insect-resistant corn have been grown for years in the United States. Several issues have been raised concerning GM foods. Some people do not want to go against Mother Nature. Even scientists may feel that because the genes in organisms have evolved over millions of years that man should not interfere. Others would argue that man has been selectively breeding plants and animals for hundreds of years, and genetic modification is just an extension of that concept. Scientists are concerned about introducing new allergens into the food supply. For example, if a gene from a peanut plant is introduced into a soybean plant, there may be a potential for allergic reactions. Proteins from microorganisms may have never been tested as allergens. Many are concerned that the genetic modifications will not be contained. Pollen from fields of genetically modified crops may be carried by insects or wind to other fields. In some cases, traits such as herbicide resistance might pass from the cultivated plants to the wild populations of those plants. Insect-resistant plants may harm insects other than those that were being targeted. For example, studies show that pollinators such as the monarch butterfly may be harmed from GM corn.

Ethical Concerns Regarding Human Cloning and Animal Cloning

Many issues are raised with the topic of human cloning and animal cloning. Disagreements arise over who would be allowed to produce human clones. Many are concerned about how clones would integrate into families and societies. Some believe that human cloning for procreation purposes should be regulated based on motivation. For example, individuals interested in raising a genetically-related child should be granted approval, but those seeking immortality or viewing cloning as a novelty should be denied. Many believe that mandatory counseling and a waiting period should be enforced. Others argue that individuals do not have a right to a genetically-related child, that cloning is not safe, and that cloning is not medically necessary. Proponents argue that cloning is needed to generate tissues and whole organs that eliminate the need for immunosuppressive drugs. Cloned tissues and organs could be used to counter the effects of aging. Others fear that this will lead to the generation of humans solely for the purpose of harvesting tissues and organs. Animal rights activists are opposed to the cloning of animals. Animals are being cloned in laboratories and in livestock production. Activists argue that many cloned animals suffer from defects before they die. Some believe that animals have moral rights and should be treated with the same ethical consideration given to humans.

Societal Concerns About Genetic Testing

Society has not fully embraced genetic testing. Many people do not consider genetic testing to be a medical test. Many feel pressure from other family members who do not want the family genes revealed. Some do not want to know of potential health problems they may face later in life. Many are concerned about the psychological impact and stigma associated with carrying gene mutations. Many fear genetic discrimination from employers if they or a near relative carries a gene for a serious health issue. They fear not being hired, losing a job, or being denied promotions. Many fear discrimination from health insurers or being denied government services. Some fear being denied educational opportunities. Many are concerned about privacy and confidentiality. For example, who owns an individual's genetic information and who has access to that information? Should courts and schools have access to that information? Genetic testing also raises philosophical issues. Do genes determine behavior? If so, then are people responsible for their behavior? Many are completely unaware of the Genetic Information

Copyright © Mometrix Media. You have been licensed one copy of this document for personal use only. Any other reproduction or redistribution is strictly prohibited. All rights reserved.

Nondiscrimination Act of 2008, which is a federal law that protects Americans from discrimination due to differences in their DNA.

Copyright © Mometrix Media. You have been licensed one copy of this document for personal use only. Any other reproduction or redistribution is strictly prohibited. All rights reserved.

Chemistry

Properties of Matter

Matter refers to substances that have **mass** and occupy **space** (or volume). The traditional definition of matter describes it as having three states: solid, liquid, and gas. These different states are caused by differences in the distances and angles between molecules or atoms, which result in differences in the energy that binds them. **Solid** structures are rigid or nearly rigid and have strong bonds. Molecules or atoms of **liquids** move around and have weak bonds, although they are not weak enough to readily break. Molecules or atoms of **gases** move almost independently of each other, are typically far apart, and do not form bonds. The current definition of matter describes it as having four states. The fourth is **plasma**, which is an ionized gas that has some electrons that are described as free because they are not bound to an atom or molecule.

The following table shows similarities and differences between solids, liquids, and gases:

	Solid	Liquid	Gas
Shape	Fixed shape	No fixed shape (assumes shape of container)	No fixed shape (assumes shape of container)
Volume	Fixed	Fixed	Changes to assume shape of container
Fluidity	Does not flow easily	Flows easily	Flows easily
Compressibility	Hard to compress	Hard to compress	Compresses

- **Mass**: Mass is a measure of the amount of substance in an object.
- **Weight**: Weight is a measure of the gravitational pull of Earth on an object.
- **Volume**: Volume is a measure of the amount of space occupied. There are many formulas to determine volume. For example, the volume of a cube is the length of one side cubed (a^3) and the volume of a rectangular prism is length times width times height ($l \cdot w \cdot h$). The volume of an irregular shape can be determined by how much water it displaces.
- **Density**: Density is a measure of the amount of mass per unit volume. The formula to find density is mass divided by volume ($D=m/V$). It is expressed in terms of mass per cubic unit, such as grams per cubic centimeter (g/cm^3).
- **Specific gravity**: This is a measure of the ratio of a substance's density compared to the density of water.

Both physical changes and chemical reactions are everyday occurrences. **Physical changes** do not result in different substances. For example, when water becomes ice it has undergone a physical change, but not a chemical change. It has changed its form, but not its composition. It is still H_2O. **Chemical properties** are concerned with the constituent particles that make up the physicality of a substance. Chemical properties are apparent when chemical changes occur. The chemical properties of a substance are influenced by its electron configuration, which is determined in part by the number of protons in the nucleus (the atomic number). Carbon, for example, has 6 protons and 6 electrons. It is an element's outermost valence electrons that mainly determine its chemical properties. **Chemical reactions** may release or consume energy.

Atomic Charge

Atomic theory is concerned with the characteristics and properties of atoms that make up matter. It deals with matter on a microscopic level as opposed to a macroscopic level. Atomic theory, for instance,

25

Copyright © Mometrix Media. You have been licensed one copy of this document for personal use only. Any other reproduction or redistribution is strictly prohibited. All rights reserved.

discusses the kinetic motion of atoms in order to explain the properties of macroscopic quantities of matter. **John Dalton** (1766-1844) is credited with making many contributions to the field of atomic theory that are still considered valid. This includes the notion that all matter consists of **atoms** and that atoms are indestructible. In other words, atoms can be neither created nor destroyed. This is also the theory behind the **conservation of matter**, which explains why chemical reactions do not result in any detectable gains or losses in matter. This holds true for chemical reactions and smaller scale processes. When dealing with large amounts of energy, however, atoms can be destroyed by **nuclear reactions.** This can happen in particle colliders or atom smashers.

Most atoms are **neutral** since the positive charge of the protons in the nucleus is balanced by the negative charge of the surrounding electrons. Electrons are transferred between atoms when they come into contact with each other. This creates a molecule or atom in which the number of electrons does not equal the number of protons, which gives it a positive or negative charge. A **negative ion** is created when an atom gains electrons, while a **positive ion** is created when an atom loses electrons. An **ionic bond** is formed between ions with opposite charges. The resulting compound is neutral. **Ionization** refers to the process by which neutral particles are ionized into charged particles. Gases and plasmas can be partially or fully ionized through ionization.

> **Review Video: Nuclear and Chemical Reactions**
> Visit mometrix.com/academy and enter code: 572819
>
> **Review Video: John Dalton**
> Visit mometrix.com/academy and enter code: 565627

Energy Transfer

Atoms interact by **transferring** or sharing the electrons furthest from the nucleus. Known as the **outer** or **valence electrons**, they are responsible for the chemical properties of an element. Bonds between atoms are created when electrons are paired up by being transferred or shared. If electrons are transferred from one atom to another, the bond is **ionic.** If electrons are shared, the bond is **covalent.** Atoms of the same element may bond together to form molecules or crystalline solids. When two or more different types of atoms bind together chemically, a **compound** is made. The physical properties of compounds reflect the nature of the interactions among their molecules. These interactions are determined by the structure of the molecule, including the atoms they consist of and the distances and angles between them.

Electrons in an atom can orbit different **levels** around the nucleus. They can absorb or release energy, which can change the location of their orbit or even allow them to break free from the atom. The outermost layer is the **valence layer**, which contains the valence electrons. The valence layer tends to have or share eight electrons. Molecules are formed by a chemical bond between atoms, a bond which occurs at the valence level. Two basic types of bonds are covalent and ionic. A **covalent bond** is formed when atoms share electrons. An **ionic bond** is formed when an atom transfers an electron to another atom. A **hydrogen bond** is a weak bond between a hydrogen atom of one molecule and an electronegative atom (such as nitrogen, oxygen, or fluorine) of another molecule. The **Van der Waals force** is a weak force between molecules. This type of force is much weaker than actual chemical bonds between atoms.

Composition of the Universe

Aside from dark energy and dark matter, which are thought to account for all but four percent of the universe, the two most abundant **elements** in the universe are hydrogen (H) and helium (He). After hydrogen and helium, the most abundant elements are oxygen, neon, nitrogen, carbon, silicon, and magnesium. The most abundant **isotopes** in the solar system are hydrogen-1 and helium-4. Measurements of the masses of elements in the Earth's crust indicate that oxygen (O), silicon (Si), and

26

Copyright © Mometrix Media. You have been licensed one copy of this document for personal use only. Any other reproduction or redistribution is strictly prohibited. All rights reserved.

aluminum (Al) are the most abundant on Earth. Hydrogen in its plasma state is the most abundant chemical element in stars in their main sequences, but is relatively rare on planet Earth.

Combustion and Species

Combustion, or burning, is a sequence of chemical reactions involving fuel and an oxidant that produces heat and sometimes light. There are many types of combustion, such as rapid, slow, complete, turbulent, microgravity, and incomplete. **Fuels** and **oxidants** determine the compounds formed by a combustion reaction. For example, when rocket fuel consisting of hydrogen and oxygen combusts, it results in the formation of water vapor. When air and wood burn, resulting compounds include nitrogen, unburned carbon, and carbon compounds. Combustion is an **exothermic process**, meaning it releases energy. **Exothermic energy** is commonly released as heat, but can take other forms, such as light, electricity, or sound.

In chemistry, **species** is a generic term that can be used to refer to any type of particle, such as atoms, ions, molecules, molecular fragments, or specific forms of elements.

> **Review Video: Combustion**
> Visit mometrix.com/academy and enter code: 592219

Important Terminology

- **Elements**: These are substances that consist of only one type of atom.
- **Compounds**: These are substances containing two or more elements. Compounds are formed by chemical reactions and frequently have different properties than the original elements. Compounds are decomposed by a chemical reaction rather than separated by a physical one.
- **Solutions**: These are homogeneous mixtures composed of two or more substances that have become one.
- **Mixtures**: Mixtures contain two or more substances that are combined but have not reacted chemically with each other. Mixtures can be separated using physical methods, while compounds cannot.
- **Heat**: Heat is the transfer of energy from a body or system as a result of thermal contact. Heat consists of random motion and the vibration of atoms, molecules, and ions. The higher the temperature is the greater the atomic or molecular motion will be.
- **Energy**: Energy is the capacity to do work.
- **Work**: Work is the quantity of energy transferred by one system to another due to changes in a system that is the result of external forces, or macroscopic variables. Another way to put this is that work is the amount of energy that must be transferred to overcome a force. Lifting an object in the air is an example of work. The opposing force that must be overcome is gravity. Work is measured in joules (J).
- **Power**: The rate at which work is performed.
- **Thermal energy**: Thermal energy is the energy present in a system due to temperature.
- **Thermal contact** refers to energy transferred to a body by a means other than work a system in thermal contact with another can exchange energy with it through the process of heat transfer. Thermal contact does not necessarily involve direct physical contact. Heat is energy that can be transferred from one body or system to another without work being done. Everything tends to become less organized and less useful over time (entropy) in all energy transfers, therefore, the overall result is that the heat is spread out so that objects are in thermodynamic equilibrium and the heat can no longer be transferred without additional work.

Copyright © Mometrix Media. You have been licensed one copy of this document for personal use only. Any other reproduction or redistribution is strictly prohibited. All rights reserved.

Structure of Atoms

All matter consists of **atoms**. Atoms consist of a nucleus and electrons. The **nucleus** consists of protons and neutrons. The properties of these are measurable; they have mass and an electrical charge. The nucleus is positively charged due to the presence of protons. **Electrons** are negatively charged and orbit the nucleus. The nucleus has considerably more mass than the surrounding electrons. Atoms can bond together to make **molecules**. Atoms that have an equal number of protons and electrons are electrically neutral. If the number of protons and electrons in an atom is not equal, the atom has a positive or negative charge and is an **ion**.

Atoms are extremely small. A **hydrogen atom** is about 5×10^{-8} mm in diameter. According to some estimates, five trillion hydrogen atoms could fit on the head of a pin. **Atomic radius** refers to the average distance between the nucleus and the outermost electron. Models of atoms that include the proton, nucleus, and electrons typically show the electrons very close to the nucleus and revolving around it, similar to how the Earth orbits the sun. However, another model relates the Earth as the nucleus and its atmosphere as electrons, which is the basis of the term "**electron cloud**." Another description is that electrons swarm around the nucleus. It should be noted that these atomic models are not to scale. A more accurate representation would be a nucleus with a diameter of about 2 cm in a stadium. The electrons would be in the bleachers.

Atom: The atom is one of the most basic units of matter. An atom consists of a central nucleus surrounded by electrons.

Nucleus: The nucleus of an atom consists of protons and neutrons. It is positively charged, dense, and heavier than the surrounding electrons. The plural form of nucleus is nuclei.

Electrons: These are atomic particles that are negatively charged and orbit the nucleus of an atom.

Protons: Along with neutrons, protons make up the nucleus of an atom. The number of protons in the nucleus determines the atomic number of an element. Carbon atoms, for example, have six protons. The atomic number of carbon is 6. The number of protons also indicates the charge of an atom. The number of protons minus the number of electrons indicates the charge of an atom.

Atomic number (proton number): The atomic number of an element refers to the number of protons in the nucleus of an atom. It is a unique identifier. It can be represented as Z. Atoms with a neutral charge have an atomic number that is equal to the number of electrons.

Neutrons: Neutrons are the uncharged atomic particles contained within the nucleus. The number of neutrons in a nucleus can be represented as "N."

Nucleon: This refers collectively to the neutrons and protons.

Element: An element is matter with one particular type of atom. It can be identified by its atomic number, or the number of protons in its nucleus. There are approximately 117 elements currently known, 94 of which occur naturally on Earth. Elements from the periodic table include hydrogen, carbon, iron, helium, mercury, and oxygen.

Atomic mass: This is also known as the mass number. The atomic mass is the total number of protons and neutrons in the nucleus of an atom. It is referred to as "A." The atomic mass (A) is equal to the number of protons (Z) plus the number of neutrons (N). This can be represented by the equation $A = Z + N$. The mass of electrons in an atom is basically insignificant because it is so small.

Copyright © Mometrix Media. You have been licensed one copy of this document for personal use only. Any other reproduction or redistribution is strictly prohibited. All rights reserved.

Atomic weight: This may sometimes be referred to as "relative atomic mass," but should not be confused with atomic mass. Atomic weight is the ratio of the average mass per atom of a sample (which can include various isotopes of an element) to 1/12 of the mass of an atom of carbon-12.

Review Video: Structure of Atoms
Visit mometrix.com/academy and enter code: 905932

Review Video: Reading Nuclear Equations
Visit mometrix.com/academy and enter code: 688890

Nuclear Reactions

The particles of an atom's nucleus (the protons and neutrons) are bound together by **nuclear force**, also known as **residual strong force**. Unlike chemical reactions, which involve electrons, nuclear reactions occur when two nuclei or nuclear particles collide. This results in the release or absorption of energy and products that are different from the initial particles. The energy released in a nuclear reaction can take various forms, including the release of kinetic energy of the product particles and the emission of very high energy photons known as **gamma rays**. Some energy may also remain in the nucleus. **Radioactivity** refers to the particles emitted from nuclei as a result of nuclear instability. There are many nuclear isotopes that are unstable and can spontaneously emit some kind of radiation. The most common types of radiation are alpha, beta, and gamma radiation, but there are several other varieties of radioactive decay.

Atomic Models and Theories

There have been many theories regarding the **structure** of atoms and their particles. Part of the challenge in developing an understanding of matter is that atoms and their particles are too small to be seen. It is believed that the first conceptualization of the atom was developed by **Democritus** in 400 B.C. Some of the more notable models are the solid sphere or billiard ball model postulated by **John Dalton**, the plum pudding or raisin bun model by **J.J. Thomson**, the planetary or nuclear model by **Ernest Rutherford**, the Bohr or orbit model by **Niels Bohr**, and the electron cloud or quantum mechanical model by **Louis de Broglie** and **Erwin Schrodinger**. Rutherford directed the alpha scattering experiment that discounted the plum pudding model. The shortcoming of the Bohr model was the belief that electrons orbited in fixed rather than changing ecliptic orbits.

Review Video: Atomic Models
Visit mometrix.com/academy and enter code: 434851

Radioactivity

Radioisotopes: Also known as radionuclides or radioactive isotopes, radioisotopes are atoms that have an unstable nucleus. This is a nucleus that has excess energy and the potential to make radiation particles within the nucleus (subatomic particles) or undergo radioactive decay, which can result in the emission of gamma rays. Radionuclides may occur naturally but can also be artificially produced.

Radioactive decay: This occurs when an unstable atomic nucleus spontaneously loses energy by emitting ionizing particles and radiation. Decay is a form of energy transfer, as energy is lost. It also

Copyright © Mometrix Media. You have been licensed one copy of this document for personal use only. Any other reproduction or redistribution is strictly prohibited. All rights reserved.

results in different products. Before decay there is one type of atom, called the **parent nuclide**. After decay there are one or more different products, called the **daughter nuclide(s)**.

Radioactivity: This refers to particles that are emitted from nuclei as a result of nuclear instability.

Review Video: Radioactivity
Visit mometrix.com/academy and enter code: 537142

Radioactive half-life is the time it takes for half of the radioactive nuclei in a sample to undergo radioactive decay. Radioactive decay rates are usually expressed in terms of half-lives. The different types of radioactivity lead to different decay paths, which transmute the nuclei into other chemical elements. **Decay products** (or daughter nuclides) make radioactive dating possible. **Decay chains** are a series of decays that result in different products. for example, uranium-238 is often found in granite. Its decay chain includes 14 daughter products. It eventually becomes a stable isotope of lead, which is why lead is often found with deposits of uranium ore. Its first half-life is equivalent to the approximate age of the earth, about 4.5 billion years. One of its products is radon, a radioactive gas. **Radiation** is when energy is emitted by one body and absorbed by another. Nuclear weapons, nuclear reactors, and radioactive substances are all examples of things that involve ionizing radiation. Acoustic and electromagnetic radiation are other types of radiation.

Stable isotopes: Isotopes that have not been observed to decay are stable, or non-radioactive, isotopes. It is not known whether some stable isotopes may have such long decay times that observing decay is not possible. Currently, 80 elements have one or more stable isotopes. There are 256 known stable isotopes in total. Carbon, for example, has three isotopes. Two (carbon-12 and carbon-13) are stable and one (carbon-14) is radioactive.

Radioactive isotopes: These have unstable nuclei and can undergo spontaneous nuclear reactions, which results in particles or radiation being emitted. It cannot be predicted when a specific nucleus will decay, but large groups of identical nuclei decay at predictable rates. Knowledge about rates of decay can be used to estimate the age of materials that contain radioactive isotopes.

Ionizing radiation is that which can cause an electron to detach from an atom. It occurs in radioactive reactions and comes in three types: alpha (α), beta (β), and gamma (γ). Alpha rays are positive, beta rays are negative, and gamma rays are neutral. **Alpha particles** are larger than beta particles and can cause severe damage if ingested. Because of their large mass, however, they can be stopped easily. Even paper can protect against this type of radiation. **Beta particles** can be beta-minus or beta-plus. Beta-minus particles contain an energetic electron, while beta-plus particles are emitted by positrons and can result in gamma photons. Beta particles can be stopped with thin metal. **Gamma rays** are a type of high energy electromagnetic radiation consisting of photons. Gamma radiation rids the decaying nucleus of excess energy after it has emitted either alpha or beta radiation. Gamma rays can cause serious damage when absorbed by living tissue, and it takes thick lead to stop them. Alpha, beta, and gamma radiation can also have positive applications.

Nuclear fission and nuclear fusion are similar in that they occur in the nucleus of an atom, can release great amounts of energy, and result in the formation of different elements (known as nuclear transmutation). They are different in that one breaks apart a nucleus and the other joins nuclei. **Nuclear fission** is the splitting of a large nucleus into smaller pieces. **Nuclear fusion** is the joining of two nuclei, which occurs under extreme temperatures and pressures. Fusion occurs naturally in stars, and is the process responsible for the release of great amounts of energy. When fusion occurs, many atomic nuclei

Copyright © Mometrix Media. You have been licensed one copy of this document for personal use only. Any other reproduction or redistribution is strictly prohibited. All rights reserved.

with like charges are joined together, forming a heavier nucleus. When this occurs, energy can be absorbed and/or released.

> **Review Video: Nuclear Fusion**
> Visit mometrix.com/academy and enter code: 381782

Radioactive waste is a waste product that is considered dangerous because of either low levels or high levels of radioactivity. Radioactive waste could include discarded clothing that was used as protection against radiation or decay products of substances used to create electricity through nuclear fission. Small amounts of radioactive material can be ingested as a method of tracing how the body distributes certain elements. Other radioactive materials are used as light sources because they glow when heated. Uncontrolled radiation or even small amounts of radioactive material can cause sickness and cancer in humans. **Gamma wave radiation** is fast moving radiation that can cause cancer and damage genetic information by crashing into DNA molecules or other cells. Low-level radiation also occurs naturally. When related to everyday occurrences, radiation is measured in millirems per hour (mrem/hr). Humans can be exposed to radiation from stone used to build houses, cosmic rays from space, x-rays and other medical devices, and nuclear energy products.

Electronegativity

Electronegativity is a measure of how capable an atom is of attracting a pair of bonding electrons. It refers to the fact that one atom exerts slightly more force in a bond than another, creating a **dipole**. If the electronegative difference between two atoms is small, the atoms will form a **polar covalent bond**. If the difference is large, the atoms will form an **ionic bond**. When there is no electronegativity, a **pure nonpolar covalent bond** is formed.

Electronegativity can be discussed as a trend in the periodic table. Fluorine (F) has the greatest electronegativity, and elements to the left and below fluorine have lower levels of electronegativity. This property of elements is often measured using the **Pauling scale**, which ranges from 4.0 (fluorine) to 0.7 (francium). Elements with high electronegativity are highly reactive because they can capture electrons. The symbols δ^+ (delta plus) and δ^- (delta minus) stand for fractional charges.

> **Review Video: Electronegativity**
> Visit mometrix.com/academy and enter code: 823348

Electrons

Electrons are subatomic particles that orbit the nucleus at various levels commonly referred to as layers, shells, or clouds. The orbiting electron or electrons account for only a fraction of the atom's mass. They are much smaller than the nucleus, are negatively charged, and exhibit wave-like characteristics. Electrons are part of the **lepton** family of elementary particles. Electrons can occupy orbits that are varying distances away from the nucleus, and tend to occupy the lowest energy level they can. If an atom has all its electrons in the lowest available positions, it has a **stable electron arrangement**. The outermost electron shell of an atom in its uncombined state is known as the **valence shell**. The electrons there are called **valence electrons**, and it is their number that determines bonding behavior. Atoms tend to react in a manner that will allow them to fill or empty their valence shells.

Electrons Shells

Chemical bonds involve a negative-positive attraction between an electron or electrons and the nucleus of an atom or nuclei of more than one atom. The attraction keeps the atom cohesive, but also enables the formation of bonds among other atoms and molecules. Each of the seven energy levels (or shells) of an atom has a maximum number of electrons it can contain. The farther away from the nucleus an electron

Copyright © Mometrix Media. You have been licensed one copy of this document for personal use only. Any other reproduction or redistribution is strictly prohibited. All rights reserved.

is, the more energy it has. The first shell, or K-shell, holds a maximum of 2 electrons; the second, L, holds 8; the third, M, holds 18; the fourth, N, holds 32; the fifth, O, holds 60; the sixth, P, holds 82; the seventh, Q, holds 108. The shells also have subshells. Chemical bonds form and break between atoms when atoms gain, lose, or share an electron in the outer (valence) shell.

Isotopes

The number of **protons** in an atom determines the element of that atom. for instance, all helium atoms have exactly two protons, and all oxygen atoms have exactly eight protons. If two atoms have the same number of protons, then they are the same element. However, the number of **neutrons** in two atoms can be different without the atoms being different elements. **Isotope** is the term used to distinguish between atoms that have the same number of protons but a different number of neutrons. The names of isotopes have the element name with the mass number. Recall that the **mass number** is the number of protons plus the number of neutrons. for example, carbon-12 refers to an atom that has 6 protons, which makes it carbon, and 6 neutrons. In other words, 6 protons + 6 neutrons = 12. Carbon-13 has six protons and seven neutrons, and carbon-14 has six protons and eight neutrons. Isotopes can also be written with the mass number in superscript before the element symbol. for example, carbon-12 can be written as ^{12}C.

Oxidation State and Oxidation Number.

Oxidation state and oxidation number are usually the same number. Even though they have different meanings, they are frequently used interchangeably. **Oxidation numbers** are Roman numerals in parentheses that are used as part of the naming scheme for inorganic compounds. **Oxidation state** refers to the hypothetical charge on an atom if all of its bonds are 100 percent ionic. They are integers that can occasionally be fractional numbers. Oxidation state is increased through oxidation (loss of electrons) and decreased through reduction (gain of electrons). The number for an oxidation state refers to a single atom or ion, and is a way to keep track of electrons. When using **Lewis diagrams**, shared electrons are generally assigned to the more electronegative element. In bonds involving two atoms of the same element, electrons are split between them. Lone pairs of electrons are assigned to the atom they are with.

Cathode Rays

The discovery of **cathode rays** in the late 1800s was basically the discovery of electrons. It was also discovered that electrons carry the negative charge of the atom and that the atom consists of smaller particles. Various scientists used different variations of cathode ray tubes containing no air or varying amounts of air. A cathode ray consists of a cathode, a negative electrode, and an anode, which has a positive charge. Modern cathode ray tubes heat a filament on the cathode end of the tube, which excites the electrons and separates them from their atoms. They travel in straight lines through the tube to the anode and back to the cathode through an electrical wire. The rays are invisible, but early scientists

Copyright © Mometrix Media. You have been licensed one copy of this document for personal use only. Any other reproduction or redistribution is strictly prohibited. All rights reserved.

discovered fluorescence when the walls of the glass glowed when electrons hit them. Cathode rays are also known as **electron beams**.

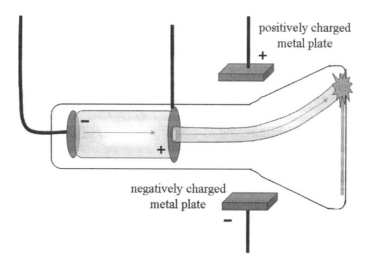

Helium Atom Vs. Hydrogen Atom

In the periodic table of elements, a **period** (also known as a row) is organized in such a way that atomic numbers (which indicate the number of protons) increase from left to right. In a single row, atomic radii decrease from left to right. The number of electrons in the outermost shell generally increases as you go left to right in a row, but varies a bit in the transition metals. In elements with more protons, the electrons are pulled in by the greater nuclear charge and the atoms become smaller because their atomic radii are shorter. Hydrogen and helium are in the same period. The most common isotope of **hydrogen** has one electron and one proton, but no neutron. The most common isotope of **helium** has two electrons, two protons, and two neutrons. The higher number of protons exerts a greater force on the electrons, which is why a helium atom is smaller than a hydrogen atom.

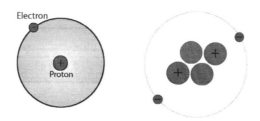

Review Video: Nuclear Charge
Visit mometrix.com/academy and enter code: 412575

Review Video: Order of Electron Filling in the Periodic Table
Visit mometrix.com/academy and enter code: 761477

Spectral Lines

Atomic spectral lines indicate change in the electrical level of an atom. This usually occurs when an electron transitions from one orbit to another. During this process, photons are absorbed or emitted. for example, an **emission line** is formed when an electron transitions to a lower energy level and a photon is emitted. An **absorption line** is formed when an electron transfers to a higher energy level and a photon is absorbed. A **photon** is an elementary particle thought to be the basic unit, or quantum, of light.

Copyright © Mometrix Media. You have been licensed one copy of this document for personal use only. Any other reproduction or redistribution is strictly prohibited. All rights reserved.

When viewed in comparison to a visible spectrum, an emission line is bright and an absorption line is dark. Spectral lines can be used to help identify atoms and determine the chemical composition of a material. Gas is usually used in spectral analysis.

Conservation of Mass Number and Charge

Mass number is the sum of neutrons and protons in the nucleus (A = N + Z). The conservation of mass number is a concept related to nuclear reactions. Two conditions are required to balance a nuclear reaction. They are **conservation of mass number** and **conservation of nuclear charge**. In a nuclear equation, the mass numbers should be equal on each side of the arrow. In this type of equation, the mass number is in superscript in front of the element and the atomic number is in subscript. The total number of nucleons is the same even though the product elements are different. for example, when a specific isotope of uranium decays into thorium and helium, the original mass number of uranium is 238. After the reaction, the mass number of thorium is 234 and the mass number of helium is 4 (238 = 234 + 4). The mass number is the same on both sides of the equation.

Atomic Radius and Ionic Radius

Atomic size is typically measured in Angstroms (A) or picometers, where 1 Angstrom is equal to 10^{-10} of a meter, or 100 picometers (pm). The **atomic radius** of a chemical element refers to the distance from the nucleus to the boundary of an electron cloud or half the distance between two bonded nuclei. It may also refer to an isolated atom, but this can be confusing since atoms can share electrons, electron clouds can overlap, and electrons may be in motion. The trend across a period is for the atomic radius to decrease since as the atomic number (number of protons) increases across a row, electrons tend to be added in the same outermost shell, which increases nuclear charge and contracts the atom. The **ionic radius** is based upon nuclei when the ions are in a crystal lattice, meaning the atoms are organized in a specific manner.

Alpha Decay of Radon

The **alpha decay of radon** (Rn) to polonium (Po), which is part of the uranium-238 decay chain, is a good example of conservation of mass number. Two protons and two neutrons are lost when a nucleus emits an alpha particle, meaning the mass number will be four less and the atomic number (Z), protons, will be 2 less. When the atomic number (Z) and mass number (A) are diagrammed in a formula, the mass number is in superscript in front of the symbol for the element and the atomic number is in subscript. When Rn, with a mass number of 222 and an atomic number of 86, emits an alpha particle, it loses four from its mass number. It becomes polonium, which has a mass number of 218 and an atomic number of 84. Since an alpha particle with two protons and two neutrons is also a result of the reaction, the mass number is **conserved**.

One rule for calculating **oxidation state** is that the oxidation state is 0 for atoms in elemental form (only one kind of atom is present and its charge is 0). for example, both S_8 and Fe have an oxidation state of 0. for a monatomic ion, the oxidation state is equal to its charge. for example, the oxidation state is -2 for S^{2-} and +3 for Al^{3+}. for all Group 1A (alkali) metals, the oxidation state is +1. It is +2 for all Group 2A (alkaline earth) metals unless they are in elemental form. Hydrogen has an oxidation state of +1 when it is bonded to a nonmetal. It can be -1 when bonded to a metal. Oxygen almost always has an oxidation state of -2, but in peroxides it is -1. There are other exceptions as well. The oxidation state for fluorine is always -1. In a neutral compound, the sum of all atoms or ions must equal zero. In a polyatomic ion, its charge is equal to the sum of all oxidation state numbers.

Important Terminology

Nuclide: A nuclide is a more inclusive term than isotope. Generally, the term nuclide refers to all the atomic nuclei containing a specified number of protons and neutrons, while isotopes are forms of a

Copyright © Mometrix Media. You have been licensed one copy of this document for personal use only. Any other reproduction or redistribution is strictly prohibited. All rights reserved.

particular atom that vary in terms of the number of protons and neutrons. In other words, all the isotopes of all the elements are nuclides.

Isotone: This refers to nuclides that have the same number of neutrons but a different number of protons. for example, carbon-14, nitrogen-15, and oxygen-16 all have eight neutrons in the nucleus. Therefore, they are all isotones of each other.

Isobar: This refers to nuclides that have the same mass number (the same number of nucleons) but differing numbers of protons and neutrons. In other words, isobars have the same total number of protons and neutrons (collectively known as the nucleon) but different numbers of each. for example, the isotopes argon-40 (which has 18 protons and 22 neutrons) and calcium-40 (which has 20 protons and 20 neutrons) are isobars.

Nuclear isomers: Atomic nuclei are long-lived, have an equal number of protons and neutrons, and differ in energy content. Nuclear isomers are excited states of atomic nuclei. Nuclear isomers are different from chemical isomers.

> **Review Video: Basics of Isomers**
> Visit mometrix.com/academy and enter code: 809623

Allotropes: Allotropes are different structures of an element. Atoms of some elements have the ability to bond to each other in more than one way. This enables an element to have multiple arrangements of atoms, which are known as allotropes. Easily recognizable allotropes of carbon are the diamond and graphite. The carbon atoms of a diamond are bonded in a tetrahedral structure. In graphite, carbon atoms are bonded in hexagonal sheets.

> **Review Video: Allotropes**
> Visit mometrix.com/academy and enter code: 259488

Quarks: Quarks are considered basic particles and fundamental components of matter. Various flavors of quarks combine to form hadrons, such as the protons and neutrons of atomic nuclei. The six flavors of quarks are up, down, charm, strange, top, and bottom.

Periodic Table

The **periodic table** groups elements with similar chemical properties together. The grouping of elements is based on **atomic structure**. It shows periodic trends of physical and chemical properties and identifies families of elements with similar properties. It is a common model for organizing and understanding elements. In the periodic table, each element has its own cell that includes varying amounts of information presented in symbol form about the properties of the element. Cells in the table are arranged in **rows** (periods) and **columns** (groups or families). A cell includes the symbol for the element and its atomic number. The cell for hydrogen, which appears first in the upper left corner, includes an "H" and a "1" above the letter. Elements are ordered by **atomic number**, left to right, top to bottom.

In the periodic table, the columns numbered 1 through 18 group elements with similar **outer electron shell configurations**. Since the configuration of the outer electron shell is one of the primary factors affecting an element's chemical properties, elements within the same group have similar chemical properties. Previous naming conventions for groups have included the use of Roman numerals and uppercase letters. Currently, the periodic table groups are: Group 1, alkali metals; Group 2, alkaline

Copyright © Mometrix Media. You have been licensed one copy of this document for personal use only. Any other reproduction or redistribution is strictly prohibited. All rights reserved.

earth metals; Groups 3-12, transition metals; Group 13, boron family; Group 14, carbon family; Group 15, pnictogens; Group 16, chalcogens; Group 17, halogens; Group 18, noble gases.

Review Video: Periodic Table
Visit mometrix.com/academy and enter code: 154828

Review Video: Metals in the Periodic Table
Visit mometrix.com/academy and enter code: 506502

Review Video: Noble Gases
Visit mometrix.com/academy and enter code: 122067

In the periodic table, there are seven **periods** (rows), and within each period there are **blocks** that group elements with the same outer electron subshell. The number of electrons in that outer shell determines which group an element belongs to within a given block. Each row's number (1, 2, 3, etc.) corresponds to the highest number electron shell that is in use. For example, row 2 uses only electron shells 1 and 2, while row 7 uses all shells from 1-7.

Atomic radii will decrease from left to right across a period (row) on the periodic table. In a group (column), there is an increase in the atomic radii of elements from top to bottom. Ionic radii will be smaller than the atomic radii for metals, but the opposite is true for non-metals. From left to right, **electronegativity**, or an atom's likeliness of taking another atom's electrons, increases. In a group, electronegativity decreases from top to bottom. **Ionization energy** or the amount of energy needed to get rid of an atom's outermost electron, increases across a period and decreases down a group. **Electron affinity** will become more negative across a period but will not change much within a group. The **melting point** decreases from top to bottom in the metal groups and increases from top to bottom in the non-metal groups.

Group→	1	2	3	4	5	6	7	8	9	10	11	12	13	14	15	16	17	18
↓Period																		
1	1 H																	2 He
2	3 Li	4 Be											5 B	6 C	7 N	8 O	9 F	10 Ne
3	11 Na	12 Mg											13 Al	14 Si	15 P	16 S	17 Cl	18 Ar
4	19 K	20 Ca	21 Sc	22 Ti	23 V	24 Cr	25 Mn	26 Fe	27 Co	28 Ni	29 Cu	30 Zn	31 Ga	32 Ge	33 As	34 Se	35 Br	36 Kr
5	37 Rb	38 Sr	39 Y	40 Zr	41 Nb	42 Mo	43 Tc	44 Ru	45 Rh	46 Pd	47 Ag	48 Cd	49 In	50 Sn	51 Sb	52 Te	53 I	54 Xe
6	55 Cs	56 Ba	*	72 Hf	73 Ta	74 W	75 Re	76 Os	77 Ir	78 Pt	79 Au	80 Hg	81 Tl	82 Pb	83 Bi	84 Po	85 At	86 Rn
7	87 Fr	88 Ra	**	104 Rf	105 Db	106 Sg	107 Bh	108 Hs	109 Mt	110 Ds	111 Rg	112 Cn	113 Uut	114 Fl	115 Uup	116 Lv	117 Uus	118 Uuo

*	57 La	58 Ce	59 Pr	60 Nd	61 Pm	62 Sm	63 Eu	64 Gd	65 Tb	66 Dy	67 Ho	68 Er	69 Tm	70 Yb	71 Lu
**	89 Ac	90 Th	91 Pa	92 U	93 Np	94 Pu	95 Am	96 Cm	97 Bk	98 Cf	99 Es	100 Fm	101 Md	102 No	103 Lr

Molar Mass, Charles's Law, and Boyle's Law

- **Molar mass**: This refers to the mass of one mole of a substance (element or compound), usually measured in grams per mole (g/mol). This differs from molecular mass in that molecular mass is the mass of one molecule of a substance relative to the atomic mass unit (amu).
- **Charles's law**: This states that gases expand when they are heated. It is also known as the law of volumes.

Copyright © Mometrix Media. You have been licensed one copy of this document for personal use only. Any other reproduction or redistribution is strictly prohibited. All rights reserved.

- **Boyle's law**: This states that gases contract when pressure is applied to them. It also states that if temperature remains constant, the relationship between absolute pressure and volume is inversely proportional. When one increases, the other decreases. Considered a specialized case of the ideal gas law, Boyle's law is sometimes known as the Boyle-Mariotte law.

Kinetic Theory of Gases

The **kinetic theory of gases** assumes that gas molecules are small compared to the distances between them and that they are in constant random motion. The attractive and repulsive forces between gas molecules are negligible. Their kinetic energy does not change with time as long as the temperature remains the same. The higher the temperature is, the greater the motion will be. As the temperature of a gas increases, so does the kinetic energy of the molecules. In other words, gas will occupy a greater volume as the temperature is increased and a lesser volume as the temperature is decreased. In addition, the same amount of gas will occupy a greater volume as the temperature increases, but pressure remains constant. At any given temperature, gas molecules have the same average kinetic energy.

Ideal Gas Law

The **ideal gas law** is used to explain the properties of a gas under ideal pressure, volume, and temperature conditions. It is best suited for describing monatomic gases (gases in which atoms are not bound together) and gases at high temperatures and low pressures. It is not well-suited for instances in which a gas or its components are close to their condensation point. All collisions are perfectly elastic and there are no intermolecular attractive forces at work. The ideal gas law is a way to explain and measure the macroscopic properties of matter. It can be derived from the kinetic theory of gases, which deals with the microscopic properties of matter. The equation for the ideal gas law is **PV = nRT**, where P is absolute **pressure**, V is absolute **volume**, and T is absolute **temperature**. R refers to the **universal gas constant**, which is 8.3145 J/mol Kelvin, and n is the number of **moles**.

Review Video: Ideal Gas Law
Visit mometrix.com/academy and enter code: 381353

Review Video: Ideal Gas vs Real Gas
Visit mometrix.com/academy and enter code: 619477

Copyright © Mometrix Media. You have been licensed one copy of this document for personal use only. Any other reproduction or redistribution is strictly prohibited. All rights reserved.

Earth Science

Astronomy

Astronomy is the scientific study of celestial objects and their positions, movements, and structures. **Celestial** does not refer to the Earth in particular, but does include its motions as it moves through space. Other objects include the Sun, the Moon, planets, satellites, asteroids, meteors, comets, stars, galaxies, the universe, and other space phenomena. The term astronomy has its roots in the Greek words "astro" and "nomos," which means "laws of the stars."

> **Review Video: Astronomy**
> Visit mometrix.com/academy and enter code: 640556

The Sun

The **Sun** is at the center of the solar system. It is composed of 70% hydrogen (H) and 28% helium (He). The remaining 2% is made up of metals. The Sun is one of 100 billion stars in the **Milky Way galaxy**. Its diameter is 1,390,000 km, its mass is 1.989×10^{30} kg, its surface temperature is 5,800 K, and its core temperature is 15,600,000 K. The Sun represents more than 99.8% of the total mass of the solar system. At the core, the temperature is 15.6 million K, the pressure is 250 billion atmospheres, and the density is more than 150 times that of water. The surface is called the **photosphere**. The **chromosphere** lies above this, and the **corona**, which extends millions of kilometers into space, is next. **Sunspots** are relatively cool regions on the surface with a temperature of 3,800 K. Temperatures in the corona are over 1,000,000 K. Its **magnetosphere**, or heliosphere, extends far beyond Pluto.

> **Review Video: The Sun**
> Visit mometrix.com/academy and enter code: 699233

The Moon

The **Moon** is the fifth largest satellite in the solar system. It orbits the Earth about every 27.3 days. The changes of the Earth, Sun, and Moon in relation to each other cause the **phases** of the Moon, which repeat every 29.5 days. The Moon's **gravitational pull** (along with the Sun's) is responsible for the tides on Earth. Its diameter is about 3,474 km and its gravity is about 17% of Earth's. The **lunar maria** (plural of mare) on the Moon's surface is dark thin layers composed of dark basalt. They were formed by ancient volcanoes. There are many impact craters on the Moon. There were numerous impact craters on Earth at one time, but they have been transformed by erosion over time. Very few are still visible.

Equinox, Solstice, Perihelion, and Aphelion

- **Equinox:** This occurs twice each year when the Sun crosses the plane of the Earth's celestial equator. During an equinox, Earth is not tilted away from or toward the Sun. The length of day and night are roughly equal. The two equinoxes are the **March equinox** and the **September equinox**.
- **Solstice:** The **summer solstice**, the day with the most amount of sunlight, occurs on June 21st in the Northern Hemisphere and on December 21st in the Southern Hemisphere. The **winter solstice**, the day with the least amount of sunlight, occurs on December 21st in the Northern Hemisphere and on June 21st in the Southern Hemisphere.
- **Perihelion:** This is the point in an object's orbit when it is closest to the Sun.
- **Aphelion:** This is the point in an object's orbit when it is farthest from the Sun.

Copyright © Mometrix Media. You have been licensed one copy of this document for personal use only. Any other reproduction or redistribution is strictly prohibited. All rights reserved.

Origin of the Universe

The **Big Bang theory**, which is widely accepted among astronomers, was developed to explain the origin of the universe. The Big Bang theory states that all the matter in the universe was once in one place. This matter underwent a huge explosion that spread the matter into space. Galaxies formed from this material and the universe is still expanding. There are other theories regarding the origin of the universe, such as the **Steady-State theory** and the **Intelligent Design theory**.

Structure of the Universe

What can be seen of the universe is believed to be at least 93 billion light years across. To put this into perspective, the Milky Way galaxy is about 100,000 light years across. Our view of matter in the universe is that it forms into clumps. Matter is organized into stars, galaxies, clusters of galaxies, superclusters, and the Great Wall of galaxies. Galaxies consist of stars, some with planetary systems. Some estimates state that the universe is about 13 billion years old. It is not considered dense, and is believed to consist of 73 percent dark energy, 23 percent cold dark matter, and 4 percent regular matter. Cosmology is the study of the universe. Interstellar medium (ISM) is the gas and dust in the interstellar space between a galaxy's stars.

Life Cycle of a Star

There are different life cycle possibilities for **stars** after they initially form and enter into the main sequence stage. Small, relatively cold **red dwarfs** with relatively low masses burn hydrogen slowly, and will remain in the main sequence for hundreds of billions of years. Massive, hot **supergiants** will leave the main sequence after just a few million years. The Sun is a mid-sized star that may be in the **main sequence** for 10 billion years. After the main sequence, the star expands to become a **red giant**. Depending upon the initial mass of the star, it can become a **white dwarf** (from a medium-sized star), and then a small, cooling **black dwarf**. Massive stars become **red supergiants** (and sometimes **blue supergiants**), explode in a supernova, and then become **neutron stars.** The largest stars can become **black holes**.

> **Review Video: Types of Stars**
> Visit mometrix.com/academy and enter code: 831934

Birth of a Star

A **nebula** is a cloud of dust and gas that is composed primarily of hydrogen (97%) and helium (3%). Gravity causes parts of the nebula to clump together. This accretion continues adding atoms to the center of an unstable **protostar**. Equilibrium between gravity pulling atoms and gas pressure pushing heat and light away from the center is achieved. A star dies when it is no longer able to maintain equilibrium. A protostar may never become a star if it does not reach a critical core temperature. It may become a **brown dwarf** or a **gas giant** instead. If nuclear fusion of hydrogen into helium begins, a star is born. The "main sequence" of a star's life involves nuclear fusion reactions. During this time, the star contracts over billions of years to compensate for the heat and light energy lost. In the star's core, temperature, density, and pressure increase as the star contracts and the cycle continues.

Black Holes, Quasars, and Blazars

- A **black hole** is a space where the gravitational field is so powerful that everything, including light, is pulled into it. Once objects enter the surface, the event horizon, they cannot escape.
- **Quasar** stands for quasi-stellar radio source, which is an energetic galaxy with an active galactic nucleus. Quasars were first identified by their emissions of large amounts of electromagnetic energy, such as radio waves and visible light. These emissions differed from those associated with other galaxies.

Copyright © Mometrix Media. You have been licensed one copy of this document for personal use only. Any other reproduction or redistribution is strictly prohibited. All rights reserved.

- A **blazar** is a compact quasar associated with galaxies containing supermassive black holes.
- Although its existence has not yet been proven, **dark matter** may account for a large proportion of the mass of the universe. It is undetectable because it does not emit any radiation, but is believed to exist because of gravitational forces exerted on visible objects.

Galaxies

Galaxies consist of stars, stellar remnants, and dark matter. **Dwarf galaxies** contain as few as 10 million stars, while **giant galaxies** contain as many as 1 trillion stars. Galaxies are gravitationally bound, meaning the stars, star systems, other gases, and dust orbit the galaxy's center. The Earth exists in the **Milky Way galaxy** and the nearest galaxy to ours is the **Andromeda galaxy**. Galaxies can be classified by their visual shape into elliptical, spiral, irregular, and starburst galaxies. It is estimated that there are more than 100 billion galaxies in the universe ranging from 1,000 to 100,000 parsecs in diameter. Galaxies can be megaparsecs apart. **Intergalactic space** consists of a gas with an average density of less than one atom per cubic meter. Galaxies are organized into clusters which form superclusters. **Dark matter** may account for up to 90% of the mass of galaxies. Dark matter is still not well understood.

> **Review Video: Galaxies**
> Visit mometrix.com/academy and enter code: 226539
>
> **Review Video: Milky Way**
> Visit mometrix.com/academy and enter code: 445889

Sidereal and Solar Days

A **sidereal day** is four minutes shorter than a solar day. A **solar day** is the time it takes the Earth to complete one revolution and face the Sun again. From noon to noon is 24 hours. A sidereal day is measured against a distant "fixed" star. As the Earth completes one rotation, it has also completed part of its revolution around the Sun, so it completes a sidereal rotation in reference to the fixed star before it completes a solar rotation. The Sun travels along the ecliptic in 365.25 days. This can be tracked day after day before dawn. After one year, the stars appear back in their original positions. As a result, different constellations are viewable at different times of the year.

Sidereal years are slightly longer than **tropical years**. The difference is caused by the precession of the equinoxes. A calendar based on the sidereal year will be out of sync with the seasons at a rate of about one day every 71 years.

Astronomical Unit, Light Years, and Parsecs

An **astronomical unit**, also known as **AU**, is a widely used measurement in astronomy. One AU is equal to the distance from the Earth to the Sun, which is 150 million km, or 93 million miles. These distances can also be expressed as 149.60×10^9 m or 92.956×10^6 mi. A **light year (ly)** is the distance that light travels in a vacuum in one year. A light year is equal to about 10 trillion km, or 64,341 AU, and is used to measure large astronomical units. Also used for measuring large distances is the **parsec (pc)**, which is the preferred unit since it is better suited for recording observational data. A parsec is the parallax of one arcsecond, and is about 31 trillion km (about 19 trillion miles), or about 3.26 light years. It is used to calculate distances by triangulation. The AU distance from the Earth to the Sun is used to form the side of a right triangle.

> **Review Video: Measures of Distance used in Astronomy**
> Visit mometrix.com/academy and enter code: 961792

Copyright © Mometrix Media. You have been licensed one copy of this document for personal use only. Any other reproduction or redistribution is strictly prohibited. All rights reserved.

Hertzsprung-Russell Diagram

A **Hertzsprung-Russell diagram (H-R diagram or HRD)** is a plot or scattergraph depicting stars' temperatures and comparing them with stars' luminosities or magnitudes. This can help determine the age and evolutionary state of a star. A Hertzsprung-Russell diagram is also known as a **color-magnitude diagram (CMD)**. It helps represent the life cycles of stars. In these plots, temperatures are plotted from highest to lowest, which aids in the comparison of H-R diagrams and observations. Hertzsprung-Russell diagrams can have many variations. Most of the stars in these diagrams lie along the line called **main sequence**, which contains stars that are fusing hydrogen. Other groupings include white dwarfs, subgiants, giants, and supergiants.

Morgan-Keenan Classification System

Stars use the **Morgan-Keenan classification system**, which is based on spectral traits that indicate the ionization of the chromosphere. The following letter designations are used to indicate **temperature**, from hottest to coolest: O, B, A, F, G, K, and M. The phrase "Oh, be a fine girl/guy, kiss me" can be used as a memory aid. Different types of stars also have different corresponding colors. O stars are blue; A stars are white; G stars are yellow; and M stars are red. The numbers 0 to 9 are used to indicate tenths between two star classes. Zero indicates 0/10 and 9 indicates 9/10. **Luminosity output** is an indicator of size, and is expressed with the Roman numerals I, II, III, IV, and V. Supergiants are included in class I, giants are included in class III, and main sequence stars are included in class V. Using the Sun as an example, the spectral type G2V could be expressed as "a yellow two-tenths towards an orange main sequence star."

Solar Systems

The **solar system** is a planetary system of objects that exist in an ecliptic plane. Objects orbit around and are bound by gravity to a star called the **Sun**. Objects that orbit around the Sun include: planets, dwarf planets, moons, asteroids, meteoroids, cosmic dust, and comets. The definition of planets has changed. At one time, there were nine planets in the solar system. There are now eight. Planetary objects in the solar system include four inner, **terrestrial planets**: Mercury, Venus, Earth, and Mars. They are relatively small, dense, rocky, lack rings, and have few or no moons. The four outer, or **Jovian, planets** are Jupiter, Saturn, Uranus, and Neptune, which are large and have low densities, rings, and moons. They are also known as **gas giants**. Between the inner and outer planets is the **asteroid belt**. Beyond Neptune is the **Kuiper belt**. Within these belts are five **dwarf planets**: Ceres, Pluto, Haumea, Makemake, and Eris.

The theory of how the solar system was created is that it started with the collapse of a cloud of interstellar gas and dust, which formed the **solar nebula**. This collapse is believed to have occurred because the cloud was disturbed. As it collapsed, it heated up and compressed at the center, forming a flatter protoplanetary disk with a **protostar** at the center. **Planets** formed as a result of accretion from the disk. Gas cooled and condensed into tiny particles of rock, metal, and ice. These particles collided and formed into larger particles, and then into objects the size of small asteroids. Eventually, some became large enough to have significant gravity.

> **Review Video: Solar System**
> Visit mometrix.com/academy and enter code: 273231

Sizes of the Earth, Sun, and Moon

The **Earth** is about 12,765 km (7,934 miles) in diameter. The **Moon** is about 3,476 km (2,160 mi) in diameter. The distance between the Earth and the Moon is about 384,401 km (238,910 mi). The diameter of the Sun is approximately 1,390,000 km (866,000 mi). The distance from the Earth to the Sun

Copyright © Mometrix Media. You have been licensed one copy of this document for personal use only. Any other reproduction or redistribution is strictly prohibited. All rights reserved.

is 149,598,000 km, also known as 1 **Astronomical Unit (AU)**. The star that is nearest to the solar system is **Proxima Centauri**. It is about 270,000 AU away.

Solar Energy

The Sun's energy is produced by **nuclear fusion reactions**. Each second, about 700,000,000 tons of hydrogen are converted (or fused) to about 695,000,000 tons of helium and 5,000,000 tons of energy in the form of gamma rays. In nuclear fusion, four hydrogen nuclei are fused into one helium nucleus, resulting in the release of energy. In the Sun, the energy proceeds towards the surface and is absorbed and re-emitted at lower and lower temperatures. Energy is mostly in the form of visible light when it reaches the surface. It is estimated that the Sun has used up about half of the hydrogen at its core since its birth. It is expected to radiate in this fashion for another 5 billion years. Eventually, it will deplete its hydrogen fuel, grow brighter, expand to about 260 times its diameter, and become a red giant. The outer layers will ablate and become a dense white dwarf the size of the Earth.

Four Innermost Planets

- **Mercury**: Mercury is the closest to the Sun and is also the smallest planet. It orbits the Sun every 88 days, has no satellites or atmosphere, has a Moon-like surface with craters, appears bright, and is dense and rocky with a large iron core.
- **Venus**: Venus is the second planet from the Sun. It orbits the Sun every 225 days, is very bright, and is similar to Earth in size, gravity, and bulk composition. It has a dense atmosphere composed of carbon dioxide and some sulfur. It is covered with reflective clouds made of sulfuric acid and exhibits signs of volcanism. Lightning and thunder have been recorded on Venus's surface.
- **Earth**: Earth is the third planet from the Sun. It orbits the Sun every 365 days. Approximately 71% of its surface is salt-water oceans. The Earth is rocky, has an atmosphere composed mainly of oxygen and nitrogen, has one moon, and supports millions of species. It contains the only known life in the solar system.
- **Mars**: Mars it the fourth planet from the Sun. It appears reddish due to iron oxide on the surface, has a thin atmosphere, has a rotational period similar to Earth's, and has seasonal cycles. Surface features of Mars include volcanoes, valleys, deserts, and polar ice caps. Mars has impact craters and the tallest mountain, largest canyon, and perhaps the largest impact crater yet discovered.

> **Review Video: The Inner Planets of Our Solar System**
> Visit mometrix.com/academy and enter code: 103427

Asteroid Belt, Kuiper Belt, and Oort Cloud

The **asteroid belt** is between Mars and Jupiter. The many objects contained within are composed of rock and metal similar to those found on the terrestrial planets.

The **Kuiper Belt** is beyond Neptune's orbit, but the influence of the gas giants may cause objects from the Kuiper Belt to cross Neptune's orbit. Objects in the Kuiper Belt are still being discovered. They are thought to be composed of the frozen forms of water, ammonia, and methane, and may be the source of short-period comets. It is estimated that there are 35,000 Kuiper Belt objects greater than 100 km in diameter and perhaps 100 million objects about 20 km in diameter.

There is also a hypothetical **Oort Cloud** that may exist far beyond the Kuiper Belt and act as a source for long-period comets.

> **Review Video: Asteroid Belt, Kuiper Belt, and Oort Cloud**
> Visit mometrix.com/academy and enter code: 208584

Copyright © Mometrix Media. You have been licensed one copy of this document for personal use only. Any other reproduction or redistribution is strictly prohibited. All rights reserved.

Four Outermost Planets

- **Jupiter**: Jupiter is the fifth planet from the Sun and the largest planet in the solar system. It consists mainly of hydrogen, and 25% of its mass is made up of helium. It has a fast rotation and has clouds in the tropopause composed of ammonia crystals that are arranged into bands sub-divided into lighter-hued zones and darker belts causing storms and turbulence. Jupiter has wind speeds of 100 m/s, a planetary ring, 63 moons, and a **Great Red Spot**, which is an anticyclonic storm.
- **Saturn**: Saturn is the sixth planet from the Sun and the second largest planet in the solar system. It is composed of hydrogen, some helium, and trace elements. Saturn has a small core of rock and ice, a thick layer of metallic hydrogen, a gaseous outer layer, wind speeds of up to 1,800 km/h, a system of rings, and 61 moons.
- **Uranus**: Uranus is the seventh planet from the Sun. Its atmosphere is composed mainly of hydrogen and helium and also contains water, ammonia, methane, and traces of hydrocarbons. With a minimum temperature of 49 K, Uranus has the coldest atmosphere. Uranus has a ring system, a magnetosphere, and 13 moons.
- **Neptune**: Neptune is the eighth planet from the Sun and is the planet with the third largest mass. It has 12 moons, an atmosphere similar to Uranus, a **Great Dark Spot**, and the strongest sustained winds of any planet (wind speeds can be as high as 2,100 km/h). Neptune is cold (about 55 K) and has a fragmented ring system.

> **Review Video: The Outer Planets of Our Solar System**
> Visit mometrix.com/academy and enter code: 683995

Phases of the Moon

It takes about one month for the Moon to go through all its phases. **Waxing** refers to the two weeks during which the Moon goes from a new moon to a full moon. About two weeks is spent **waning**, going from a full moon to a new moon. The lit part of the Moon always faces the Sun. The **phases of waxing** are: new moon, during which the Moon is not illuminated and rises and sets with the Sun; crescent moon, during which a tiny sliver is lit; first quarter, during which half the Moon is lit and the phase of the Moon is due south on the meridian; gibbous, during which more than half of the Moon is lit and has a shape similar to a football; right side, during which the Moon is lit; and full moon, during which the Moon is fully illuminated, rises at sunset, and sets at sunrise. After a full moon, the Moon is waning. The **phases of waning** are: gibbous, during which the left side is lit and the Moon rises after sunset and sets after sunrise; third quarter, during which the Moon is half lit and rises at midnight and sets at noon; crescent, during which a tiny sliver is lit; and new moon, during which the Moon is not illuminated and rises and sets with the Sun.

Earth-Moon-Sun System

The **Earth-Moon-Sun system** is responsible for **eclipses**. From Earth, the Sun and the Moon appear to be about the same size. An **eclipse of the Sun** occurs during a new Moon, when the side of the Moon facing the Earth is not illuminated. The Moon passes in front of the Sun and blocks its view from Earth. Eclipses do not occur every month because the orbit of the Moon is at about a 5° angle to the plane of Earth's orbit. An **eclipse of the Moon** happens during the full Moon phase. The Moon passes through the shadow of the Earth and blocks sunlight from reaching it, which temporarily causes darkness. During a lunar eclipse, there are two parts to the shadow. The **umbra** is the dark, inner region. The sun is completely blocked in this area. The **penumbra** is a partially lighted area around the umbra. Earth's shadow is four times longer than the Moon's shadow.

> **Review Video: Lunar Eclipse**
> Visit mometrix.com/academy and enter code: 908819

Copyright © Mometrix Media. You have been licensed one copy of this document for personal use only. Any other reproduction or redistribution is strictly prohibited. All rights reserved.

Meteoroids

A **meteoroid** is the name for a rock from space before it enters the Earth's atmosphere. Most meteoroids burn up in the atmosphere before reaching altitudes of 80 km. A **meteor** is the streak of light from a meteoroid in the Earth's atmosphere, and is also known as a shooting star. Meteor showers are associated with comets, happen when the Earth passes through the debris of a comet, and are associated with a higher than normal number of meteors. **Meteorites** are rocks that reach the Earth's surface from space. **Fireballs** are very bright meteors with trails that can last as long as 30 minutes. A **bolide** is a fireball that burns up when it enters Earth's atmosphere. There are many types of meteorites, and they are known to be composed of various materials. Iron meteorites consist of iron and nickel with a criss-cross, or Widmanstatten, internal metallic crystalline structure. Stony iron meteorites are composed of iron, nickel, and silicate materials. Stony meteorites consist mainly of silicate and also contain iron and nickel.

> **Review Video:** Meteoroids, Meteors, and Meteorites
> Visit mometrix.com/academy and enter code: 454866

Comets

A **comet** consists of frozen gases and rocky, metallic materials. Comets are usually small and typically have long tails. A comet's tail is made of ionized gases. It points away from the Sun and follows the comet as it approaches the Sun. The tail precedes the head as the comet moves away from the Sun. It is believed that as many as 100 billion comets exist. About 12 new ones are discovered each year. Their orbits are elliptical, not round. Some scientists theorize that short-period comets originate from the **Kuiper Belt** and long-period comets originate from the **Oort Cloud**, which is thought to be 100,000 AU away. Comets orbit the Sun in time periods varying from a few years to hundreds of thousands of years. A well-known comet, **Halley's Comet**, has an orbit of 76 years. It is 80 percent water, and consists of frozen water, carbon dioxide (dry ice), ammonia, and methane.

Natural Satellites

There are about 335 **moons**, or **satellites**, that orbit the planets and objects in the solar system. Many of these satellites have been recently discovered, a few are theoretical, some are asteroid moons (moons orbiting asteroids), some are moonlets (small moons), and some are moons of dwarf planets and objects that have not been definitively categorized, such as trans-Neptunian objects. Mercury and Venus do not have any moons. There are several moons larger than the dwarf planet Pluto and two larger than Mercury. Some consider the Earth and Moon a pair of double planets rather than a planet and a satellite. Some satellites may have started out as asteroids. They were eventually captured by a planet's gravity and became moons.

Types of Orbit

A **geosynchronous orbit** around the Earth has an orbital period matching the Earth's sidereal rotation period. **Sidereal rotation** is based on the position of a fixed star, not the Sun, so a sidereal day is slightly shorter than a 24-hour solar day. A satellite in a geosynchronous orbit appears in the same place in the sky at the same time each day. Technically, any object with an orbit time period equal to the Earth's rotational period is geosynchronous. A **geostationary orbit** is a geosynchronous orbit that is circular and at zero inclination, which means the object is located directly above the equator. Geostationary orbits are useful for communications satellites because they are fixed in the same spot relative to the Earth. A **semisynchronous orbit** has an orbital period of half a sidereal day.

Copyright © Mometrix Media. You have been licensed one copy of this document for personal use only. Any other reproduction or redistribution is strictly prohibited. All rights reserved.

Piloted Space Missions

The Soviet space program successfully completed the first space flight by orbiting **Yuri Gagarin** in 1961 on Vostok 1. His orbit lasted 1 hour, 48 minutes. Later in 1961, the U.S. completed its first piloted space flight by launching **Alan Shepard** into space in the Mercury-Redstone 3. This space mission was suborbital. The first woman in space was **Valentina Tereshkova**, who orbited the Earth 48 times aboard Vostok 6 in 1963. The first space flight with more than one person and also the first that didn't involve space suits took place on the Voskhod in 1964. The first person on the Moon was American **Neil Armstrong**. In 1969, he traveled to the Moon on Apollo 11, which was the 11th manned space flight completed in the Apollo program, which was conducted from 1968 to 1972. In 2003, **Yang Liwei** became the first person from China to go into space. He traveled onboard the Shenzhou 5. The **Space Shuttle Orbiter** has included piloted space shuttles from 1981 until the present. The program was suspended after two space shuttle disasters: **Challenger** in 1986 and **Columbia** in 2003.

Noteworthy Satellites

The first satellite to orbit the Earth was the Soviet Union's **Sputnik 1** in 1957. Its two radio transmitters emitted beeps that were received by radios around the world. Analysis of the radio signals was used to gather information about the electron density of the ionosphere. Soviet success escalated the American space program. In 1958, the U.S. put **Explorer 1** into orbit. The **Osumi** was the first Japanese satellite, which was put into orbit in 1970. The **Vanguard 1** is the satellite that has orbited the Earth the longest. It was put into orbit in 1958 and was still in orbit in October 2016. The **Mir Space Station** orbited Earth for 11 years, and was assembled in space starting in 1986. It was almost continuously occupied until 1999. The **International Space Station** began being assembled in orbit in 1998. At 43,000 cubic feet, it is the largest manned object sent into space. It circles the Earth every 90 minutes.

Limitations of Space Exploration

There are many limitations of space exploration. The main limitation is **knowledge**. Space exploration is currently time-consuming, dangerous, and costly. Manned and unmanned missions, even within the solar system, take years of planning and years to complete. The associated **financial costs** are great. **Technological advances** are needed before interstellar and intergalactic missions can be carried out. By some estimates, it would take more than 70 years to travel to Proxima Centauri (the nearest star) using the fastest rocket technology available. It would take much longer using less advanced technologies. Space travel is **dangerous** for many reasons. Rocket fuel is highly explosive. Non-Earth environments are uninhabitable for humans. Finally, astronauts are exposed to larger than usual amounts of radiation.

Unpiloted Space Missions

The first artificial object to reach another space object was **Luna 2**. It crashed on the Moon in 1959. The first automatic landing was by **Luna 9**. It landed on the Moon in 1966. **Mariner 2**'s flyby of Venus in 1962 was the first successful interplanetary flyby. **Venera 7** landing on and transmitting data from Venus was the first interplanetary surface landing, which took place in 1970. The first soft landing on Mars was in 1971. Unpiloted spacecraft have also made successful soft landings on the asteroids Eros and Itokawa, as well as Titan, a moon of Saturn. The first flyby of Jupiter was in 1973 by **Pioneer 10**. Pioneer 10 was also the first craft of its kind to leave the solar system. The first flyby of Mercury was in 1974 by **Mariner**. The first flyby of Saturn was in 1979 by **Pioneer 11**. The first flyby of Uranus was in 1986 by **Voyager 2**, which also flew by Neptune in 1989.

Evidence of Water

Much of the search for life on other planets has centered on the search for **water**. This is because water is a vital resource for life on Earth and could potentially support life on other planets.

45

Copyright © Mometrix Media. You have been licensed one copy of this document for personal use only. Any other reproduction or redistribution is strictly prohibited. All rights reserved.

Scientists have long speculated that water once covered a large portion of the planet **Mars**. The Curiosity Rover recently found evidence of liquid water in the soil of Mars.

Scientists also believe that there may be liquid water beneath the crusts of three of **Jupiter's moons** (Europa, Ganymede, and Callisto) and two of Saturn's moons (Enceladus and Titan). Titan is also thought to have lakes of liquid hydrocarbon.

Radioactive Dating

Radioactive dating, also known as **radiometric dating**, is a technique that can be used to determine the **age** of rocks and even the Earth itself. The process compares the amount of radioactive material in a rock to the amount of material that has "decayed." **Decay** refers to the fact that the nuclide of an element loses subatomic particles over time. The process includes a parent element that undergoes changes to create a daughter element, also known as the decay product. The daughter element can also be unstable and lose particles, creating another daughter element. This is known as a **decay chain**. Decay occurs until all the elements are stable. Three types of dating techniques are radiocarbon dating, potassium-argon dating, and uranium-lead dating. These techniques can be used to date a variety of natural and manmade materials, including archaeological artifacts.

Theory of Mass Extinction

Mass extinction, also known as an **extinction event**, is a decrease in the number of species over a short period of time. While there are many theories as to the causes of mass extinction, it occurs when a relatively large number of species die off or when fewer species evolve than expected. Extinction events are classified as major and minor. It is generally accepted that there have been five **major extinction events** in Earth's history. The five most significant mass extinction events are Ordovician-Silurian, Permian-Triassic, Late Devonian, Triassic-Jurassic, and Cretaceous-Tertiary.

Uniformitarianism, Catastrophism, and Superposition

- **Uniformitarianism**: Also known as gradualism, uniformitarianism is the belief that the forces, processes, and laws that we see today have existed throughout geologic time. It involves the belief that the present is the key to the past, and that relatively slow processes have shaped the geological features of Earth.
- **Catastrophism**: This is the belief that the Earth was shaped by sudden, short-term catastrophic events.
- **Superposition**: In geology, the law of superposition is that underground layers closer to the surface were deposited more recently.

Geologic Time Scale

One year is 365.25 days long. The **International System of Units (SI)** uses the symbol "a" for a standard year or **annum**. The prefixes "M" for **mega** and "G" for **giga** are used to refer to one million and one billion years, respectively. Ma stands for a **megannum** (10^6 years) and Ga stands for a **gigannum** (10^9 years). For example, it can be said that the Earth was formed 4.5 billion years ago, or 4.5 Ga. Use of the abbreviation "mya" for millions of years (ago) is discouraged, but it is still occasionally used. The abbreviation "BP" stands for "before present." The "present" is defined as January 1, 1950, since present changes from year to year. Another abbreviation used is BCE, which stands for "Before the Common Era."

Geologists use the **geologic time scale** when discussing Earth's chronology and the formation of rocks and minerals. Age is calculated in millions of years before the present time. Units of time are often delineated by geologic or paleontologic events. Smaller units of time such as **eras** are distinguished by the abundance and/or extinction of certain plant and animal life. For example, the extinction of the

Copyright © Mometrix Media. You have been licensed one copy of this document for personal use only. Any other reproduction or redistribution is strictly prohibited. All rights reserved.

dinosaurs marks the end of the Mesozoic era and the beginning of the Cenozoic, the present, era. We are in the Holocene epoch. The **supereon** encompasses the greatest amount of time. It is composed of eons. Eons are divided into eras, eras into periods, and periods into epochs. Layers of rock also correspond to periods of time in geochronology. Current theory holds that the Earth was formed 4.5 billion years ago.

History of Time Scale

The first known observations of **stratigraphy** were made by **Aristotle**, who lived before the time of Christ. He observed seashells in ancient rock formations and on the beach, and concluded that the fossilized seashells were similar to current seashells. **Avicenna**, a Persian scholar from the 11th century, also made early advances in the development of stratigraphy with the concept of superposition. **Nicolas Steno**, a Danish scientist from the 17th century, expounded upon this with the belief that layers of rock are piled on top of each other. In the 18th century, **Abraham Werner** categorized rocks from four different periods: the Primary, Secondary, Tertiary, and Quaternary periods. This fell out of use when the belief emerged that rock layers containing the same fossils had been deposited at the same time, and were therefore from the same age. British geologists created the names for many of the time divisions in use today. For example, the Devonian period was named after the county of Devon, and the Permian period was named after Perm, Russia.

Relative and Absolute Time

A **numerical**, or "**absolute**," age is a specific number of years, such as 150 million years ago. A "**relative**" age refers to a time range, such as the Mesozoic era. It is used to determine whether one rock formation is older or younger than another formation. Radioactive dating is a form of **absolute dating** and stratigraphy is a form of **relative dating**. Radioactive dating techniques have provided the most information about the absolute age of rocks and other geological features. Together, geochronologists have created a geologic time scale. **Biostratigraphy** uses plant and animal fossils within rock to determine its relative age.

Paleozoic Era

The **Paleozoic era** began about 542 Ma and lasted until 251 Ma. It is further divided into six periods. The Paleozoic era began after the supercontinent Pannotia started to break up and at the end of a global ice age. By the end of the era, the supercontinent Pangaea had formed. The beginning of the Paleozoic era is marked by **Cambrian Explosion**, a time when there were abundant life forms according to the fossil record. The end of the era is marked by one of the major extinction events, the Permian extinction, during which almost 90 percent of the species living at the time became extinct. Many plant and animal forms appeared on the land and in the sea during this era. It is also when large land plants first appeared in the fossil record. There are many invertebrates found in the fossil record of the Paleozoic era, and fish, amphibians, and reptiles also first appeared in the fossil record during this era. There were also large swamps and forests, some of which were formed into coal deposits that exist today.

Mesozoic Era

The **Mesozoic era** is known as the **Age of the Dinosaurs**. It is also the era during which the dinosaurs became extinct. The fossil record also shows the appearance of mammals and birds. Trees that existed included gymnosperms, which have uncovered seeds and are mostly cone bearing, and angiosperms, which have covered seeds and are flowering plants. The angiosperm group is currently the dominant plant group. It was also during this era that the supercontinent **Pangaea** divided into the continental pieces that exist today. During the **Cretaceous period**, sea levels rose until one-third of the Earth's present land mass was underwater, and then receded. This period created huge marine deposits and chalk. The extinction of the dinosaurs occurred about 65 Ma, and was believed to have been triggered by the impact of an asteroid.

47

Copyright © Mometrix Media. You have been licensed one copy of this document for personal use only. Any other reproduction or redistribution is strictly prohibited. All rights reserved.

Cenozoic Era

The **Cenozoic era** began about 65.5 Ma and continues to the present. It is marked by the **Cretaceous-Tertiary extinction event** (extinction of the dinosaurs as well as many invertebrates and plants). The Cenozoic era is further divided into the Paleogene, Neogene, and Quaternary periods. During the Cenozoic era, Pangaea continued to drift, and the plates eventually moved into their present positions. The **Pleistocene Ice Age**, also known as Quaternary glaciation or the current ice age began about 2.58 Ma and includes the glaciation occurring today. Mammals continued to evolve and other plants and animals came into existence during this era. The fossil record includes the ancestors of the horse, rhinoceros, and camel. It also includes the first dogs and cats and the first humanlike creatures. The first humans appeared less than 200,000 years ago.

Stratigraphy

Stratigraphy is a branch of geology that involves the study of rock layers and layering. **Sedimentary rocks** are the primary focus of stratigraphy. Subfields include **lithostratigraphy**, which is the study of the vertical layering of rock types, and **biostratigraphy**, which is the study of fossil evidence in rock layers. **Magnetostratigraphy** is the study of changes in detrital remnant magnetism (DRM), which is used to measure the polarity of Earth's magnetic field at the time a stratum was deposited. **Chronostratigraphy** focuses on the relative dating of rock strata based on the time of rock formation. **Unconformity** refers to missing layers of rock.

Fossil

Fossils are preservations of plants, animals, their remains, or their traces that date back to about 10,000 years ago. Fossils and where they are found in rock strata makes up the fossil record. Fossils are formed under a very specific set of conditions. The fossil must not be damaged by predators and scavengers after death, and the fossil must not decompose. Usually, this happens when the organism is quickly covered with sediment. This sediment builds up and molecules in the organism's body are replaced by minerals. Fossils come in an array of sizes, from single-celled organisms to large dinosaurs.

Fossils provide a wealth of information about the past, particularly about the flora and fauna that once occupied the Earth, but also about the geologic history of the Earth itself and how Earth and its inhabitants came to be. Some fossilized remains in the **geohistorical record** exemplify ongoing processes in the Earth's environment, such as weathering, glaciation, and volcanism. These have all led to evolutionary changes in plants and animals. Other fossils support the theory that **catastrophic events** caused drastic changes in the Earth and its living creatures. One example of this type of theory is that a meteor struck the Earth and caused dinosaurs to become extinct. Both types of fossils provide scientists with a way to hypothesize whether these types of events will happen again.

Formation of the Earth

Earth's early development began after a **supernova** exploded. This led to the formation of the **Sun** out of hydrogen gas and interstellar dust. These same elements swirled around the newly-formed Sun and formed the **planets**, including Earth. Scientists theorize that about 4.5 billion years ago, Earth was a chunk of rock surrounded by a cloud of gas. It is believed it lacked water and the type of atmosphere that exists today. Heat from radioactive materials in the rock and pressure in the Earth's interior melted the interior. This caused the heavier materials, such as iron, to sink. Lighter silicate-type rocks rose to the Earth's surface. These rocks formed the Earth's earliest crust. Other chemicals also rose to the Earth's surface, helping to form the water and atmosphere.

Copyright © Mometrix Media. You have been licensed one copy of this document for personal use only. Any other reproduction or redistribution is strictly prohibited. All rights reserved.

Formation of the Atmosphere

It is generally believed that the Earth's **atmosphere** evolved into its present state. Some believe Earth's early atmosphere contained hydrogen, helium, methane, ammonia, and some water vapor. These elements also played a role in planet formation. Earth's early atmosphere was developed before the emergence of living organisms as we know them today. Eventually, the hot hydrogen and helium escaped Earth's gravity and drifted off. Others believe the early atmosphere contained a large amount of carbon dioxide. Either way, there was probably little oxygen at the time.

Another theory is that a second stage of the atmosphere evolved over several hundred million years through a process during which methane, ammonia, and water vapor broke down and reformed into nitrogen, hydrogen, and carbon dioxide. About two billion years ago, higher levels of oxygen were found in the atmosphere, which is indicated by large deposits of iron ore. At the same time, iron ores created in oxygen-poor environments stopped forming. The oxygen in the atmosphere today comes mainly from plants and microorganisms such as algae.

> **Review Video: Earth's Atmosphere**
> Visit mometrix.com/academy and enter code: 417614

Deposition

Deposition, or **sedimentation**, is the geological process in which previously eroded material is transported or added to a land form or land mass. Erosion and sedimentation are complementary geological processes. **Running water** causes a substantial amount of deposition of transported materials in both fresh water and coastal areas. Examples include gravity transporting material down the slope of a mountain and depositing it at the base of the slope. Another example is when sandstorms deposit particles in other locations. When glaciers melt and retreat, it can result in the deposition of sediments. **Evaporation** is also considered to cause deposition since dissolved materials are left behind when water evaporates. Deposition can include the buildup of **organic materials**. For example, chalk is partially made up of the small calcium carbonate skeletons of marine plankton, which helps create more calcium carbonate from chemical processes.

Weathering

There are two basic types of **weathering**: mechanical and chemical. Weathering is a very prominent process on the Earth's surface. Materials weather at different rates, which are known as differential weathering. Mechanical and chemical weathering is interdependent. For example, **chemical weathering** can loosen the bonds between molecules and allow mechanical weathering to take place. **Mechanical weathering** can expose the surfaces of land masses and allow chemical weathering to take place. Impact, abrasion, frost wedging, root wedging, salt wedging, and uploading are types of mechanical weathering.

Types of chemical weathering are dissolution, hydration, hydrolysis, oxidation, biological, and carbonation. The primary type of chemical weathering is caused by **acid rain**. Carbonic and sulfuric acids can enter rain when they are present in the atmosphere. This lowers the pH value of rain, making it more acidic. Normal rain water has a pH value of 5.5. Acid rain has a pH value of 4 or less.

Erosion

Erosion is the wearing-away of rock materials from the Earth's surface. Erosion can be classified as natural geologic erosion and erosion due to human activity. **Natural geologic erosion** occurs due to weathering and gravity. Factors involved in natural geologic erosion are typically long term forces. **Human activities** such as development, farming, and deforestation occur over shorter periods of time. Soil, which supports plant growth, is the topmost layer of organic material. One type of erosion is **sheet**

Copyright © Mometrix Media. You have been licensed one copy of this document for personal use only. Any other reproduction or redistribution is strictly prohibited. All rights reserved.

erosion, which is the gradual and somewhat uniform removal of surface soil. **Rills** are small rivulets that cut into soil. **Gullies** are rills that have become enlarged due to extended water run-off. **Sandblows** are caused by wind blowing away particles. Negative effects of erosion include sedimentation in rivers, which can pollute water and damage ecosystems. Erosion can also result in the removal of topsoil, which destroys crops and prevents plants from growing. This reduces food production and alters ecosystems.

Physical Properties

Physical properties (as opposed to chemical structures) used to identify **minerals** are hardness, luster, color, cleavage, and streak. Senses other than sight, such as touch, taste, and smell, may be used to observe physical properties. **Hardness** is the resistance a mineral has to scratches. The *Mohs Hardness Scale* is used to rate hardness from 1 to 10. **Color** can often not be determined definitively as some minerals can be more than one color. **Luster** is determined by reflected light. Luster can be described as metallic (shiny), sub-metallic (dull), non-metallic (vitreous, like glass), or earthy (like dirt or powder). **Streak** is the true color of the mineral in powdered form. It can be determined by rubbing the specimen across an unglazed porcelain tile. Fracture or **cleavage** is how a mineral reacts to stress, such as being struck with a hammer. Other properties that can be used to identify rocks and minerals include magnetism, a salty taste, or a pungent odor in a streak test.

Rocks and Minerals

Minerals are naturally occurring, inorganic solids with a definite chemical composition and an orderly internal crystal structure. A **polymorph** is two minerals with the same chemical composition, but a different crystal structure. **Rocks** are aggregates of one or more minerals, and may also contain **mineraloids** (minerals lacking a crystalline structure) and organic remains. The three types of rocks are sedimentary, igneous, and metamorphic. Rocks are classified based on their formation and the minerals they contain. Minerals are classified by their chemical composition.

> **Review Video: Rocks vs. Minerals**
> Visit mometrix.com/academy and enter code: 947587

Geology, Petrology, and Mineralogy

- **Geology** is the study of the planet Earth as it pertains to the composition, structure, and origin of its rocks.
- **Petrology** is the study of rocks, including their composition, texture, structure, occurrence, mode of formation, and history.
- **Mineralogy** is the study of minerals.

Mineral Classification

Minerals are **classified** by chemical composition and internal crystalline structure. They are organized into **classes**. Native elements such as gold and silver are not classified in this manner. The eight classes are sulfides, oxides\hydroxides, halides, carbonates, sulfates, phosphates, and silicates. These classes are based on the dominant **anion** (negatively charged ion) or anionic group. Minerals are classified in this way for three main reasons. First, minerals with the same anion have unmistakable resemblances. Second, minerals with the same anion are often found in the same geologic environment. For example, calcite and dolomite, which belong to the same group, are often found together. Last, this method is similar to the naming convention used to identify inorganic compounds in chemistry. Minerals can be further separated into groups on the basis of **internal structure**.

Copyright © Mometrix Media. You have been licensed one copy of this document for personal use only. Any other reproduction or redistribution is strictly prohibited. All rights reserved.

Sedimentary Rocks

Sedimentary rocks are formed by the process of **lithification**, which involves compaction, the expulsion of liquids from pores, and the cementation of the pre-existing rock. It is pressure and temperature that are responsible for this process. Sedimentary rocks are often formed in layers in the presence of water, and may contain organic remains, such as fossils. Sedimentary rocks are organized into three groups: detrital, biogenic, and chemical. **Texture** refers to the size, shape, and grains of sedimentary rock. Texture can be used to determine how a particular sedimentary rock was created. **Composition** refers to the types of minerals present in the rock. The **origin** of sedimentary rock refers to the type of water that was involved in its creation. Marine deposits, for example, likely involved ocean environments, while continental deposits likely involved dry land and lakes.

Metamorphic Rocks

Metamorphic rock is that which has been changed by great heat and pressure. This results in a variety of outcomes, including deformation, compaction, destruction of the characteristics of the original rock, bending, folding, formation of new minerals because of chemical reactions, and changes in the size and shape of the mineral grain. For example, the igneous rock ferromagnesian can be changed into schist and gneiss. The sedimentary rock carbonaceous can be changed into marble. The texture of metamorphic rocks can be classified as foliated and unfoliated. **Foliation**, or layering, occurs when rock is compressed along one axis during recrystallization. This can be seen in schist and shale. **Unfoliated** rock does not include this banding. Rocks that are compressed equally from all sides or lack specific minerals will be unfoliated. An example is marble.

Igneous Rocks

Igneous rock is formed from **magma**, which is molten material originating from beneath the Earth's surface. Depending upon where magma cools, the resulting igneous rock can be classified as intrusive, plutonic, hypabyssal, extrusive, or volcanic. Magma that solidifies at a depth is **intrusive**, cools slowly, and has a coarse grain as a result. An example is granite. Magma that solidifies at or near the surface is **extrusive**, cools quickly, and usually has a fine grain. An example is basalt. Magma that actually flows out of the Earth's surface is called **lava**. Some extrusive rock cools so quickly that crystals do not have time to form. These rocks have a glassy appearance. An example is obsidian. **Hypabyssal** rock is igneous rock that is formed at medium depths.

> **Review Video: Igneous, Sedimentary, and Metamorphic Rocks**
> Visit mometrix.com/academy and enter code: 689294

Granite and Basalt

Both granite and basalt are plentiful igneous rocks, but granite is intrusive and basalt is extrusive. Intrusive rocks come from **magma** within the Earth's crust and cool slowly. Extrusive rocks are formed from **lava** on the Earth's surface and cool more quickly than intrusive rocks. **Granite** is an igneous rock with a medium to coarse texture that is formed from magma. It can be a variety of colors. It is intrusive, massive, hard, and coarse grained. It forms a major part of continental crust. It can be composed of potassium feldspar, plagioclase feldspar, and quartz, as well as various amounts of muscovite, biotite, and hornblende-type amphiboles. **Basalt** is extrusive and usually colored gray to black. It has a fine grain due to quicker cooling. Basalt is porphyritic, meaning it contains larger crystals in a fine matrix. Basalt is usually composed of amphibole and pyroxene, and sometimes of plagioclase, feldspathoids, and olivine.

Copyright © Mometrix Media. You have been licensed one copy of this document for personal use only. Any other reproduction or redistribution is strictly prohibited. All rights reserved.

Soil Profiles

A **soil profile** depicts the parallel layers of rock and soil in the earth's crust. The layers are:

- **O** (organic matter) – consists of non-decomposed organic material
- **A** (surface soil) – organic substances mixed with minerals
- **B** (subsoil) – clay and organic substances
- **C** (parent rock) – large, unbroken rock layer
- **R** (bedrock) – layer of primarily unbroken rock

Earth's Structure and Layers

The Earth is **ellipsoid**, not perfectly spherical. This means the diameter is different through the poles and at the equator. Through the poles, the Earth is about 12,715 km in diameter. The approximate center of the Earth is at a depth of 6,378 km. The Earth is divided into a crust, mantle, and core. The **core** consists of a solid inner portion. Moving outward, the molten outer core occupies the space from about a depth of 5,150 km to a depth of 2,890 km. The **mantle** consists of a lower and upper layer. The lower layer includes the D' (D prime) and D" (D double-prime) layers. The solid portion of the upper mantle and crust together form the **lithosphere**, or rocky sphere. Below this, but still within the mantle, is the **asthenosphere**, or weak sphere. These layers are distinguishable because the lithosphere is relatively rigid, while the asthenosphere resembles a thick liquid.

The Earth's **core** consists of hot iron and forms of nickel. The **mantle** consists of different materials, including iron, magnesium, and calcium. The **crust** covers the mantle, consists of a thin layer of much lighter rocks, and is further subdivided into continental and oceanic portions. The **continental portion** consists mainly of silicates, such as granite. The **oceanic portion** consists of heavier, volcanic rocks, such as basalt. The upper 10 miles of the lithosphere layer (the crust and part of the mantle) is made up of 95% igneous rock (or its metamorphic equivalent), 4% shale, 0.75% sandstone, and 0.25% limestone. There are over 4,000 known minerals, but only about 20 make up some 95% of all rocks. There are, however, more than 3,000 individual kinds of minerals in the Earth's crust. **Silicates** are the largest group of minerals.

Mountains

Orogeny refers to the formation of mountains, particularly the processes of folding and faulting caused by plate tectonics. **Folding** is when layers of sedimentary rock are pressed together by continental plate movements. Sections of rock that are folded upward are called **anticlines**. Sections of rock that are folded downward are called **synclines**. Examples of folded mountains are the Alps and the Himalayans. **Fault-block mountains** are created when tectonic plate movement produces tension that results in displacement. Mountains in the Southwest United States are examples of fault-blocking mountains. Mountains can also be caused by **volcanic activity** and **erosion**.

Maps

Traditional maps represent land in two dimensions, while **topographic maps** represent elevation through the use of contour lines. **Contour lines** help show changes to elevations above the surface of the Earth and on the ocean floor. They also help show the shape of Earth's surface features. The United States Geological Survey (USGS) produces frequently used quadrangle maps in various scales. A **quadrangle topographic map** is bounded by two lines of latitude and two lines of longitude. A **7.5-minute map** shows an area that spans 7.5 minutes of latitude and 7.5 minutes of longitude. The name of the quadrangle map appears at the top, and usually indicates the name of a prominent feature. Topographic maps that show much less detail are also available. They might show a much larger area, such as a country or state. USGS quad maps also refer to **adjacent quad maps**. Other information

52

Copyright © Mometrix Media. You have been licensed one copy of this document for personal use only. Any other reproduction or redistribution is strictly prohibited. All rights reserved.

contained on quad maps includes the projection and grid used, scale, contour intervals, and magnetic declination, which is the difference between true north and magnetic north.

Plate Tectonics

The **theory of plate tectonics** states that the lithosphere, the solid portion of the mantle and Earth's crust, consists of **major and minor plates**. These plates are on top of and move with the viscous upper mantle, which is heated because of the **convection cycle** that occurs in the interior of the Earth. There are different estimates as to the exact number of major and minor plates. The number of major plates is believed to be between 9 and 15, and it is thought that there may be as many as 40 minor plates. The United States is atop the North American plate. The Pacific Ocean is atop the Pacific plate. The point at which these two plates slide horizontally along the San Andreas fault is an example of a **transform plate boundary**. The other two types of boundaries are **divergent** (plates that are spreading apart and forming new crust) and **convergent** (the process of subduction causes one plate to go under another). The movement of plates is what causes other features of the Earth's crust, such as mountains, volcanoes, and earthquakes.

Heat is transferred through the process of **convection**, which is a cycle. Hot material rises and spreads, cooling as it spreads. The cool material then sinks, where it is heated again. The process of convection can be seen in a pot of boiling water. It is believed this same process is happening deep within the Earth. Greater depths are associated with more pressure and heat. The weight of all the rocks causes the increase in pressure, while the decay of heavy radioactive elements such as uranium produces heat. This creates hot areas of molten material that find their way upward and to the surface in an effort to **equalize**, which means pressure and temperature are reduced. This causes the processes involved in **plate tectonics**.

> **Review Video: Plate Tectonic Theory**
> Visit mometrix.com/academy and enter code: 535013

Volcanoes and Plate Tectonics

Volcanoes can occur along any type of tectonic plate boundary. At a **divergent boundary**, as plates move apart, magma rises to the surface, cools, and forms a ridge. An example of this is the mid-Atlantic ridge. **Convergent boundaries**, where one plate slides under another, are often areas with a lot of volcanic activity. The **subduction process** creates magma. When it rises to the surface, volcanoes can be created. Volcanoes can also be created in the middle of a plate over hot spots. **Hot spots** are locations where narrow plumes of magma rise through the mantle in a fixed place over a long period of time. The Hawaiian Islands and Midway are examples. The plate shifts and the island moves. Magma continues to rise through the mantle, however, which produces another island. Volcanoes can be active, dormant, or extinct. **Active volcanoes** are those that are erupting or about to erupt. **Dormant volcanoes** are those that might erupt in the future and still have internal volcanic activity. **Extinct volcanoes** are those that will not erupt.

Seafloor-Spreading

Seafloor spreading is the result of underwater volcanic activity. It is a process in which new oceanic crust is formed through volcanic activity at a mid-ocean ridge and then moves away from the ridge. This process provides a mechanism for continental drift.

Volcanoes

The three types of volcanoes are shield, cinder cone, and composite. A **shield volcano** is created by a long-term, relatively gentle eruption. This type of volcanic mountain is created by each progressive lava flow that occurs over time. A **cinder cone volcano** is created by explosive eruptions. Lava is spewed out

Copyright © Mometrix Media. You have been licensed one copy of this document for personal use only. Any other reproduction or redistribution is strictly prohibited. All rights reserved.

of a vent into the air. As it falls to the ground, the lava cools into cinders and ash, which build up around the volcano in a cone shape. A **composite volcano** is a combination of the other two types of volcanoes. In this type, there are layers of lava flows and layers of ash and cinder.

Earthquakes

Most **earthquakes** are caused by tectonic plate movement. They occur along fractures called **faults** or **fault zones**. Friction in the faults prevents smooth movement. Tension builds up over time, and the release of that tension results in earthquakes. Faults are grouped based on the type of slippage that occurs. The types of faults are dip-slip, strike-slip, and oblique-slip. A **dip-slip fault** involves vertical movement along the fault plane. In a normal dip-slip fault, the wall that is above the fault plane moves down. In a reverse dip-slip fault, the wall above the fault plane moves up. A **strike-slip fault** involves horizontal movement along the fault plane. **Oblique-slip faults** involve both vertical and horizontal movement. The **Richter magnitude scale** measures how much seismic energy was released by an earthquake. The **epicenter** is the area on the earth's surface that is directly above the point where an earthquake originates.

> **Review Video: Earthquakes**
> Visit mometrix.com/academy and enter code: 252531
>
> **Review Video: Measuring Earthquakes**
> Visit mometrix.com/academy and enter code: 393730

Seismic Deformation

There are two types of deformations created by an earthquake fault rupture: static and dynamic. **Static deformation** permanently displaces the ground. Examples are when a road or railroad track becomes distorted by an earthquake. Plate tectonics stresses the fault by creating tension with slow plate movements. An earthquake releases the tension. Plate tectonics also cause a second type of deformation. This type results in dynamic motions that take the form of **seismic waves**. These sound waves can be **compression waves**, also known as primary or P waves, or **shear waves**, also known as secondary or S waves. P waves travel fastest, with speeds ranging between 1.5 and 8 kilometers per second. Shear waves are slower. P waves shake the ground in the direction they are propagating. S waves shake perpendicularly or transverse to the direction of propagation. **Seismographs** use a simple pendulum to record earthquake movement in a record called a **seismogram**. A seismogram can help seismologists estimate the distance, direction, Richter magnitude, and type of faulting of an earthquake.

Hydrologic Cycle

The **hydrologic**, or **water**, **cycle** refers to water movement on, above, and in the Earth. Water can be in any one of its three states during different phases of the cycle. The three states of water are liquid water, frozen ice, and water vapor. Processes involved in the hydrologic cycle include precipitation, canopy interception, snow melt, runoff, infiltration, subsurface flow, evaporation, sublimation, advection, condensation, and transpiration. **Precipitation** occurs when condensed water vapor falls to Earth. Examples include rain, fog drip, and various forms of snow, hail, and sleet. **Canopy interception** occurs when precipitation lands on plant foliage instead of falling to the ground and evaporating. **Snowmelt** is runoff produced by melting snow. **Infiltration** occurs when water flows from the surface into the ground. **Subsurface flow** refers to water that flows underground. **Evaporation** occurs when water in a liquid state changes to a gas. **Sublimation** occurs when water in a solid state (such as snow or ice) changes to water vapor without going through a liquid phase. Advection is the movement of water through the atmosphere. **Condensation** occurs when water vapor changes to liquid water. **Transpiration** occurs when water vapor is released from plants into the air.

Copyright © Mometrix Media. You have been licensed one copy of this document for personal use only. Any other reproduction or redistribution is strictly prohibited. All rights reserved.

Environmental Science

Layers of the Atmosphere

The **atmosphere** consists of 78% nitrogen, 21% oxygen, and 1% argon. It also includes traces of water vapor, carbon dioxide and other gases, dust particles, and chemicals from Earth. The atmosphere becomes thinner the farther it is from the Earth's surface. It becomes difficult to breathe at about 3 km above sea level. The atmosphere gradually fades into space.

The main layers of the Earth's atmosphere (from lowest to highest) are:

- **Troposphere** (lowest layer): where life exists and most weather occurs; elevation 0–15 km
- **Stratosphere**: has the ozone layer, which absorbs UV radiation from the sun; hottest layer; where most satellites orbit; elevation 15–50 km
- **Mesosphere**: coldest layer; where meteors will burn up; elevation 50–80 km
- **Thermosphere**: where the international space station orbits; elevation 80–700 km
- **Exosphere** (outermost layer): consists mainly of hydrogen and helium; extends to ~10,000 km

Tropospheric Circulation

Most weather takes place in the **troposphere**. Air circulates in the atmosphere by convection and in various types of "cells." Air near the equator is warmed by the Sun and rises. Cool air rushes under it, and the higher, warmer air flows toward Earth's poles. At the poles, it cools and descends to the surface. It is now under the hot air, and flows back to the equator. Air currents coupled with ocean currents move heat around the planet, creating winds, weather, and climate. Winds can change direction with the seasons. For example, in Southeast Asia and India, summer monsoons are caused by air being heated by the Sun. This air rises, draws moisture from the ocean, and causes daily rains. In winter, the air cools, sinks, pushes the moist air away, and creates dry weather.

Meteorology, Weather, and Climate

Meteorology is the study of the atmosphere, particularly as it pertains to forecasting the weather and understanding its processes. **Weather** is the condition of the atmosphere at any given moment. Most weather occurs in the troposphere. Weather includes changing events such as clouds, storms, and temperature, as well as more extreme events such as tornadoes, hurricanes, and blizzards. **Climate** refers to the average weather for a particular area over time, typically at least 30 years. Latitude is an indicator of climate. Changes in climate occur over long time periods.

> **Review Video: Climate and Weather**
> Visit mometrix.com/academy and enter code: 455373

Common Weather Phenomenon

Common atmospheric conditions that are frequently measured are temperature, precipitation, wind, and humidity. These weather conditions are often measured at permanently fixed **weather stations** so weather data can be collected and compared over time and by region. Measurements may also be taken by ships, buoys, and underwater instruments. Measurements may also be taken under special circumstances. The measurements taken include temperature, barometric pressure, humidity, wind speed, wind direction, and precipitation. Usually, the following instruments are used: A **thermometer** is used for measuring temperature; a **barometer** is used for measuring barometric/air pressure; a **hygrometer** is used for measuring humidity; an **anemometer** is used for measuring wind speed; a

Copyright © Mometrix Media. You have been licensed one copy of this document for personal use only. Any other reproduction or redistribution is strictly prohibited. All rights reserved.

ISARUWU-OGAEORSCANNERUWU-CANARY

weather vane is used for measuring wind direction; and a **rain gauge** is used for measuring precipitation.

Latitude

Latitude is a measurement of the distance from the equator. The distance from the equator indicates how much **solar radiation** a particular area receives. The equator receives more sunlight, while polar areas receive less. The Earth tilts slightly on its **rotational axis**. This tilt determines the seasons and affects weather. There are eight **biomes** or **ecosystems** with particular climates that are associated with latitude. Those in the high latitudes, which get the least sunlight, are tundra and taiga. Those in the mid latitudes are grassland, temperate forest, and chaparral. Those in latitudes closest to the equator are the warmest. The sixth and seventh biomes are desert and tropical rain forest. The eighth biome is the ocean, which is unique because it consists of water and spans the entire globe. Insolation refers to incoming solar radiation. **Diurnal variations** refer to the daily changes in **insolation**. The greatest insolation occurs at noon.

Tilt of the Earth

The **tilt of the Earth** on its axis is 23.5°. This tilt causes the **seasons** and affects the **temperature** because it affects the amount of Sun the area receives. When the Northern or Southern Hemispheres are tilted toward the Sun, the hemisphere tilted toward the sun experiences summer and the other hemisphere experiences winter. This reverses as the Earth revolves around the Sun. Fall and spring occur between the two extremes. The **equator** gets the same amount of sunlight every day of the year, about 12 hours, and doesn't experience seasons. Both poles have days during the winter when they are tilted away from the Sun and receive no daylight. The opposite effect occurs during the summer. There are 24 hours of daylight and no night. The **summer solstice**, the day with the most amount of sunlight, occurs on June 21st in the Northern Hemisphere and on December 21st in the Southern Hemisphere. The **winter solstice**, the day with the least amount of sunlight, occurs on December 21st in the Northern Hemisphere and on June 21st in the Southern Hemisphere.

> **Review Video: Tilt of Earth and Seasons**
> Visit mometrix.com/academy and enter code: 602892

Sea and Land Breezes

Sea breezes and land breezes help influence an area's prevailing **winds**, particularly in areas where the wind flow is light. **Sea breezes**, also called onshore breezes, are the result of the different capacities for absorbing heat of the ocean and the land. The sea can be warmed to a greater depth than the land. It warms up more slowly than the land's surface. Land heats air above it as its temperature increases. This heated, warmer air is less dense and rises as a result. The cooler air above the sea and higher sea level pressure create a wind flow in the direction of the land. Coastal areas often receive these cooler breezes. Land cools slower at night than the ocean, and coastal breezes weaken at this time. When the land becomes so cool that it is cooler than the sea surface, the pressure over the ocean is lower than the land. This creates a **land breeze**. This can cause rain and thunderstorms over the ocean.

Causes of Wind and Wind Belts

Winds are the result of air moving by **convection**. Masses of warm air rise, and cold air sweeps into their place. The warm air also moves, cools, and sinks. The term "**prevailing wind**" refers to the wind that usually blows in an area in a single direction. **Dominant winds** are the winds with the highest speeds. Belts or bands that run latitudinally and blow in a specific direction are associated with convection cells. **Hadley cells** are formed directly north and south of the equator. The **Farrell cells** occur at about 30° to 60°. The **jet stream** runs between the Farrell cells and the polar cells. At the higher and lower latitudes, the direction is easterly. At mid latitudes, the direction is westerly. From the North

Copyright © Mometrix Media. You have been licensed one copy of this document for personal use only. Any other reproduction or redistribution is strictly prohibited. All rights reserved.

Pole to the south, the surface winds are Polar High Easterlies, Subpolar Low Westerlies, Subtropical High or Horse Latitudes, North-East Trade winds, Equatorial Low or Doldrums, South-East Trades, Subtropical High or Horse Latitudes, Subpolar Low Easterlies, and Polar High.

Local Atmospheric Variations

Terrain affects several local **atmospheric conditions**, including temperature, wind speed, and wind direction. When there are land forms, heating of the ground can be greater than the heating of the surrounding air than it would be at the same altitude above sea level. This creates a thermal low in the region and amplifies any existing thermal lows. It also changes the wind circulation. Terrain such as hills and valleys increase friction between the air and the land, which disturbs the air flow. This physical block deflects the wind, and the resulting air flow is called a barrier jet. Just as the heating of the land and air affects sea and land breezes along the coast, rugged terrain affects the wind circulation between mountains and valleys.

Thunderstorms

A **thunderstorm** is one of the many weather phenomena that can be created during the ongoing process of heat moving through Earth's atmosphere. Thunderstorms form when there is moisture to form rain clouds, unstable air, and lift. Unstable air is usually caused by warm air rising quickly through cold air. Lift can be caused by fronts, sea breezes, and elevated terrain, such as mountains. **Single cell thunderstorms** have one main draft. **Multicell clusters** have clusters of storms. **Multicell lines** have severe thunderstorms along a squall line. **Supercell thunderstorms** are large and severe, and have the capacity to produce destructive tornadoes. **Thunder** is a sonic shock wave caused by the rapid expansion of air around lightning. **Lightning** is the discharge of electricity during a thunderstorm. Lightning can also occur during volcanic eruptions or dust storms.

Cyclones

Cyclones generally refer to large air masses rotating in the same direction as the Earth. They are formed in low pressure areas. Cyclones vary in size. Some are **mesoscale systems**, which vary in size from about 5 km to hundreds of kilometers. Some are **synoptic scale systems**, which are about 1,000 km in size. The size of subtropical cyclones is somewhere in between. Cold-core polar and extratropical cyclones are synoptic scale systems. Warm-core tropical, polar low, and mesocyclones are mesoscale systems. Extratropical cyclones, sometimes called mid-latitude cyclones or wave cyclones, occur in the middle latitudes. They have neither tropical nor polar characteristics. Extratropical cyclones are everyday phenomena which, along with anticyclones, drive the weather over much of the Earth. They can produce cloudiness, mild showers, heavy gales, and thunderstorms. **Anticyclones** occur when there is a descending pocket of air of higher than average pressure. Anticyclones are usually associated with clearing skies and drier, cooler air.

Tornados

During a **tornado**, wind speeds can be upward of 300 miles per hour. Tornados are rotating funnel-like clouds. They have a very high energy density, which means they are very destructive to a small area. They are also short-lived. About 75% of the world's tornadoes occur in the United States, mostly in an area of the Great Plains known as **Tornado Alley**. If there are two or more columns of air, it is referred to as a **multiple vortex tornado**. A **satellite tornado** is a weak tornado that forms near a larger one within the same mesocyclone. A **waterspout** is a tornado over water. The severity of tornadoes is measured using the **Enhanced Fujita Scale**. An EF-0 rating is associated with a 3-second wind gust

Copyright © Mometrix Media. You have been licensed one copy of this document for personal use only. Any other reproduction or redistribution is strictly prohibited. All rights reserved.

between 65 and 85 miles per hour, while an EF-5 is associated with wind speeds of greater than 200 mph.

Review Video: Tornadoes
Visit mometrix.com/academy and enter code: 540439

Hurricanes

A **hurricane** is one of the three weather phenomena that can occur as a result of a tropical cyclone. Hurricanes appear well-organized and sometimes have a recognizable eye with strong rotation. Its wind speed is more than 73 mph. Hurricanes are classified using the **Saffir-Simpson Scale**, which ranges from category 1 to category 5. A category 5 hurricane has wind speeds greater than 155 mph. Hurricanes are named alphabetically through the season starting with "A." The letters "Q," "U," "X," "Y," and "Z" are not used. There are six lists of names that are used from year to year. The names of devastating hurricanes are retired from the list.

Humidity

Humidity refers to water vapor contained in the air. The amount of moisture contained in air depends upon its **temperature**. The higher the air temperature, the more moisture it can hold. These higher levels of moisture are associated with higher humidity. **Absolute humidity** refers to the total amount of moisture air is capable of holding at a certain temperature. **Relative humidity** is the ratio of water vapor in the air compared to the amount the air is capable of holding at its current temperature. As temperature decreases, absolute humidity stays the same and relative humidity increases. A **hygrometer** is a device used to measure humidity. The **dew point** is the temperature at which water vapor condenses into water at a particular humidity.

Precipitation

After clouds reach the dew point, **precipitation** occurs. Precipitation can take the form of a liquid or a solid. It is known by many names, including rain, snow, ice, dew, and frost. **Liquid** forms of precipitation include rain and drizzle. Rain or drizzle that freezes on contact is known as freezing rain or freezing drizzle. **Solid** or frozen forms of precipitation include snow, ice needles or diamond dust, sleet or ice pellets, hail, and graupel or snow pellets. **Virga** is a form of precipitation that evaporates before reaching the ground. It usually looks like sheets or shafts falling from a cloud. The amount of rainfall is measured with a **rain gauge**. Intensity can be measured according to how fast precipitation is falling or by how severely it limits visibility. Precipitation plays a major role in the **water cycle** since it is responsible for depositing much of the Earth's fresh water.

Review Video: Hydrologic Cycle
Visit mometrix.com/academy and enter code: 426578

Heat Waves

A **heat wave** is a stretch of hotter than normal weather. Some heat waves may involve high humidity and last longer than a week. Heat waves can form if a **warm high-pressure weather system** stalls in an area. The **jet stream** is a flow that moves air through the middle latitudes. If the jet stream shifts, it can bring a pattern of unusually warm weather into a region, creating a heat wave. Heat can be trapped by cities. If there is no rain or clouds to help cool the weather, the heat wave can linger. In humans, heat waves can lead to heat stroke, heat exhaustion, cramps, dehydration, and even death. Plants can dry up and crops can fail. There is also a greater threat of **fires** during a heat wave in dry areas.

Copyright © Mometrix Media. You have been licensed one copy of this document for personal use only. Any other reproduction or redistribution is strictly prohibited. All rights reserved.

Formation of Clouds

Clouds **form** when air cools and warm air is forced to give up some of its **water vapor** because it can no longer hold it. This vapor condenses and forms tiny droplets of water or ice crystals called clouds. Particles, or aerosols, are needed for water vapor to form water droplets. These are called **condensation nuclei**. Clouds are created by surface heating, mountains and terrain, rising air masses, and weather fronts. Clouds precipitate, returning the water they contain to Earth. Clouds can also create atmospheric optics. They can scatter light, creating colorful phenomena such as rainbows, colorful sunsets, and the green flash phenomenon.

> **Review Video: Clouds**
> Visit mometrix.com/academy and enter code: 803166

Cloud Types

Most clouds can be classified according to the altitude of their base above Earth's surface. **High clouds** occur at altitudes between 5,000 and 13,000 meters. **Middle clouds** occur at altitudes between 2,000 and 7,000 meters. **Low clouds** occur from the Earth's surface to altitudes of 2,000 meters. Types of high clouds include cirrus (Ci), thin wispy mare's tails that consist of ice; cirrocumulus (Cc), small, pillow-like puffs that often appear in rows; and cirrostratus (Cs), thin, sheet-like clouds that often cover the entire sky. Types of middle clouds include altocumulus (Ac), gray-white clouds that consist of liquid water; and altostratus (As), grayish or blue-gray clouds that span the sky. Types of low clouds include stratus (St), gray and fog-like clouds consisting of water droplets that take up the whole sky; stratocumulus (Sc), low-lying, lumpy gray clouds; and nimbostratus (Ns), dark gray clouds with uneven bases that indicate rain or snow. Two types of clouds, cumulus (Cu) and cumulonimbus (Cb), are capable of great vertical growth. They can start at a wide range of altitudes, from the Earth's surface to altitudes of 13,000 meters.

Contrails, or condensation trails, are thin white streaks caused by jets. These are created from water vapor condensing and freezing the jet's exhaust particles. Contrails can be further classified as short-lived, persistent non-spreading, and persistent. **Lenticular** or lee wave clouds are created by an air current over an obstacle, such as a mountain. They appear to be stationary, but are actually forming, dissipating, and reforming in the same place. **Kelvin-Helmholtz** clouds are formed by winds with different speeds or directions. They look like ocean waves. **Mammatus** clouds hang down from the base of a cloud, usually a cumulonimbus cloud. They often occur during the warmer months.

Air Masses

Air masses are large volumes of air in the troposphere of the Earth. They are categorized by their temperature and by the amount of water vapor they contain. Arctic and Antarctic air masses are cold. Polar air masses are cool. Tropical and equatorial air masses are hot. Other types of air masses include maritime and monsoon, both of which are moist and unstable. There are also continental and superior air masses, which are dry. A **weather front** separates two masses of air of different densities. It is the principal cause of meteorological phenomena. Air masses are quickly and easily affected by the land they are above. They can have certain characteristics, and then develop new ones when they get blown over a different area.

Pressure Systems

The concept of atmospheric pressure involves the idea that air exerts a force. An imaginary column of air 1 square inch in size rising through the atmosphere would exert a force of 14.7 pounds per square inch (psi). Both temperature and altitude affect atmospheric pressure. Low and high **pressure systems** tend to want to equalize. Air tends to move from areas of high pressure to areas of low pressure. When air moves into a low pressure system, the air that was there gets pushed up, creating lower temperatures

Copyright © Mometrix Media. You have been licensed one copy of this document for personal use only. Any other reproduction or redistribution is strictly prohibited. All rights reserved.

and pressures. Water vapor condenses and forms clouds and possibly rain and snow. A **barometer** is used to measure air pressure.

> **Review Video:** Rotation of Low Pressure Systems
> Visit mometrix.com/academy and enter code: 258356

Frontal Systems

A **cold front** is a mass of cold air, usually fast moving and dense, that moves into a warm air front, producing clouds. This often produces a temperature drop and rain, hail (frozen rain), thunder, and lightning. A **warm front** is pushed up by a fast-moving cold front. It is often associated with high wispy clouds, such as cirrus and cirrostratus clouds. A **stationary front** forms when a warm and cold front meet, but neither is strong enough to move the other. Winds blowing parallel to the fronts keep the front stationary. The front may remain in the same place for days until the wind direction changes and both fronts become a single warm or cold front. In other cases, the entire front dissipates. An **occluded front** forms when a cold front pushes into a warm front. The warm air rises and the two masses of cool air join. These types of fronts often occur in areas of low atmospheric pressure.

Short and Long-term Weather Forecasting

Short and long-term **weather forecasting** is important because the day-to-day weather greatly affects humans and human activity. Severe weather and natural events can cause devastating harm to humans, property, and sources of livelihood, such as crops. The **persistence method** of forecasting can be used to create both short and long-term forecasts in areas that change very little or change slowly. It assumes that the weather tomorrow will be similar to the weather today. **Barometric pressure** is measured because a change in air pressure can indicate the arrival of a cold front that could lead to precipitation. **Long-term forecasts** based on climate data are useful to help people prepare for seasonal changes and severe events such as hurricanes.

Weather Fronts and Weather Maps

A **weather front** is the area between two differing masses of air that affects weather. **Frontal movements** are influenced by the jet stream and other high winds. Movements are determined by the type of front. **Cold fronts** move up to twice as fast as **warm fronts**. It is in the turbulent frontal area where weather events take place. This area also creates temperature changes. Weather phenomena include rain, thunderstorms, high winds, tornadoes, cloudiness, clear skies, and hurricanes. Different fronts can be plotted on weather maps using a set of designated symbols. **Surface weather maps** can also include symbols representing clouds, rain, temperature, air pressure, and fair weather.

The Ozone Layer, the Ionosphere, the Homosphere, and the Heterosphere

- The **ozone layer**, although contained within the stratosphere, is determined by ozone (O_3) concentrations. It absorbs the majority of ultraviolet light from the Sun.
- The **ionosphere** encompasses the mesosphere, thermosphere, and parts of the exosphere. The has molecules in this layer are partially ionized by solar radiation. It affects radio wave transmission and auroras.
- The **homosphere** encompasses the troposphere, stratosphere, and mesosphere. Gases in the homosphere are considered well mixed.
- The **heterosphere** encompasses the thermosphere and exosphere. In this layer, the distance that particles can move without colliding is large. As a result, gases are **stratified** according to their molecular weights. Heavier gases such as oxygen and nitrogen occur near the bottom of the heterosphere, while hydrogen, the lightest element, is found at the top.

Copyright © Mometrix Media. You have been licensed one copy of this document for personal use only. Any other reproduction or redistribution is strictly prohibited. All rights reserved.

Hydrosphere

Much of Earth is covered by a layer of water or ice called the **hydrosphere**. Most of the hydrosphere consists of ocean water. The **water cycle** and the many processes involved in it take place in the hydrosphere.

There are several theories regarding how the Earth's hydrosphere was formed. Earth contains more surface water than other planets in the inner solar system. **Outgassing**, the slow release of trapped water vapor from the Earth's interior, is one theory used to explain the existence of water on Earth. This does not really account for the quantity of water on Earth, however. Another hypothesis is that the early Earth was subjected to a period of bombardment by **comets** and **water-rich asteroids**, which resulted in the release of water into the Earth's environment. If this is true, much of the water on the surface of the Earth today originated from the outer parts of the solar system beyond Neptune.

Frontal Systems and Weather Maps

Cold fronts are represented on weather maps as a blue line. Solid blue triangles are used to indicate the direction of movement. **Warm fronts** are represented with a red line. Solid red semi-circles are used to indicate the direction of the front. The cold and warm front symbols are merged and alternated to point in opposite directions to indicate a **stationary front**. An **occluded front** is represented by a purple line with alternating solid purple triangles and semi-circles. A **surface trough** is represented by an orange dashed line. A **squall** or **shear line** is represented by a red line. Two dots and a dash are alternated to form the line. A **dry line** is represented by an orange line with semi-circles in outline form. A **tropical wave** is represented by a straight orange line. An "L" is used to indicate an area of **low atmospheric pressure** and an "H" is used to indicate an area of **high atmospheric pressure**.

Bergeron Classification System

The **Bergeron classification system** uses three sets of letters to identify the following characteristics of air masses: moisture content, thermal characteristics from where they originated, and the stability of the atmosphere. "**Moisture content**" abbreviations are as follows: "c" represents the dry continental air masses and "m" stands for the moist maritime air masses. "**Thermal characteristics**" abbreviations are as follows: "T" indicates the air mass is tropical in origin; "P" indicates the air mass is polar in origin; "A" indicates the air mass is Antarctic in origin; "M" stands for monsoon; "E" indicates the air mass is equatorial in origin; and "S" is used to represent superior air, which is dry air formed by a downward motion. "**Stability of the Atmosphere**" abbreviations are as follows: "k" indicates the mass is colder than the ground below it, while "w" indicates the mass is warmer than the ground. For example, cP is a continental polar air mass, while cPk is a polar air mass blowing over the Gulf Stream, which is warmer than the mass.

Shearline, Dry Line, Squall Line, and Tropical Waves

- **Shearline**: This evolves from a stationary front that has gotten smaller. Wind direction shifts over a short distance.
- **Dry line or dew point line**: This separates two warm air masses of differing moisture content. At lower altitudes, the moist air mass wedges under the drier air. At higher altitudes, the dry air wedges under the moist air. This is a frequent occurrence in the Midwest and Canada, where the dry air of the Southwest and the moister air of the Gulf of Mexico meet. This can lead to extreme weather events, including tornadoes and thunderstorms.

Copyright © Mometrix Media. You have been licensed one copy of this document for personal use only. Any other reproduction or redistribution is strictly prohibited. All rights reserved.

- **Squall line**: Severe thunderstorms can form at the front of or ahead of a cold front. In some cases, severe thunderstorms can also outrun cold fronts. A squall line can produce extreme weather in the form of heavy rain, hail, lightning, strong winds, tornadoes, and waterspouts.
- **Tropical waves or easterly waves**: These are atmospheric troughs or areas of low air pressure that travel westward in the tropics, causing clouds and thunderstorms.

Latitude, Longitude, and the Equator

For the purposes of tracking time and location, the Earth is divided into sections with imaginary lines. Lines that run vertically around the globe through the poles are lines of **longitude**, sometimes called meridians. The **Prime Meridian** is the longitudinal reference point of 0. Longitude is measured in 15-degree increments toward the east or west. Degrees are further divided into 60 minutes, and each minute is divided into 60 seconds. Lines of **latitude** run horizontally around the Earth parallel to the equator, which is the 0-reference point and the widest point of the Earth. Latitude is the distance north or south from the equator, and is also measured in degrees, minutes, and seconds.

Tropic of Cancer, Tropic of Capricorn, Antarctic, and Arctic Circles

- **Tropic of Cancer**: This is located at 23.5 degrees north. The Sun is directly overhead at noon on June 21st in the Tropic of Cancer, which marks the beginning of summer in the Northern Hemisphere.
- **Tropic of Capricorn**: This is located at 23.5 degrees south. The Sun is directly overhead at noon on December 21st in the Tropic of Capricorn, which marks the beginning of winter in the Northern Hemisphere.
- **Arctic Circle**: This is located at 66.5 degrees north, and marks the start of when the Sun is not visible above the horizon. This occurs on December 21st, the same day the Sun is directly over the Tropic of Capricorn.
- **Antarctic Circle**: This is located at 66.5 degrees south, and marks the start of when the Sun is not visible above the horizon. This occurs on June 21st, which marks the beginning of winter in the Southern Hemisphere and is when the Sun is directly over the Tropic of Cancer.

Properties of Water

Water contains an extensive network of **hydrogen bonds**. As a result, water has a high **heat capacity**, meaning that it can absorb a large amount of heat without changing temperature, and a high **heat of vaporization**, meaning that it can absorb a large amount of heat before it transforms from a liquid to a gas state. One result of these properties is that water helps to regulate the Earth's climate by absorbing **thermal radiation**.

The presence of hydrogen bonds is also responsible for **capillary action**, which allows water to rise into a narrow tube against the force of gravity. This is part of the reason that water can be transported into the body of trees.

When water freezes, it becomes less dense and **expands**, allowing ice to float on water. This **insulates** the water below, preventing a lake from freezing from the bottom up. If a lake froze from the bottom up, it might destroy life in the lake, and might not completely thaw during the summer.

> **Review Video: Properties of Water**
> Visit mometrix.com/academy and enter code: 279526

Ocean

The **ocean** is a salty body of water that covers 71% of the Earth's surface. Geographically, the ocean is divided into three large oceans: the **Pacific Ocean**, the **Atlantic Ocean**, and the **Indian Ocean**. There are

Copyright © Mometrix Media. You have been licensed one copy of this document for personal use only. Any other reproduction or redistribution is strictly prohibited. All rights reserved.

also other divisions, such as gulfs, bays, and various types of seas, including Mediterranean and marginal seas. The ocean's depth is greatest at **Challenger Deep** in the Mariana Trench (10,924 meters below sea level).

Salinity is a measure of the amount of dissolved salts in ocean water. It is defined in terms of conductivity. Salinity is influenced by the geologic formations in the area, with igneous formations leading to lower salinity and sedimentary formations leading to higher salinity. Dryer areas with greater rates of evaporation also have higher salt concentrations. Areas where fresh water mixes with ocean water have lower salt concentrations. Hydrogen and oxygen make up about 96.5% of sea water. The major constituents of the dissolved solids of sea water at an atomic level are chlorine (55.3%), sodium (30.8%), magnesium (3.7%), sulfur (2.6%), calcium (1.2%), and potassium (1.1%). The salinity of ocean water is fairly constant, ranging from 34.60 to 34.80 parts per thousand, which is 200 parts per million. Measuring variation on this small of a scale requires instruments that are accurate to about one part per million.

Ocean Floor

The **ocean floor** includes features similar to those found on land, such as mountains, ridges, plains, and canyons. Other features of the ocean floor are as follows:

- The oceanic **crust** is a thin, dense layer that is about 10 km thick.
- A **seamount** is an undersea volcanic peak that rises to a height of at least 1,000 meters.
- A **guyot** is a seamount with a flat top.
- A **mid-ocean ridge** is a continuous undersea mountain chain.
- **Sills** are low parts of ridges separating ocean basins or other seas.
- **Trenches** are long, narrow troughs.

Gyres and Coriolis Effect

Gyres are surface ocean currents that form large circular patterns. In the Northern Hemisphere, they flow clockwise. In the Southern Hemisphere, they flow counterclockwise. These directions are caused by the **Coriolis effect**. The Coriolis effect occurs due to the fact that the Earth is a rotating object. In the Northern Hemisphere, currents appear to be curving to the right. In the Southern Hemisphere, currents appear to be curving to the left. Gyres tend to flow in the opposite direction near the Earth's poles. In the portion of the Pacific Ocean north of the equator, the major currents are North Pacific, California, North Equatorial, and Kuroshio. In the South Pacific, they are South Equatorial, East Australia, South Pacific, and Peru. In the North Atlantic, they are the North Atlantic Drift, Canary, North Equatorial, and Gulf Stream. In the South Atlantic, they are South Equatorial, Brazil, South Atlantic, and Benguela.

Ocean Currents

Surface currents are caused by winds. **Subsurface currents**, which occur deep beneath the ocean's surface, are caused by land masses and the Earth's rotation. The density of ocean water can also affect currents. Sea water with a higher salinity is denser than sea water with a lower salinity. Water from denser areas flows to areas with water that is less dense. Currents are classified by **temperature**. Colder polar sea water flows south towards warmer water, forming **cold currents**. **Warm water currents** swirl around the basins and equator. In turn, heat lost and gained by the ocean creates winds. Ocean currents play a significant role in transferring this heat toward the poles, which aids in the development of many types of weather phenomena.

Upwelling and Ekman Transport

Upwelling occurs where wind blows parallel to a coast. This causes the ocean surface to move away from the coast. Deep-sea water, which is usually cold and rich in nutrients, rises to takes its place.

Copyright © Mometrix Media. You have been licensed one copy of this document for personal use only. Any other reproduction or redistribution is strictly prohibited. All rights reserved.

Ekman transport refers to the impact of the Coriolis effect when wind moves water. Wind blowing in one direction tries to move the surface layer of water in a straight line, but the rotation of the Earth causes water to move in a curved direction. The wind continues to blow the surface of the water and the surface water turns slightly. Below the surface, the water turns even more, eventually creating a spiral. This creates water movement at a right angle to the wind direction. The importance of upwelling is that it brings the nutrient-rich dead and rotting sea creatures closer to the ocean's surface. Here, they are consumed by **phytoplankton**, which is in turn eaten by **zooplankton**. Fish eat the zooplankton, and larger creatures and humans eat the fish. **Downwelling** is the opposite of upwelling.

Deep Sea Currents and Ocean Waves

Deep sea currents are often likened to a conveyor belt because they circumnavigate the entire ocean, albeit weakly, and slowly mix deeper and shallower water. In the winter, deep circulation carries cold water from high latitudes to lower latitudes throughout the world. This takes place in areas where most water is at a depth of between 4 and 5 km. This water mass can reach temperatures of 4°C or lower. Surface ocean temperatures average about 17°C, but can vary from 2°C to 36°C. The vast cold mass of sea water is also dense and has a high saline content, which forces it to sink at high latitudes. It spreads out, stratifies, and fills the ocean basins. Deep mixing occurs and then the water upwells. The manner in which deep sea currents move can be described as **abyssal circulation**.

Most waves in the ocean are formed by winds. The stronger the winds are, the larger the waves will be. The highest point of a wave is the **crest**. The lowest point of a wave is the **trough**. The **wavelength** is measured from crest to crest. The wave **height** is measured from the trailing trough to the peak of the crest. The wave **frequency** refers to the number of wave crests passing a designated point each second. A wave **period** is the time it takes for a wave crest to reach the point of the wave crest of the previous wave. The **energy** in the wave runs into the shallow sea floor. This causes the wave to become steeper and then fall over, or break.

Waves that reach the shore are not all the same size. They can be larger or smaller than average. About once an hour, there is usually a wave that is twice the size of others. There are even larger, but rare, **rogue waves**, which often travel alone and in a different direction from other waves. **Swells** are waves that have traveled a great distance. These types of waves are usually large waves with flatter crests. They are very regular in shape and size.

Tides

The sea level slowly rises and falls over the period of a day. These types of waves on the sea surface are known as **tides**. Tides have wavelengths of thousands of kilometers. They differ from other wave types in that they are created by slow and very small changes in gravity due to the motion of the Sun and the Moon relative to Earth.

The **gravitational pull** of the Sun and Moon causes the oceans to rise and fall each day, creating high and low tides. Most areas have two high tides and two low tides per day. Because the Moon is closer to the Earth than the Sun, its gravitational pull is much greater. The water on the side of the Earth that is closest to the Moon and the water on the opposite side experience **high tide**. The two **low tides** occur on the other sides. This changes as the Moon revolves around the Earth. **Tidal range** is the measurement of the height difference between low and high tide. Tidal range also changes with the location of the Sun and Moon throughout the year, creating spring and neap tides. When all these bodies are aligned, the combined gravitational pull is greater and the tidal range is also greater. This is what

Copyright © Mometrix Media. You have been licensed one copy of this document for personal use only. Any other reproduction or redistribution is strictly prohibited. All rights reserved.

creates the **spring tide**. The **neap tide** is when the tidal range is at its lowest, which occurs when the Sun and Moon are at right angles.

> **Review Video: Moon and Sun on Ocean Tides**
> Visit mometrix.com/academy and enter code: 902956

Seismic Sea Waves

Seismic sea waves or **tsunamis** (sometimes mistakenly called tidal waves) are formed by **seismic activity**. A tsunami is a series of waves with long wavelengths and long periods. Far out at sea, the heights of these waves are typically less than one meter. The wavelength may be 100 km and the wave period may range from five minutes to one hour. However, as seismic sea waves approach the shoreline, the bottom of the wave is slowed down by the shallower sea floor. The top is not slowed as much, and wave height increases to as much as 20 meters. These waves can hit the shore at speeds of up to 30 miles per hour. Tsunamis are caused by earthquakes, submarine landslides, and volcanic eruptions.

Rift Valleys

Rift valleys occur both on land and in the ocean. They are a result of **plate tectonics** and occur when plates are spreading apart. In the ocean, this is part of the crust development cycle in which new crust is created at mid-ocean ridges and old crust is lost at the trenches. The Mid-Atlantic Ridge is an example of this. It occurs at divergent Eurasian and North American plates and in the South Atlantic, African, and South American plates. The East Pacific Rise is also a mid-oceanic ridge. The most extensive rift valley is located along the crest of the mid-ocean ridge system. It is a result of sea floor spreading.

Shorelines and Coastal Processes

The area where land meets the sea is called the **shoreline**. This marks the average position of the ocean. Longshore currents create **longshore drift** or **transport** (also called beach drift). This is when ocean waves move toward a beach at an angle, which moves water along the coast. Sediment is eroded from some areas and deposited in others. In this way, it is moved along the beach. **Rip currents** are strong, fast currents that occur when part of longshore current moves away from the beach. Hard, man-made structures built perpendicular to the beach tend to trap sand on the up-current side. Erosion occurs on the down-current side. Features formed by the sediment deposited by waves include spits, bay-mouth bars, tombolos, barrier islands, and buildups. **Sand** is composed of weather-resistant, granular materials like quartz and orthoclase. In some locations, it is composed of rock and basalt.

Weathering erodes rock and soil into sand. Other parts of the soil such as clay and silt are deposited in areas of the continental shelf. The larger sand particles get deposited in the form of a **beach**. This includes a **near shore**, which is underwater, a **fore shore**, the area typically considered the beach, and a **back shore**. The **offshore** starts about 5 meters from the shoreline and extends to about 20 meters. The beach also includes wet and dry parts and a fore dune and rear dune. Waves typically move sand from the sea to the beach, and gravity and wave action move it back again. Wind gradually pushes sand particles uphill in a jumping motion called saltation. Sand stays deposited in the form of **dunes** and the dunes appear as if they roll backward. Storms can both erode a beach and provide additional deposition.

Black Smokers

A **black smoker** is a type of hydrothermal vent formed when superheated water from below Earth's crust emerges from the ocean floor. This hot water is also rich in sulfides and other minerals from the Earth's crust. When the hot water comes in contact with the cold ocean water, it creates a black chimney-like structure around the vent. Water temperatures around black smokers have been recorded at 400°C. However, water pressure is too great on the sea floor to allow for boiling. The water is also

Copyright © Mometrix Media. You have been licensed one copy of this document for personal use only. Any other reproduction or redistribution is strictly prohibited. All rights reserved.

very acidic (twice that of vinegar). It is estimated that the yearly volume of water passing through black smokers is 1.4×10^{14} kg.

Carbon Cycle, Phytoplankton, and Zooplankton

- The **carbon and nutrient cycles** of the ocean are processes that are due in part to the deep currents, mixing, and upwelling that occur in the ocean. **Carbon dioxide** (CO_2) from the atmosphere is dissolved into the ocean at higher latitudes and distributed to the denser deep water. Where upwelling occurs, CO_2 is brought back to the surface and emitted into the tropical air.
- **Phytoplankton** are typically single-celled organisms that are nourished by the Sun. They are photosynthetic autotrophs, meaning they convert water, carbon dioxide, and solar energy into food. They drift with the currents, produce oxygen as a byproduct, and serve as a food source. Zooplankton feed on phytoplankton.
- **Zooplankton** are heterotrophic organisms, meaning they do not synthesize their own food. Zooplankton can be single-celled creatures or much larger organisms, such as jellyfish, mollusks, and crustaceans.

El Niño-Southern Oscillation (ENSO)

The **El Niño-Southern Oscillation (ENSO)** is a climate pattern of the Pacific Ocean area that lasts 6 to 18 months and causes weather that is different from the expected seasonal patterns and variations. There are two sets of events associated with ENSO: El Niño and La Niña. The usual weather patterns for the Pacific Ocean involve the movement of sea water by winds from the eastern part of the tropical Pacific to the western part of the Pacific Ocean. This pattern causes cold deep water upwells in the eastern Pacific. This creates wet weather and is considered a low-pressure system. Conversely, the eastern Pacific is a dry, high-pressure system. **El Niño** weakens upwelling because equalization in air pressure leads to less wind, which leads to more water staying in the eastern Pacific. **La Niña** increases upwelling because winds grow stronger because of higher air pressures across the Pacific. Both El Niño and La Niña cause extreme weather events such as droughts, heavy rain, and flooding.

North Atlantic Oscillation (NAO)

The **North Atlantic Oscillation** is a climatic occurrence that affects winter weather in the Northern Hemisphere, particularly in the east coast regions of the United States, Europe, and North Africa. Atmospheric pressure over the North Atlantic caused by the Icelandic Low and the high pressure Azores leads to the North Atlantic Oscillation. There is both a "**positive**" and "**negative**" phase of the NAO. The positive phase is when strong winds caused by a large difference in air pressure send wet winter storms from eastern North America to northern Europe. Weaker winds associated with a smaller difference in air pressure cause eastern North America and northern Europe to have fewer winter storms. Instead, the weather is rainy in southern Europe and North Africa.

Beaufort Wind Scale

The **Beaufort wind scale** assigns a numerical value to wind conditions and the appearance of the sea. **Zero** represents a calm, mirror-like sea with no measurable wind. **Twelve** is the maximum on the Beaufort scale, and represents hurricane force winds with speeds of 35.2 meters per second (m/s). Visibility is greatly reduced, the sea air is filled with foam, and the sea is completely white with driving spray. The scale is as follows: 1 is light wind with a speed of 1.2 m/s; 2 is a light breeze of 2.8 m/s; 3 is a gentle breeze of 4.9 m/s; 4 is a moderate breeze of 7.7 m/s; and 5 is a fresh breeze of 10.5 m/s. At 5, there are moderate waves, many white caps, and some spray. Six is a strong breeze of 13.1 m/s; 7 is a near gale with wind speeds of 15.8 m/s; 8 is gale force winds of 18.8 m/s; 9 is strong gales of 22.1 m/s; 10 is considered a storm with wind speeds of 25.9 m/s; and 11 is a violent storm.

Copyright © Mometrix Media. You have been licensed one copy of this document for personal use only. Any other reproduction or redistribution is strictly prohibited. All rights reserved.

Physics

Energy Transformation

Energy is constantly changing forms and being transferred back and forth. A pendulum swinging is an example of both a kinetic to potential and a potential to kinetic **energy transformation**. When a pendulum is moved from its center point (the point at which it is closest to the ground) to the highest point before it returns, it is an example of a kinetic to potential transformation. When it swings from its highest point toward the center, it is considered a potential to kinetic transformation. The sum of the potential and kinetic energy is known as the **total mechanical energy**. Stretching a rubber band gives it potential energy. That potential energy becomes kinetic energy when the rubber band is released.

> **Review Video:** Energy
> Visit mometrix.com/academy and enter code: 677735

Mechanics

Mechanics is the study of matter and motion, and the topics related to matter and motion, such as force, energy, and work. Discussions of mechanics will often include the concepts of vectors and scalars. **Vectors** are quantities with both magnitude and direction, while **scalars** have only magnitude. **Scalar quantities** include length, area, volume, mass, density, energy, work, and power. **Vector quantities** include displacement, velocity, acceleration, momentum, and force.

Velocity and Accelerations

There are two types of velocity to consider: average velocity and instantaneous velocity. Unless an object has a constant velocity or we are explicitly given an equation for the velocity, finding the **instantaneous velocity** of an object requires the use of calculus. If we want to calculate the **average velocity** of an object, we need to know two things: the displacement, or the distance it has covered, and the time it took to cover this distance. The formula for average velocity is simply the distance traveled divided by the time required. In other words, the average velocity is equal to the change in position divided by the change in time. Average velocity is a vector and will always point in the same direction as the displacement vector (since time is a scalar and always positive).

Acceleration is the change in the velocity of an object. Typically, the acceleration will be a constant value. Like position and velocity, acceleration is a vector quantity and will therefore have both magnitude and direction.

> **Review Video:** Speed and Velocity
> Visit mometrix.com/academy and enter code: 645590
>
> **Review Video:** Velocity and Acceleration
> Visit mometrix.com/academy and enter code: 671849

Newton's First Law of Motion

An object at rest or in motion will remain at rest or in motion unless acted upon by an external force.

This phenomenon is commonly referred to as **inertia**, the tendency of a body to remain in its present state of motion. In order for the body's state of motion to change, it must be acted on by an unbalanced force.

Copyright © Mometrix Media. You have been licensed one copy of this document for personal use only. Any other reproduction or redistribution is strictly prohibited. All rights reserved.

Newton's Second Law of Motion

An object's **acceleration** is directly proportional to the **net force** acting on the object, and inversely proportional to the object's **mass**.

It is generally written in equation form $F = ma$, where F is the net force acting on a body, m is the mass of the body, and a is its acceleration. Note that since the mass is always a positive quantity, the acceleration is always in the same direction as the force.

Newton's Third Law of Motion

For every force, there is an equal and opposite force.

When a hammer strikes a nail, the nail hits the hammer just as hard. If we consider two objects, A and B, then we may express any contact between these two bodies with the equation $F_{AB} = -F_{BA}$, where the order of the subscripts denotes which body is exerting the force. At first glance, this law might seem to forbid any movement at all since every force is being countered with an equal opposite force, but these equal opposite forces are acting on different bodies with different masses, so they will not cancel each other out.

> **Review Video:** Newton's First Law of Motion
> Visit mometrix.com/academy and enter code: 590367
>
> **Review Video:** Newton's Second Law of Motion
> Visit mometrix.com/academy and enter code: 737975
>
> **Review Video:** Newton's Third Law of Motion
> Visit mometrix.com/academy and enter code: 838401

Kinetic and Potential Energy

The two types of energy most important in mechanics are potential and kinetic energy. **Potential energy** is the amount of energy an object has stored within itself because of its position or orientation. There are many types of potential energy, but the most common is **gravitational potential energy**. It is the energy that an object has because of its height (h) above the ground. It can be calculated as $PE = mgh$, where m is the object's mass and g is the acceleration of gravity. **Kinetic energy** is the energy of an object in motion, and is calculated as $KE = mv^2/2$, where v is the magnitude of its velocity. When an object is dropped, its potential energy is converted into kinetic energy as it falls. These two equations can be used to calculate the velocity of an object at any point in its fall.

> **Review Video:** Potential and Kinetic Energy
> Visit mometrix.com/academy and enter code: 491502

Weight, Mass, and Acceleration

The **weight** of an object is the force of gravity on the object, and may be defined as the mass times the acceleration of gravity: $w = mg$. **Mass** is the amount of matter an object contains. When an object falls, it will **accelerate** at the same speed regardless of its mass, provided that gravity is the only force working on the object. Where mass can come into play is when there is significant **air resistance**. The force due to air resistance is a function of the object's size, shape, and velocity, but not mass. Thus, the air resistance force on two identically sized and shaped objects of different masses will be the same, but the heavier object will not be as affected, since it requires a greater force to overcome its momentum.

68

Copyright © Mometrix Media. You have been licensed one copy of this document for personal use only. Any other reproduction or redistribution is strictly prohibited. All rights reserved.

Work

Work can be thought of as the amount of energy expended in accomplishing some goal. The simplest equation for **mechanical work** (W) is $W = Fd$, where F is the force exerted and d is the displacement of the object on which the force is exerted. This equation requires that the force be applied in the same direction as the displacement. If this is not the case, then the work may be calculated as $W = Fd\cos(\theta)$, where θ is the angle between the force and displacement vectors. If force and displacement have the same direction, then work is positive; if they are in opposite directions, then work is negative; and if they are perpendicular, the work done by the force is zero.

If a man pushes a block horizontally across a surface with a constant force of 10 N for a distance of 20 m, the work done by the man is 200 N-m or 200 J. If instead the block is sliding and the man tries to slow its progress by pushing against it, his work done is -200 J, since he is pushing in the direction opposite the motion. If the man pushes vertically downward on the block while it slides, his work done is zero, since his force vector is perpendicular to the displacement vector of the block.

> **Review Video: Work**
> Visit mometrix.com/academy and enter code: 681834

Acceleration

When an object is thrown upward the acceleration throughout its flight is 9.8 meters per second squared (m/s^2) downward. This is Earth's **gravity** (g) close to its surface. It is the acceleration of all objects when there is no resistance, such as that of air.

If an object is held **stationary**, there is no work performed. This is because the formula for work performed is equal to the force times distance, or **displacement** ($W = F \times d[\cos\theta]$). Displacement is a vector measurement, and there must be displacement for work to be done. If an object is being held up, forces are at work, but are canceling each other out. No work is being done.

Density

A key property determining whether an object will float or sink in water is its **density**. The general rule is that if an object is less dense than water, it floats; if it is denser than water, it sinks. The density of an object is equal to its mass divided by its volume ($d = m/v$). It is important to note the difference between an **object's** density and a **material's** density. Water has a density of one gram per cubic centimeter, while steel has a density approximately eight times that. Despite having a much higher material density, an object made of steel may still float. A hollow steel sphere, for instance, will float easily because the density of the object includes the air contained within the sphere. An object may also float only in certain orientations. An ocean liner that is placed in the water upside down, for instance, may not remain afloat. An object will float only if it can displace a mass of water equal to its own mass.

> **Review Video: Mass, Weight, Volume, Density, and Specific Gravity**
> Visit mometrix.com/academy and enter code: 920570

Archimedes's Principle

Archimedes's principle states that a buoyant (upward) force on a submerged object is equal to the weight of the liquid displaced by the object. Water has a density of one gram per cubic centimeter. Anything that floats in water has a lower effective density, and anything that sinks has a higher effective density. This principle of buoyancy can also be used to calculate the volume of an irregularly shaped object. The mass of the object (m) minus its apparent mass in the water (m_a) divided by the density of water (ρ_w), gives the object's volume: $V = (m - m_a)/\rho_w$.

69

Copyright © Mometrix Media. You have been licensed one copy of this document for personal use only. Any other reproduction or redistribution is strictly prohibited. All rights reserved.

Projectile, Circular, and Periodic Motion

- **Projectile motion**: occurs where an object thrown into the air near the earth's surface moves along an arched path under the effect of gravity alone
- **Circular motion**: movement of an object in a rotating circular path
- **Periodic motion**: motion that is repeated at recurring intervals, such as the swinging of a pendulum

Collision and Conservation of Momentum

- **Elastic collision**: collision in which the total kinetic energy between two bodies before the collision equals the total kinetic energy after the collision. An example would be a collision between two gas molecules, in which the two molecules only change direction after a collision, but not kinetic energy.
- **Inelastic collision**: collision in which the total kinetic energy between two bodies increases or decreases after a collision. An example would be a collision in which a moving car strikes a parked car, resulting in a single body with a different kinetic energy than either of the original two bodies. In this case, kinetic energy could be lost because of friction between the tires and the road or changes in the car bodies because of the collision.
- **Law of conservation of momentum**: for a collision between two bodies with no external forces, the vector sum of the momentums is not affected by the interaction and remains constant.

Types of Energy Transformation

Other examples of energy transformations include:

- Electric to mechanical: Ceiling fan
- Chemical to heat: burning coal
- **Chemical to light**: Phosphorescence and luminescence (which allow objects to glow in the dark) occur because energy is absorbed by a substance (charged) and light is re-emitted comparatively slowly
- **Heat to electricity**: Examples include thermoelectric, geothermal, and ocean thermal.
- Heat to mechanical: steam engine
- **Nuclear to heat**: Examples include nuclear reactors and power plants.
- **Mechanical to sound**: Playing a violin or almost any instrument
- Sound to electric: Microphone
- Light to electric: Solar panels
- Electric to light: Light bulbs

Motion and Displacement

Motion is a change in the location of an object, and is the result of an unbalanced net force acting on the object. Understanding motion requires the understanding of three basic quantities: displacement, velocity, and acceleration.

When something moves from one place to another, it has undergone **displacement**. Displacement along a straight line is a very simple example of a vector quantity. If an object travels from position x = -5 cm to x = 5 cm, it has undergone a displacement of 10 cm. If it traverses the same path in the opposite direction, its displacement is -10 cm. A vector that spans the object's displacement in the direction of travel is known as a **displacement vector**.

> **Review Video: Displacement**
> Visit mometrix.com/academy and enter code: 236197

Copyright © Mometrix Media. You have been licensed one copy of this document for personal use only. Any other reproduction or redistribution is strictly prohibited. All rights reserved.

Gravitational Force and Friction

Gravitational force is a universal force that causes every object to exert a force on every other object. The gravitational force between two objects can be described by the formula, $F = Gm_1m_2/r^2$, where m_1 and m_2 are the masses of two objects, r is the distance between them, and G is the gravitational constant, $G = 6.672 \times 10^{-11}$ N-m²/kg². In order for this force to have a noticeable effect, one or both of the objects must be extremely large, so the equation is generally only used in problems involving planetary bodies. For problems involving objects on the earth being affected by earth's gravitational pull, the force of gravity is simply calculated as $F = mg$, where g is 9.8 m/s² toward the ground.

Friction is a force that arises as a resistance to motion where two surfaces are in contact. The maximum magnitude of the **frictional force** (f)can be calculated as $f = F_c\mu$, where F_c is the contact force between the two objects and μ is a **coefficient of friction** based on the surfaces' material composition. Two types of friction are static and kinetic. To illustrate these concepts, imagine a book resting on a table. The force of its weight (W) is equal and opposite to the force of the table on the book, or the normal force (N). If we exert a small force (F) on the book, attempting to push it to one side, a frictional force (f) would arise, equal and opposite to our force. At this point, it is a **static frictional force** because the book is not moving. If we increase our force on the book, we will eventually cause it to move. At this point, the frictional force opposing us will be a **kinetic frictional force**. Generally, the kinetic frictional force is lower than static frictional force (because the frictional coefficient for static friction is larger), which means that the amount of force needed to maintain the movement of the book will be less than what was needed to start it moving.

> **Review Video: Friction**
> Visit mometrix.com/academy and enter code: 716782

Simple Machines

Simple machines include the inclined plane, lever, wheel and axle, and pulley. These simple machines have no internal source of energy. More complex or compound machines can be formed from them. Simple machines provide a force known as a mechanical advantage and make it easier to accomplish a task. The inclined plane enables a force less than the object's weight to be used to push an object to a greater height. A lever enables a multiplication of force. The wheel and axle allows for movement with less resistance. Single or double pulleys allow for easier direction of force. The wedge and screw are forms of the inclined plane. A wedge turns a smaller force working over a greater distance into a larger force. The screw is similar to an incline that is wrapped around a shaft.

> **Review Video: Simple Machines**
> Visit mometrix.com/academy and enter code: 950789

Mechanical Advantage

A certain amount of **work** is required to move an object. The amount cannot be reduced, but by changing the way the work is performed a **mechanical advantage** can be gained. A certain amount of work is required to raise an object to a given vertical height. By getting to a given height at an angle, the effort required is reduced, but the distance that must be traveled to reach a given height is increased. An example of this is walking up a hill. One may take a direct, shorter, but steeper route, or one may take a more meandering, longer route that requires less effort. Examples of wedges include doorstops, axes, plows, zippers, and can openers.

> **Review Video: Mechanical Advantage**
> Visit mometrix.com/academy and enter code: 482323

Copyright © Mometrix Media. You have been licensed one copy of this document for personal use only. Any other reproduction or redistribution is strictly prohibited. All rights reserved.

Levers

A **lever** consists of a bar or plank and a pivot point or fulcrum. Work is performed by the bar, which swings at the pivot point to redirect the force. There are three types of levers: first, second, and third class. Examples of a **first-class lever** include balances, see-saws, nail extractors, and scissors (which also use wedges). In a **second-class lever** the fulcrum is placed at one end of the bar and the work is performed at the other end. The weight or load to be moved is in between. The closer to the fulcrum the weight is, the easier it is to move. Force is increased, but the distance it is moved is decreased. Examples include pry bars, bottle openers, nutcrackers, and wheelbarrows. In a **third-class lever** the fulcrum is at one end and the positions of the weight and the location where the work is performed are reversed. Examples include fishing rods, hammers, and tweezers.

> **Review Video: Levers**
> Visit mometrix.com/academy and enter code: 103910

Wheel and Axle

The center of a **wheel and axle** can be likened to a fulcrum on a rotating lever. As it turns, the wheel moves a greater distance than the axle, but with less force. Obvious examples of the wheel and axle are the wheels of a car, but this type of simple machine can also be used to exert a greater force. For instance, a person can turn the handles of a winch to exert a greater force at the turning axle to move an object. Other examples include steering wheels, wrenches, faucets, waterwheels, windmills, gears, and belts. **Gears** work together to change a force. The four basic types of gears are spur, rack and pinion, bevel, and worm gears. The larger gear turns slower than the smaller, but exerts a greater force. Gears at angles can be used to change the direction of forces.

> **Review Video: Simple Machines**
> Visit mometrix.com/academy and enter code: 950789

Pulleys

A **single pulley** consists of a rope or line that is run around a wheel. This allows force to be directed in a downward motion to lift an object. This does not decrease the force required, just changes its direction. The load is moved the same distance as the rope pulling it. When a **combination pulley** is used, such as a double pulley, the weight is moved half the distance of the rope pulling it. In this way, the work effort is doubled. Pulleys are never 100% efficient because of friction. Examples of pulleys include cranes, chain hoists, block and tackles, and elevators.

> **Review Video: Pulley**
> Visit mometrix.com/academy and enter code: 495865

Conductors and Insulators

- **Conductor**: This is a material that provides little resistance to heat transfer between its particles.
- **Insulator**: This is a material that provides resistance to heat transfer between its particles.

Valence Electrons and Conduction

When studying atoms at a microscopic level, it can be seen that some materials such as metals have properties that allow electrons to flow easily. Metals are good **conductors** of electricity because their valence electrons are loosely held in a network of atoms. This is because the valence shells of metal atoms have weak attractions to their nuclei. This results in a "sea of electrons," and electrons can flow between atoms with little resistance. In **insulating** materials such as glass, they hardly flow at all. In

Copyright © Mometrix Media. You have been licensed one copy of this document for personal use only. Any other reproduction or redistribution is strictly prohibited. All rights reserved.

between materials can be called **semiconducting materials**, and have intermediate conducting behavior. At low temperatures, some materials become superconductors and offer no resistance to the flow of electrons. **Thermal conductivity** refers to a material's capacity to conduct heat.

> **Review Video: Resistance of Electric Currents**
> Visit mometrix.com/academy and enter code: 668423

Electric Motors

An **electric motor** converts electric energy into **mechanical energy**. Energy can be provided by an AC or DC source. The power provided has many practical applications. The basic premise of a motor is that the electric current passing through a wire or coil creates a magnetic field that opposes the poles of a permanent magnet. The repelling forces between one pole of the electromagnet and the opposing pole of the fixed magnet cause the coil to move about ½ a turn. As it approaches the pole of like attraction, the coil would normally stop moving. In a motor, however, the current is reversed at this time, which reverses the poles and again forces rotation. In a **DC motor**, a switch or commuter can be used to reverse the charge. In an **AC motor**, the charge alternates on its own. The coil is attached to a shaft that is rotated, which provides the mechanical energy necessary to do work.

Electrical Generators and Electric Potential

An **electrical generator** is the opposite of a motor in that it transforms magnetic force into electrical energy. Like a motor, however, it uses an electromagnetic field and a permanent magnet to achieve electromagnetic induction. Generators do not create electricity, but rather convert mechanical energy into electric energy. Smaller gas generators are used as backup or primary power sources of electricity for equipment, homes, and other small-scale applications. Larger generators may use mechanical energy from many different sources, including water, steam, wind, compressed air, or even a hand crank.

The current does not flow through the bird because it and the wire have the same **electric potential**. Therefore, there is no reason for current to move from the wire to the bird. If the bird touched something else in addition to the wire and became grounded, the electrons would flow through the bird and electrocute it.

Static Electricity

Static electricity occurs when the net electric charge is non-zero, motionless, and produces an electrostatic discharge in two objects brought together. The objects' charges are changed to achieve a balance. **Polarization** is when there is a zero net charge that is unevenly distributed, which leads to a bound charge. The motion of charged particles in a given direction is known as **electric current**. It does not produce a net loss or gain of charge.

> **Review Video: Static Electricity**
> Visit mometrix.com/academy and enter code: 113722

Friction

A glass rod and a plastic rod can illustrate the concept of static electricity due to **friction**. Both start with no charge. A glass rod rubbed with silk produces a positive charge, while a plastic rod rubbed with fur produces a negative charge. The **electron affinity** of a material is a property that helps determine how easily it can be charged by friction. Materials can be sorted by their affinity for electrons into a **triboelectric series**. Materials with greater affinities include celluloid, sulfur, and rubber. Materials with lower affinities include glass, rabbit fur, and asbestos. In the example of a glass rod and a plastic one, the glass rod rubbed with silk acquires a positive charge because glass has a lower affinity for

Copyright © Mometrix Media. You have been licensed one copy of this document for personal use only. Any other reproduction or redistribution is strictly prohibited. All rights reserved.

electrons than silk. The electrons flow to the silk, leaving the rod with fewer electrons and a positive charge. When a plastic rod is rubbed with fur, electrons flow to the rod and result in a negative charge.

Power, Watt, and Transformer

- **Power**: Measured in watts, electric power refers to the rate at which electrical energy is transferred by an electric circuit. It can be calculated using **Joule's law**: $P = VI$, where P is power, V is the potential difference (in volts) and I is current (in amps). Power can be generated, transmitted, and converted into various forms of light.
- **Watt**: A watt is the unit used to measure power. One watt is equal to one joule of energy per second.
- **Transformer**: A transformer is a device that uses induction to transfer current from one circuit to another. Two wound coils act as a pair of **inductors**. Voltage can be modified to be transferred to another circuit (as in transmission lines) or to a load, such as an electrical device plugged into a socket.

Models Explaining Electric Current

Models that can be used to explain the flow of **electric current**, potential, and circuits include water, gravity, and roller coasters. For example, just as gravity is a force and a mass can have a potential for energy based on its location, so can a charge within an electrical field. Just as a force is required to move an object uphill, a force is also required to move a charge from a low to high potential. Another example is water. Water does not flow when it is level. If it is lifted to a point and then placed on a downward path, it will flow. A roller coaster car requires work to be performed to transport it to a point where it has potential energy (the top of a hill). Once there, gravity provides the force for it to flow (move) downward. If either path is broken, the flow or movement stops or is not completed.

Electric Charge and Atomic Structure

The attractive force between the electrons and the nucleus is called the **electric force**. A positive (+) charge or a negative (-) charge creates a field of sorts in the empty space around it, which is known as an **electric field**. The direction of a positive charge is away from it and the direction of a negative charge is towards it. An electron within the force of the field is pulled towards a positive charge because an electron has a negative charge. A particle with a positive charge is pushed away, or repelled, by another positive charge. Like charges repel each other and opposite charges attract. **Lines of force** show the paths of charges. The **magnitude** of the force is directly proportional to the magnitude of the charges (q) and inversely proportional to the square of the distance (r) between the two objects: $F = kq_1q_2/r^2$, where $k = 9 \times 10^9$ N-m^2/C^2. This relationship is known as **Coulomb's Law**. Electric charge is measured with the unit Coulomb (C). It is the amount of charge moved in one second by a steady current of one ampere (1C = 1A × 1s).

> **Review Video:** Electric Charge
> Visit mometrix.com/academy and enter code: 323587
>
> **Review Video:** Electric Force
> Visit mometrix.com/academy and enter code: 717639

Induction and Insulators

Insulators are materials that prevent the movement of electrical charges, while conductors are materials that allow the movement of electrical charges. This is because conductive materials have free electrons that can move through the entire volume of the conductor. This allows an external charge to change the charge distribution in the material. In **induction**, a neutral conductive material, such as a sphere, can become charged by a positively or negatively charged object, such as a rod. The charged object is placed close to the material without touching it. This produces a force on the free electrons,

74

Copyright © Mometrix Media. You have been licensed one copy of this document for personal use only. Any other reproduction or redistribution is strictly prohibited. All rights reserved.

which will either be attracted to or repelled by the rod, polarizing (or separating) the charge. The sphere's electrons will flow into or out of it when touched by a ground. The sphere is now charged. The charge will be opposite that of the charging rod.

Conduction and Law of Conservation of Charge

Charging by **conduction** is similar to charging by induction, except that the material transferring the charge actually touches the material receiving the charge. A negatively or positively charged object is touched to an object with a neutral charge. Electrons will either flow into or out of the neutral object and it will become charged. Insulators cannot be used to conduct charges. Charging by conduction can also be called charging by **contact**. The **law of conservation of charge** states that the total number of units before and after a charging process remains the same. No electrons have been created. They have just been moved around. The removal of a charge on an object by conduction is called grounding.

Dielectric, Electroscope, and Van de Graaff Generator

- **Dielectric**: This refers to a nonconducting substance of electric current that can usually sustain an electric field or maintain polarization. It differs from an insulator, which is typically defined as a material used to prevent the flow of current.
- **Electroscope**: This refers to an instrument used to detect a charge on another object. One somewhat low-tech type is the gold foil electroscope. It includes a conducting part connected to thin leaves of gold or aluminum foil which separate when a charged object is touched with the conducting part. The reason for this separation is that like charges repel each other. Electroscopes require high levels of voltage and are used with high voltage sources, such as static electricity and electrostatic machines. An electroscope cannot be used to determine whether a charge is positive or negative.
- **Van de Graaff generator**: This device, typically composed of a hollow metal ball and belt, is used to produce static electricity or high-voltage electricity with a low current.

Electric Potential

Electric potential, or electrostatic potential or voltage, is an expression of potential energy per unit of charge. It is measured in volts (V) as a scalar quantity. The formula used is $V = E/Q$, where V is voltage, E is electrical potential energy, and Q is the charge. **Voltage** is typically discussed in the context of electric potential difference between two points in a circuit. Voltage can also be thought of as a measure of the rate at which energy is drawn from a source in order to produce a flow of electric charge.

Circuits and Current

A **circuit** is a closed path along which electrons can travel with minimal resistance except at particular locations. **Electric current** is the sustained flow of electrons that are part of an electric charge moving along a path in a circuit. This differs from a **static electric charge**, which is a constant non-moving charge rather than a continuous flow. The rate of flow of electric charge is expressed using the ampere (amp or A) and can be measured using an ammeter. A current of 1 ampere means that 1 coulomb of charge passes through a given area every second. Electric charges typically only move from areas of high electric potential to areas of low electric potential.

Ohm's Law

Electric currents experience **resistance** as they travel through a circuit. Resistance is the hindrance to the flow of an electric charge. Different objects have different levels of resistance. The **ohm** (Ω) is the measurement unit of electric resistance. The symbol is the Greek letter omega. **Ohm's Law**, which is expressed as $I = V/R$, states that current flow (I, measured in amps) through an object is equal to the potential difference from one side to the other (V, measured in volts) divided by resistance (R, measured

75

Copyright © Mometrix Media. You have been licensed one copy of this document for personal use only. Any other reproduction or redistribution is strictly prohibited. All rights reserved.

in ohms). An object with a higher resistance will have a lower current flow through it given the same potential difference.

Simple Circuits

Movement of electric charge along a path between areas of high electric potential and low electric potential, with a resistor or load device between them, is the definition of a **simple circuit**. It is a closed conducting path between the high and low potential points, such as the positive and negative terminals on a battery. One example of a circuit is the flow from one terminal of a car battery to the other. The electrolyte solution of water and sulfuric acid provides work in chemical form to start the flow. A frequently used classroom example of circuits involves using a D cell (1.5 V) battery, a small light bulb, and a piece of copper wire to create a circuit to light the bulb.

Series Circuits

Series circuits are circuits in which there is only one path through which electrons can flow. An example of a series circuit is a string of old-fashioned Christmas tree lights. If a load in this type of circuit is removed, disabled, or switched off, the circuit is open and electricity does not flow. In the series circuit below, three resistors are in series, and their equivalent resistance is:

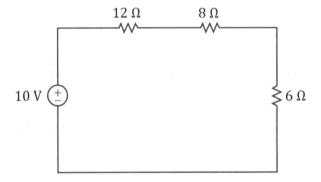

$$R_{eq} = R_1 + R_2 + \cdots + R_n = 12 + 8 + 6 = 26\Omega$$

Parallel Circuit

A **parallel circuit** is one in which there is more than one path through which electrons can travel. In a parallel circuit, the same voltage exists across all parallel paths, though the current may be vastly different among them. For the parallel circuit below, the equivalent resistance is:

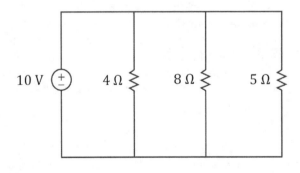

$$R_{eq} = \cfrac{1}{\cfrac{1}{R_1} + \cfrac{1}{R_2} + \cdots + \cfrac{1}{R_n}} = \cfrac{1}{\cfrac{1}{4} + \cfrac{1}{8} + \cfrac{1}{5}}$$

Copyright © Mometrix Media. You have been licensed one copy of this document for personal use only. Any other reproduction or redistribution is strictly prohibited. All rights reserved.

Short Circuit, Breakers, and Fuses

Short circuit: This refers to a low-resistance connection between two nodes of an electrical circuit, which results in an excessive electric current, or overcurrent. For example, a D cell battery with no load (such as a light bulb within the circuit) would result in a high rate of charge flow between terminals. This could cause unwanted or unintended high temperatures or rapid energy loss. Other short circuit circumstances could lead to circuit damage, fire, or explosion.

Because of the risks, circuit **breakers** are used as safety features to prevent overcurrent. Once a fault is detected, the circuit breaker acts like a switch to interrupt flow. It can be reset once the condition is corrected.

A **fuse** has a component that melts, which interrupts the flow of charges. Fuses differ from breakers in that fuses are one-time interrupters that must be replaced before the circuit can be restored.

Direct and Alternating Current

Direct current (DC) is the flow of an electric charge in one direction. Batteries and solar cells typically use direct current.

Alternating current (AC) is current that periodically reverses direction. AC is typically used in houses and other buildings.

Diodes and Inverters

A **diode** is an electronic device used to conduct electric current in one direction. The process of conduction in one direction is known as **rectification**. A rectifier is used to convert alternating current to direct current. Diodes are also used to remove modulation from radio signals.

An **inverter** is the opposite of a rectifier in that it converts direct current to alternating current. **Electromotive force (emf)** is what causes electrons to move when there is potential difference between two points (voltage). Devices that can provide emf include batteries, voltaic cells, thermoelectric devices, solar cells, electrical generators, transformers, and Van de Graaff generators.

Circuit Terminology

Circuit breaker: stops the flow of an electric charge through a circuit by creating a break in the path. A fuse also creates a break.

Resistor: a device used in a circuit that opposes the flow of an electric charge.

Transistor: a device made of a semiconductive material that can amplify or switch an electric charge.

Semiconductor: a material with conductivity between an insulator and a conductor. These materials replaced earlier electric devices such as vacuum tubes.

Solid State Devices

Solid state device: Used in modern circuits, solid state devices are solid materials in which the charge carriers, or electrons, are contained entirely within the material. Examples include transistors, microprocessors, integrated circuits, light-emitting diodes (LEDs), and liquid-crystal displays (LCDs).

Magnets and Magnetism

A **magnet** is a piece of metal, such as iron, steel, or magnetite (lodestone) that can affect another substance within its field of force that has like characteristics. Magnets can either attract or repel other

Copyright © Mometrix Media. You have been licensed one copy of this document for personal use only. Any other reproduction or redistribution is strictly prohibited. All rights reserved.

substances. Magnets have two **poles**: north and south. Like poles repel and opposite poles (pairs of north and south) attract. The magnetic field is a set of invisible lines representing the paths of attraction and repulsion.

Magnetism can occur naturally, or ferromagnetic materials can be magnetized. Certain matter that is magnetized can retain its magnetic properties indefinitely and become a permanent magnet. Other matter can lose its magnetic properties. For example, an iron nail can be temporarily magnetized by stroking it repeatedly in the same direction using one pole of another magnet. Once magnetized, it can attract or repel other magnetically inclined materials, such as paper clips. Dropping the nail repeatedly will cause it to lose its magnetic properties.

Magnetic Fields and Atomic Structure

The motions of subatomic structures (nuclei and electrons) produce a **magnetic field**. It is the direction of the spin and orbit that indicate the direction of the field. The strength of a magnetic field is known as the magnetic moment. As electrons spin and orbit a nucleus, they produce a magnetic field.

Pairs of electrons that spin and orbit in opposite directions cancel each other out, creating a **net magnetic field** of zero. Materials that have an unpaired electron are magnetic. Those with a weak attractive force are referred to as **paramagnetic materials**, while **ferromagnetic materials** have a strong attractive force. A **diamagnetic material** has electrons that are paired, and therefore does not typically have a magnetic moment. There are, however, some diamagnetic materials that have a weak magnetic field.

A magnetic field can be formed not only by a magnetic material, but also by electric current flowing through a wire. When a coiled wire is attached to the two ends of a battery, for example, an **electromagnet** can be formed by inserting a ferromagnetic material such as an iron bar within the coil. When electric current flows through the wire, the bar becomes a magnet. If there is no current, the magnetism is lost. A **magnetic domain** occurs when the magnetic fields of atoms are grouped and aligned. These groups form what can be thought of as miniature magnets within a material. This is what happens when an object like an iron nail is temporarily magnetized. Prior to magnetization, the organization of atoms and their various polarities are somewhat random with respect to where the north and south poles are pointing. After magnetization, a significant percentage of the poles are lined up in one direction, which is what causes the magnetic force exerted by the material.

> **Review Video: Magnetic Field Part I**
> Visit mometrix.com/academy and enter code: 953150
>
> **Review Video: Magnetic Field Part II**
> Visit mometrix.com/academy and enter code: 710249

Wave Types

Waves are divided into types based on the direction of particle motion in a medium and the direction of wave propagation.

- **Longitudinal waves**: These are waves that travel in the same direction as the particle movement. They are sometimes called pressure, compression, or density waves. Longitudinal sound waves are the easiest to produce and have the highest speed. A longitudinal wave consists of compressions and rarefactions, such as those seen by extending and collapsing a Slinky toy.
- **Shear or transverse waves**: These types of waves move perpendicular to the direction of the particle movement. For example, if the particles in a medium move up and down, a transverse wave will move forward. Transverse waves are possible only in solids and are slower than longitudinal waves.

Copyright © Mometrix Media. You have been licensed one copy of this document for personal use only. Any other reproduction or redistribution is strictly prohibited. All rights reserved.

- **Surface (circular) waves**: These waves travel at the surface of a material and move in elliptical orbits. They are a little slower than shear waves.
- **Plate waves**: These waves move in elliptical orbits and only occur in very thin pieces of material.

Wave Interactions

Waves can be in phase or out of phase, which is similar to the concept of being in sync or out of sync. For example, if two separate waves originate from the same point and the peaks (crests) and valleys (troughs) are exactly aligned, they are said to be **in phase**. If the peak of a wave aligns with the valley of another wave, they are **out of phase**. When waves are in phase their displacement is doubled. If they are out of phase they cancel each other out. If they are somewhere in between being completely in phase and completely out of phase, the wave interaction is a wave that is the sum of the **amplitudes** of all points along the wave. If waves originate from different points, the amplitude of particle displacement is the combined sum of the particle displacement amplitude of each individual wave.

Waveforms

Waveforms refer to the shapes and forms of waves as they are depicted on graphs. Forms include sinusoidal, square, triangle, and sawtooth. **Sinusoidal** refers to a waveform in which the amplitude (displacement from the rest position) is proportional to the sine (side opposite of angle/hypotenuse) of a variable such as time. Square, triangle, and sawtooth waveforms are **non-sinusoidal**, and are usually based on formulas. **Square waves** are used to depict digital information. **Pulse waves**, also known as rectangular waves, are a non-sinusoidal form similar to square waves, and are found in synthesizer programming. **Triangle waves**, like square waves, only have odd harmonics. The harmonic of a wave is the integer multiple of a base frequency. **Sawtooth waves** have both even and odd harmonics, and produce a sound particularly suited for synthesizing bowed string instruments.

Wave Interference

When waves traveling in the same medium interact, it is known as **wave interference**. While a single wave generally remains the same in terms of waveform, frequency, amplitude, and wavelength, several waves traveling through particles in a medium take on a more complicated appearance after they interact. The final properties of a wave are dependent on many factors, such as the points of origin of waves and whether they are in phase, out of phase, or somewhere in between. **Constructive interference** refers to what happens when two crests or two troughs of a wave meet. The resulting amplitude of the crest or trough is doubled. **Destructive interference** is what happens when the crest of one wave and the trough of another that are the same shape meet. When this occurs, the two waves cancel each other out.

Transfer of Energy in Waves

Waves have **energy** and can transfer energy when they interact with matter. Although waves transfer energy, they do not transport **matter**. They are a disturbance of matter that transfers energy from one particle to an adjacent particle. There are many types of waves, including sound, seismic, water, light, micro, and radio waves. The two basic categories of waves are mechanical and electromagnetic. **Mechanical waves** are those that transmit energy through matter. **Electromagnetic waves** can transmit energy through a vacuum. A **transverse wave** provides a good illustration of the features of a wave, which include crests, troughs, amplitude, and wavelength.

Copyright © Mometrix Media. You have been licensed one copy of this document for personal use only. Any other reproduction or redistribution is strictly prohibited. All rights reserved.

Wave Terminology

- **Frequency** is a measure of how often particles in a medium vibrate when a wave passes through the medium with respect to a certain point or node. Usually measured in Hertz (Hz), frequency might refer to cycles per second, vibrations per second, or waves per second. One Hz is equal to one cycle per second.
- **Period** is a measure of how long it takes to complete a cycle. It is the inverse of frequency; where frequency is measure in cycles per second, period can be thought of as seconds per cycle, though it is measured in units of time only.
- **Speed** refers to how fast or slow a wave travels. It is measured in terms of distance divided by time. While frequency is measured in terms of cycles per second, speed might be measured in terms of meters per second.
- **Amplitude** is the maximum amount of displacement of a particle in a medium from its rest position, and corresponds to the amount of energy carried by the wave. High-energy waves have greater amplitudes; low energy waves have lesser amplitudes. Amplitude is a measure of a wave's strength.
- **Rest position**, also called equilibrium, is the point at which there is neither positive nor negative displacement.
- **Crest**, also called the peak, is the point at which a wave's positive or upward displacement from the rest position is at its maximum.
- **Trough**, also called a valley, is the point at which a wave's negative or downward displacement from the rest position is at its maximum.
- A **wavelength** is one complete wave cycle. It could be measured from crest to crest, trough to trough, rest position to rest position, or any point of a wave to the corresponding point on the next wave.

Phenomenon of Sound

Sound is a pressure disturbance that moves through a medium in the form of mechanical waves. Sound requires a medium to travel through, such as air, water, or other matter since it is the vibrations that transfer energy to adjacent particles, not the actual movement of particles over a great distance. Sound is transferred through the movement of atomic particles, which can be atoms or molecules. Waves of sound energy move outward in all directions from the source. **Sound waves** consist of **compressions** (particles are forced together) and **rarefactions** (particles move farther apart and their density decreases). A wavelength consists of one compression and one rarefaction. Different sounds have different wavelengths. Sound is a form of kinetic energy.

Pitch, Loudness, Timbre, and Oscillation

- **Pitch**: Pitch is the quality of sound determined by frequency. For example, a musical note can be tuned to a specific frequency. Humans can detect frequencies between about 20 Hz to 20,000 Hz.
- **Loudness**: Loudness is a human's perception of sound intensity.
- **Sound intensity**: Sound intensity is measured as the sound power per unit area, and can be expressed in decibels.
- **Timbre**: This is a human's perception of the type or quality of sound.
- **Oscillation**: This is a measurement, usually of time, against a basic value, equilibrium, or rest point.

Doppler Effect

The **Doppler effect** refers to the effect the relative motion of the source of the wave and the location of the observer has on waves. The Doppler effect is easily observable in sound waves. What a person hears when a train approaches or a car honking its horn passes by are examples of the Doppler effect. The pitch of the sound is different not because the *emitted frequency* has changed, but because the *received frequency* has changed. The frequency is higher (as is the pitch) as the train approaches, the same as

Copyright © Mometrix Media. You have been licensed one copy of this document for personal use only. Any other reproduction or redistribution is strictly prohibited. All rights reserved.

emitted just as it passes, and lower as the train moves away. This is because the wavelength changes. A **redshift** occurs when light or radiation is increased in wavelength. A **blueshift** is a decrease in wavelength.

Electromagnetic Spectrum

The **electromagnetic spectrum** is defined by frequency (f) and wavelength (λ). Frequency is typically measured in hertz and wavelength is usually measured in meters. Because light travels at a fairly constant speed, **frequency** is inversely proportional to **wavelength**, a relationship expressed by the formula $f = c/\lambda$, where c is the speed of light (about 300 million meters per second). Frequency multiplied by wavelength equals the speed of the wave; for electromagnetic waves, this is the speed of light, with some variance for the medium in which it is traveling. Electromagnetic waves include (from largest to smallest wavelength) radio waves, microwaves, infrared radiation (radiant heat), visible light, ultraviolet radiation, x-rays, and gamma rays. The energy of electromagnetic waves is carried in packets that have a magnitude inversely proportional to the wavelength. **Radio waves** have a range of wavelengths, from about 10^{-3} to 10^5 meters, while their frequencies range from about 10^3 to 10^{11} Hz.

> **Review Video: Electromagnetic Radiation Waves**
> Visit mometrix.com/academy and enter code: 135307
>
> **Review Video: Electromagnetic Spectrum**
> Visit mometrix.com/academy and enter code: 771761

Visible Light

Light is the portion of the electromagnetic spectrum that is visible because of its ability to stimulate the **retina**. It is absorbed and emitted by electrons, atoms, and molecules that move from one energy level to another. **Visible light** interacts with matter through molecular electron excitation (which occurs in the human retina) and through plasma oscillations (which occur in metals). Visible light is between ultraviolet and infrared light on the spectrum. The wavelengths of visible light cover a range from 380 nm (violet) to 760 nm (red). Different wavelengths correspond to different colors. **Dispersion** is the action of distributing radiation according to wavelength, such as light into colors.

> **Review Video: Light**
> Visit mometrix.com/academy and enter code: 900556

Color in Rainbows

A rainbow is an example of the separation of light. The water molecules act as a separator, relying on both *refraction* and *reflection*. Rainbows include the colors of the visible light spectrum: red, orange, yellow, green, blue, indigo, and violet, which can be remembered using the acronym Roy G. Biv. The observer is at the center of the rainbow with the sun at his back, but only an arc of the rainbow circle is visible from the ground.

Perception of Color

The human brain interprets or perceives visible light, which is emitted from the sun and other stars, as **color**. For example, when the entire wavelength reaches the retina, the brain perceives the color white. When no part of the wavelength reaches the retina, the brain perceives the color black. The particular color of an object depends upon what is **absorbed** and what is **transmitted** or **reflected**. For example, a leaf consists of chlorophyll molecules, the atoms of which absorb all wavelengths of the visible light spectrum except for green, which is why a leaf appears green. Certain wavelengths of visible light can be absorbed when they interact with matter. Wavelengths that are not absorbed can be transmitted by transparent materials or reflected by opaque materials.

Copyright © Mometrix Media. You have been licensed one copy of this document for personal use only. Any other reproduction or redistribution is strictly prohibited. All rights reserved.

Light and Solid Objects

When light waves encounter an object, the light waves are reflected, transmitted, or absorbed. If the light is **reflected** from the surface of the object, the angle at which it contacts the surface will be the same as the angle at which it leaves, on the other side of the perpendicular. If the ray of light is perpendicular to the surface, it will be reflected back in the direction from which it came. When light is **transmitted** through the object, its direction may be altered upon entering the object. This is known as refraction. When light waves are refracted, or bent, an image can appear distorted. The degree to which the light is refracted depends on the speed at which light travels in the object. Light that is neither reflected nor transmitted will be **absorbed** by the surface and stored as heat energy. Nearly all instances of light hitting an object will involve a combination of two or even all three of these.

> **Review Video: Reflection, Transmission, and Absorption of Light**
> Visit mometrix.com/academy and enter code: 109410

Diffraction

Diffraction refers to the bending of waves around small objects and the spreading out of waves past small openings. The narrower the opening, the greater the level of diffraction will be. Larger wavelengths also increase diffraction. A **diffraction grating** can be created by placing a number of slits close together, and is used more frequently than a prism to separate light. Different wavelengths are diffracted at different angles.

> **Review Video: Diffraction of Light Waves**
> Visit mometrix.com/academy and enter code: 785494

Light Waves and Changing Media

When light waves pass from water to air, the frequency stays the same even though the speed and wavelength increase. This is because frequency is equal to speed (velocity) divided by wavelength ($f = v/\lambda$). In this case, there are two different mediums (water and air), which have different **refractive indexes**. Air has a smaller refractive index. The smaller the refractive index, the faster light moves through the medium. The refractive index of a medium can affect the speed and direction of travel of transmitted light. In air, both the speed and wavelength of the light increase, but the frequency (the number of cycles in a given unit of time) is the same. The **speed** of a wave is equal to its frequency times its wavelength ($v = f \times \lambda$). **Nodes** of a wave are the points at which the amplitude is at its minimum. **Wavelength** is measured as the distance between nodes.

Applications of the Properties of Light

The various properties of light have numerous **real life applications**. For example, polarized sunglasses have lenses that help reduce glare, while non-polarized sunglasses reduce the total amount of light that reaches the eyes. Polarized lenses consist of a chemical film of molecules aligned in parallel. This allows the lenses to block wavelengths of light that are intense, horizontal, and reflected from smooth, flat surfaces. The "fiber" in fiber optics refers to a tube or pipe that channels light. Because of the composition of the fiber, light can be transmitted greater distances before losing the signal. The fiber consists of a core, cladding, and a coating. Fibers are bundled, allowing for the transmission of large amounts of data.

Geometric Optics

Geometric optics uses the concept of rays to determine how light will propagate. **Ray diagrams** can illustrate the path of light through a lens. Different types of lenses refract light, either convergently or divergently, to form images. After passing through a lens, rays converge at a focal point. **Collimated**

Copyright © Mometrix Media. You have been licensed one copy of this document for personal use only. Any other reproduction or redistribution is strictly prohibited. All rights reserved.

rays are nearly parallel, and can be thought of as having no focal point. There are many types and combinations of lenses. **Convergent lenses**, also called positive lenses, are thicker in the middle and thinner at the edges. Rays are focused to a point. **Divergent lenses**, also called negative lenses, are thicker at the ends and thinner in the middle. Rays are spread apart, or diverged. A **convex lens** is bowed outward, either at one vertical surface or both. A convex lens with two convex surfaces may also be termed biconvex or double convex. A **concave lens** is bowed inward, while a planar lens is flat.

Theory of Relativity

Albert Einstein proposed two theories of relativity: the general theory of relativity (1916) and the special theory of relativity (1905). **Special relativity** is based on two basic premises. The first is that the laws of physics are the same for all observers in uniform motion relative to one another. This is also known as the principle of relativity. The second is that the speed of light in a vacuum is also the same for all observers and their relative motion or the motion of the source of the light does not affect this. **General relativity** is the generally accepted explanation of gravity as a property of space and time, or spacetime. Einstein was born in Germany in 1879 and received the Nobel Prize in Physics in 1921. He died in April of 1955.

Copyright © Mometrix Media. You have been licensed one copy of this document for personal use only. Any other reproduction or redistribution is strictly prohibited. All rights reserved.

Biochemistry, Cells, and Energetics

Prokaryotes and Eukaryotes

Sizes and Metabolism

Cells of the domains of Bacteria and Archaea are prokaryotes. Bacteria cells and Archaea cells are much smaller than cells of eukaryotes. Prokaryote cells are usually only 1 to 2 micrometers in diameter, but eukaryotic cells are usually at least 10 times and possibly 100 times larger than prokaryotic cells. Eukaryotic cells are usually 10 to 100 micrometers in diameter. Most prokaryotes are unicellular organisms, although some prokaryotes live in colonies. Because of their large surface-area-to-volume ratios, prokaryotes have a very high metabolic rate. Eukaryotic cells are much larger than prokaryotic cells. Due to their larger sizes, they have a much smaller surface-area-to-volume ratio and consequently have much lower metabolic rates.

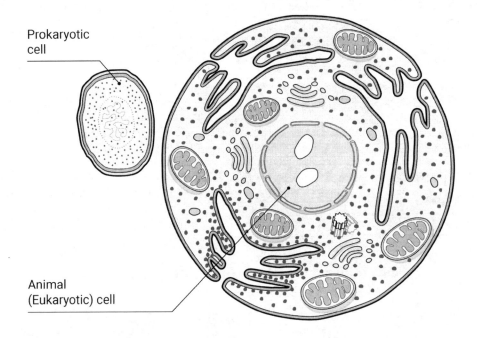

Prokaryotic cell

Animal (Eukaryotic) cell

Review Video: Eukaryotic and Prokaryotic
Visit mometrix.com/academy and enter code: 231438

Membrane-Bound Organelles

Prokaryotic cells are much simpler than eukaryotic cells. Prokaryote cells do not have a nucleus due to their small size. Their DNA is located in the center of the cell in a region referred to as a nucleoid. Eukaryote cells have a nucleus bound by a double membrane. Eukaryotic cells typically have hundreds or thousands of additional membrane-bound organelles that are independent of the cell membrane. Prokaryotic cells do not have any membrane-bound organelles that are independent of the cell membrane. Once again, this is probably due to the much larger size of the eukaryotic cells. The organelles of eukaryotes give them much higher levels of intracellular division than is possible in prokaryotic cells.

Cell Walls

Not all cells have cell walls. Most prokaryotes have cell walls. The cell walls of organisms from the domain Bacteria differ from the cell walls of the organisms from the domain Archaea. Some eukaryotes,

84

Copyright © Mometrix Media. You have been licensed one copy of this document for personal use only. Any other reproduction or redistribution is strictly prohibited. All rights reserved.

such as some fungi, some algae, and plants, have cell walls that differ from the cell walls of the Bacteria and Archaea domains. Most bacteria have cell walls outside of the plasma membrane that contains the molecule peptidoglycan. Peptidoglycan is a large polymer of amino acids and sugars. The peptidoglycan helps maintain the strength of the cell wall. Some of the Archaea cells have cell walls containing the molecule pseudopeptidoglycan, which differs in chemical structure from the peptidoglycan but basically provides the same strength to the cell wall. Some fungi cell walls contain chitin. The cell walls of diatoms, a type of yellow algae, contain silica. Plant cell walls contain cellulose, and woody plants are further strengthened by lignin. Some algae also contain lignin. Animal cells do not have cell walls.

Chromosome Structure

Prokaryote cells have DNA arranged in a circular structure that should not be referred to as a chromosome. Due to the small size of a prokaryote cell, the DNA material is simply located near the center of the cell in a region called the nucleoid. A prokaryotic cell may also contain tiny rings of DNA called plasmids. Prokaryote cells lack histone proteins, and therefore the DNA is not actually packaged into chromosomes. Prokaryotes reproduce by binary fission. The DNA in a eukaryotic cell is located in the membrane-bound nucleus. Eukaryote cells have linear chromosomes and histone proteins. During mitosis, the chromatin is tightly wound on the histone proteins and packaged as a chromosome. Eukaryotic cells may contain several large DNA molecules or chromosomes. Eukaryotes reproduce by mitosis.

> **Review Video: Chromosomes**
> Visit mometrix.com/academy and enter code: 132083

Cells and Organelles of Plant Cells and Animal Cells

Plant cells and animal cells both have a nucleus, cytoplasm, cell membrane, ribosomes, mitochondria, endoplasmic reticulum, Golgi apparatus, and vacuoles. Plant cells have only one or two extremely large vacuoles. Animal cells typically have several small vacuoles. Plant cells have chloroplasts for photosynthesis because plants are autotrophs. Animal cells do not have chloroplasts because they are

Copyright © Mometrix Media. You have been licensed one copy of this document for personal use only. Any other reproduction or redistribution is strictly prohibited. All rights reserved.

heterotrophs. Plant cells have a rectangular shape due to the cell wall, and animal cells have more of a circular shape. Animal cells have centrioles, but only some plant cells have centrioles.

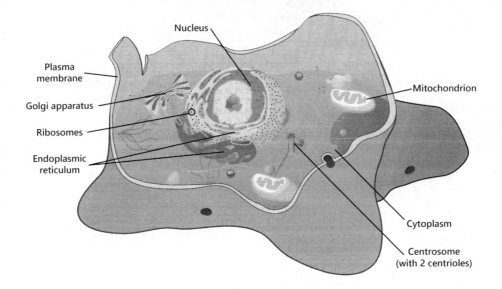

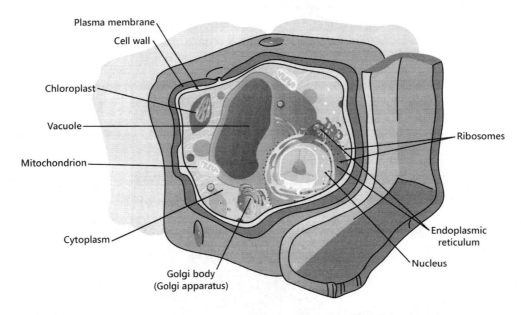

Review Video: <u>Plant and Animal Cells</u>
Visit mometrix.com/academy and enter code: 115568

Cell Membranes

The cell membrane, also referred to as the plasma membrane, is a thin semipermeable membrane of lipids and proteins. The cell membrane isolates the cell from its external environment while still enabling the cell to communicate with that outside environment. It consists of a phospholipid bilayer, or double layer, with the hydrophilic ends of the outer layer facing the external environment, the inner layer facing the inside of the cell, and the hydrophobic ends facing each other. Cholesterol in the cell membrane adds stiffness and flexibility. Glycolipids help the cell to recognize other cells of the organisms. The proteins in the cell membrane help give the cells shape. Special proteins help the cell

Copyright © Mometrix Media. You have been licensed one copy of this document for personal use only. Any other reproduction or redistribution is strictly prohibited. All rights reserved.

communicate with its external environment. Other proteins transport molecules across the cell membrane.

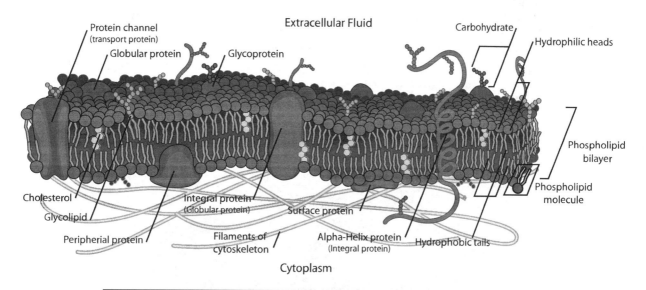

Review Video: Plasma Membrane
Visit mometrix.com/academy and enter code: 943095

Nucleus

Typically, a eukaryote has only one nucleus that takes up approximately 10% of the volume of the cell. Components of the nucleus include the nuclear envelope, nucleoplasm, chromatin, and nucleolus. The nuclear envelope is a double-layered membrane with the outer layer connected to the endoplasmic reticulum. The nucleus can communicate with the rest of the cell through several nuclear pores. The chromatin consists of deoxyribonucleic acid (DNA) and histones that are packaged into chromosomes during mitosis. The nucleolus, which is the dense central portion of the nucleus, manufactures ribosomes. Functions of the nucleus include the storage of genetic material, production of ribosomes, and transcription of ribonucleic acid (RNA).

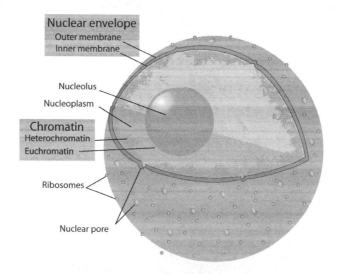

Review Video: Nucleic Acids
Visit mometrix.com/academy and enter code: 503931

Copyright © Mometrix Media. You have been licensed one copy of this document for personal use only. Any other reproduction or redistribution is strictly prohibited. All rights reserved.

Chloroplasts

Chloroplasts are large organelles that are enclosed in a double membrane. Discs called thylakoids are arranged in stacks called grana (singular, granum). The thylakoids have chlorophyll molecules on their surfaces. Stromal lamellae separate the thylakoid stacks. Sugars are formed in the stroma, which is the inner portion of the chloroplast. Chloroplasts perform photosynthesis and make food in the form of sugars for the plant. The light reaction stage of photosynthesis occurs in the grana, and the dark reaction stage of photosynthesis occurs in the stroma. Chloroplasts have their own DNA and can reproduce by fission independently.

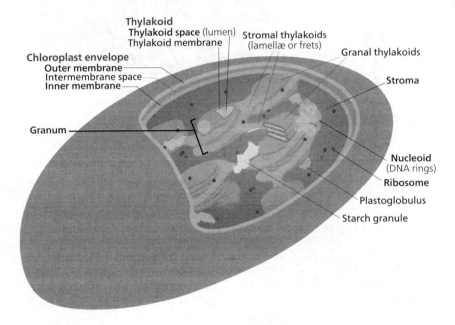

Plastids

Plastids are major organelles found in plants and algae. Because plastids can differentiate, there are many forms of plastids. Specialized plastids can store pigments, starches, fats, or proteins. Two examples of plastids are amyloplasts and chloroplasts. Amyloplasts are the plastids that store the starch formed from long chains of glucose produced during photosynthesis. Amyloplasts synthesize and store the starch granules through the polymerization of glucose. When needed, amyloplasts also convert these starch granules back into sugar. Fruits and potato tubers have large numbers of amyloplasts. Chloroplasts can synthesize and store starch. Interestingly, amyloplasts can redifferentiate and transform into chloroplasts.

Mitochondria

Mitochondria break down sugar molecules and produce energy in the form of molecules of adenosine triphosphate (ATP). Plant and animal cells contain mitochondria. Mitochondria are enclosed in a bilayer semimembrane of phospholipids and proteins. The intermembrane space is the space between the two layers. The outer membrane has proteins called porins, which allow small molecules through. The inner membrane contains proteins that aid in the synthesis of ATP. The matrix consists of enzymes that help synthesize ATP. Mitochondria have their own DNA and can reproduce by fission independently.

Copyright © Mometrix Media. You have been licensed one copy of this document for personal use only. Any other reproduction or redistribution is strictly prohibited. All rights reserved.

Mitochondria also help to maintain calcium concentrations, form blood components and hormones, and are involved in activating cell death pathways.

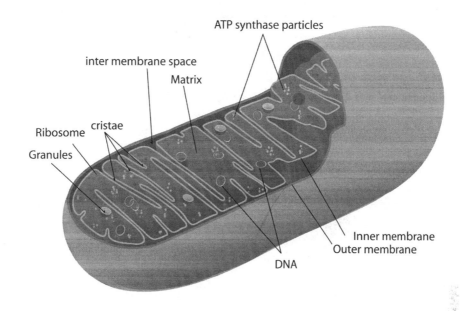

Review Video: Mitochondria
Visit mometrix.com/academy and enter code: 444287

Ribosomes

A ribosome consists of RNA and proteins. The RNA component of the ribosome is known as ribosomal RNA (rRNA). Ribosomes consist of two subunits, a large subunit and a small subunit. Few ribosomes are free in the cell. Most of the ribosomes in the cell are embedded in the rough endoplasmic reticulum located near the nucleus. Ribosomes are protein factories. Ribosomes translate the code of DNA into proteins by assembling long chains of amino acids. Messenger RNA (mRNA) is used by the ribosome to

Copyright © Mometrix Media. You have been licensed one copy of this document for personal use only. Any other reproduction or redistribution is strictly prohibited. All rights reserved.

generate a specific protein sequence. Transfer RNA (tRNA) collects the needed amino acids and delivers them to the ribosome.

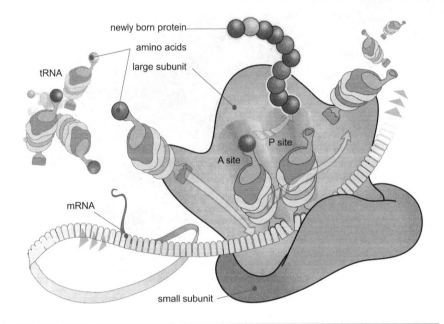

Review Video: RNA
Visit mometrix.com/academy and enter code: 888852

Golgi Apparatus

The Golgi apparatus, also called the Golgi body or Golgi complex, is a stack of flattened membranes called *cisternae* that package, ship, and distribute macromolecules in shipping containers called vesicles. Most Golgi apparatuses have six to eight cisternae. Each Golgi apparatus has four regions: the cis region, the endo region, the medial region, and the trans region. Transfer vesicles from the rough endoplasmic reticulum (ER) enter at the cis region, and secretory vesicles leave the Golgi apparatus from the trans

Copyright © Mometrix Media. You have been licensed one copy of this document for personal use only. Any other reproduction or redistribution is strictly prohibited. All rights reserved.

region. The Golgi apparatus directs the movement of carbohydrates, proteins, and lipids throughout the cell. Also, the Golgi apparatus helps modify proteins and lipids before they are shipped.

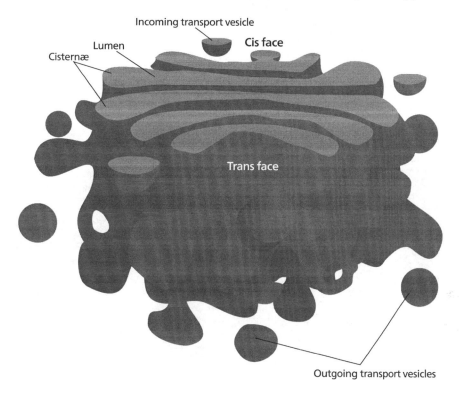

Cytoskeleton

The cytoskeleton is a scaffolding system located in the cytoplasm. The cytoskeleton consists of elongated organelles made of proteins called microtubules, microfilaments, or actin filaments and intermediate filaments. These organelles provide the shape and the needed support for the cell. They can also give cells the ability to move. These structures assist in moving the chromosomes during mitosis.

91

Copyright © Mometrix Media. You have been licensed one copy of this document for personal use only. Any other reproduction or redistribution is strictly prohibited. All rights reserved.

Microtubules and microfilaments help transport materials throughout the cell and are the major components in cilia and flagella.

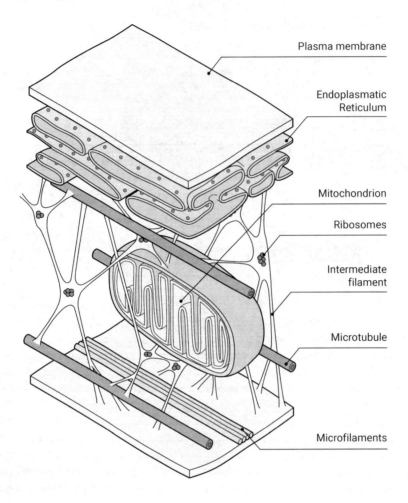

Plasma membrane

Endoplasmatic Reticulum

Mitochondrion

Ribosomes

Intermediate filament

Microtubule

Microfilaments

Selective Permeability

The cell membrane, or plasma membrane, has selective permeability with regard to size, charge, and solubility. With regard to molecule size, the cell membrane allows only small molecules to diffuse through it. Oxygen and water molecules are small and typically can pass through the cell membrane. The charge of the ions on the cell's surface also either attracts or repels ions. Ions with like charges are repelled, and ions with opposite charges are attracted to the cell's surface. Molecules that are soluble in phospholipids can usually pass through the cell membrane. Many molecules are not able to diffuse the cell membrane, and, if needed, those molecules must be moved through by active transport and vesicles.

Copyright © Mometrix Media. You have been licensed one copy of this document for personal use only. Any other reproduction or redistribution is strictly prohibited. All rights reserved.

Active and Passive Transport

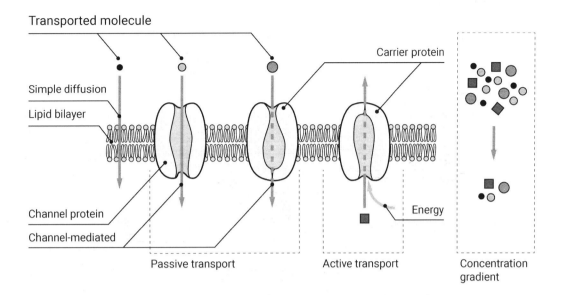

Cells can move materials in and out through the cell membrane by active and passive transport. In passive transport, the molecules diffuse across the cell membrane by osmosis. These molecules are moving from a region where they have a high concentration to a region where the concentration is lower. In passive transport, the molecules move across the cell membrane without the cell expending any extra energy. Diffusion and facilitated diffusion are considered passive transport. Facilitated diffusion occurs when molecules are helped across the membrane by certain proteins called channel proteins or carrier proteins. Because facilitated diffusion is still from a region of high to low concentration, it does not require additional energy and is therefore a type of passive transport. In active transport, molecules are forcibly moved from regions where the concentration is low into a region where the concentration is higher. Carrier proteins must carry these ions and molecules, and this requires an expenditure of energy. Some ions are actively pumped across the cell membrane by proteins. Sodium ions are pumped out of cell, and potassium ions are pumped into the cell in this manner.

> **Review Video: Passive Transport: Diffusion and Osmosis**
> Visit mometrix.com/academy and enter code: 642038

Water Movement to Maintain Internal Environments of Cells

Cells must maintain their water balance for homeostasis. If cells have too little water, wastes and poisons can build up in the cells. If cells have too much water, the chemicals in the cells may be diluted. Water is moved in and out of cells by osmosis. Because osmosis is a type of passive transport, the cell cannot actually control this diffusion of water in and out of the cells. The amount of water that diffuses into or out of cells depends on the cell's environment. When the cell's concentration of water and dissolved solids equals that of its environment, the cells are isotonic with their environment. Cells with a lower concentration of water than their environment tend to rapidly gain water by osmosis. These cells are hypotonic with their environment. Cells with a higher concentration of water than their

93

Copyright © Mometrix Media. You have been licensed one copy of this document for personal use only. Any other reproduction or redistribution is strictly prohibited. All rights reserved.

environment tend to rapidly lose water by osmosis. The cells are hypertonic with their environment. If cells are hypotonic or hypertonic, they must expend energy to maintain the proper water balance.

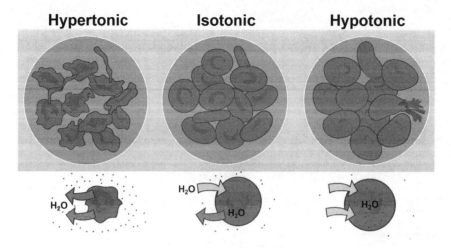

Use of Cell Surface Proteins and Cell Communication

In order to maintain a stable internal environment, cells need to send and receive signals from the external environment. Cells have specialized surface proteins called receptors embedded in the cell membrane that allow them to communicate with this external environment. Some surface proteins are exposed to the external side of the membrane. Some surface proteins allow entry to specific materials, and others trigger chemical signals inside the cell. Because these proteins have attached carbohydrates, they are called glycoproteins. Due to the cholesterol in the cell membrane, fat-soluble materials can pass straight through the membrane, but water-soluble materials cannot diffuse. Sodium, calcium, and potassium must use these specialized surface proteins to gain entry to the cell. These surface proteins bind to specific chemicals in the materials seeking access to the cell. This triggers a chemical signal to the interior of the cell.

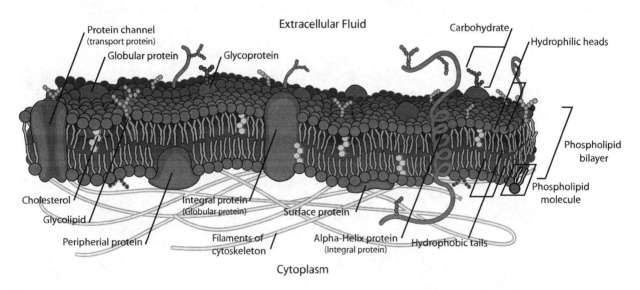

Copyright © Mometrix Media. You have been licensed one copy of this document for personal use only. Any other reproduction or redistribution is strictly prohibited. All rights reserved.

Exocytosis and Endocytosis

Larger particles or groups of particles can be transported whole across the cell membrane by being packaged in a piece of cell membrane. Endocytosis is the process by which large particles are moved into the cell, and exocytosis is the process by which large molecules are moves out of the cell. Three main types of endocytosis are phagocytosis, pinocytosis, and receptor-mediated endocytosis. Phagocytosis, or "cell eating," is the process by which large solid particles are engulfed. Pinocytosis, or "cell drinking," is the process by which liquids and dissolved substances are surrounded by small sacs of cell membrane. Receptor-mediated endocytosis is the process by which molecules enter cells through receptor molecules on the cell membrane.

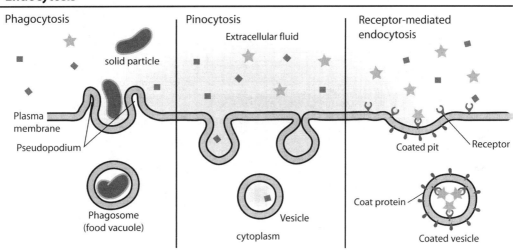

Hormone Action and Feedback

In order to maintain homeostasis, the endocrine system often employs negative-feedback inhibition or positive-feedback regulation. In negative-feedback inhibition, an increase in an output of a reaction to a stimulus triggers a decrease in the stimulus, which in turn causes a decrease in the original output. In positive-feedback regulation, an increase in an output leads to further increase of the stimulus. An

95

Copyright © Mometrix Media. You have been licensed one copy of this document for personal use only. Any other reproduction or redistribution is strictly prohibited. All rights reserved.

example of negative-feedback inhibition is the release of the hormones insulin and glucagon to maintain the level of glucose in the blood.

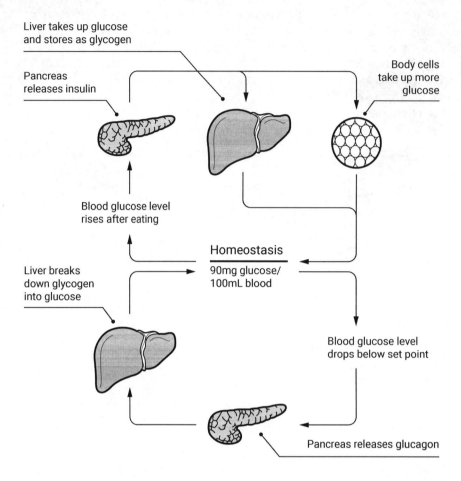

Cell Cycle Stages

The cell cycle consists of three stages: interphase, mitosis, and cytokinesis. Interphase is the longest stage of the cell cycle. Cells typically spend more than 90% of the cell cycle in interphase. Interphase includes two growth phases called G1 and G2. The order of interphase is the first growth cycle, GAP 1 (G1 phase), followed by the synthesis phase (S), followed by the second growth phase, GAP 2 (G2 phase). During the G1 phase of interphase, the cell increases the number of organelles by forming diploid cells. During the S phase of interphase, the DNA is replicated, and the chromosomes are doubled. During the G2 phase of interphase, the cell synthesizes needed proteins and continues to increase in size. During mitosis, the cell completes four phases: prophase, metaphase, anaphase, and telophase. During mitosis, the two sets of DNA that are arranged as the duplicated chromosomes are separated. Organelles such as chloroplasts and mitochondria also divide. During cytokinesis, the parent cell divides to form two

Copyright © Mometrix Media. You have been licensed one copy of this document for personal use only. Any other reproduction or redistribution is strictly prohibited. All rights reserved.

identical daughter cells. After cytokinesis, the daughter cells begin interphase and the cell cycle starts again.

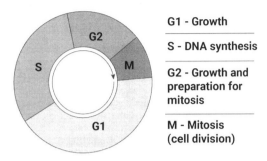

G1 - Growth

S - DNA synthesis

G2 - Growth and preparation for mitosis

M - Mitosis (cell division)

Mitosis

Mitosis is the asexual process of cell division. During mitosis, one parent cell divides into two identical daughter cells. Mitosis is used for growth, repair, and replacement of cells. Some unicellular organisms reproduce asexually by mitosis. Some multicellular organisms can reproduce by fragmentation or budding, which involves mitosis. Mitosis consists of four phases: prophase, metaphase, anaphase, and telophase. During prophase, the spindle fibers appear, and the DNA is condensed and packaged as chromosomes that become visible. The nuclear membrane breaks down, and the nucleolus disappears. During metaphase, the spindle apparatus is formed and the centromeres of the chromosomes line up on the equatorial plane. During anaphase, the centromeres divide and the two chromatids separate and are

Copyright © Mometrix Media. You have been licensed one copy of this document for personal use only. Any other reproduction or redistribution is strictly prohibited. All rights reserved.

pulled toward the opposite poles of the cell. During telophase, the spindle fibers disappear, the nuclear membrane reforms, and the DNA in the chromatids is decondensed.

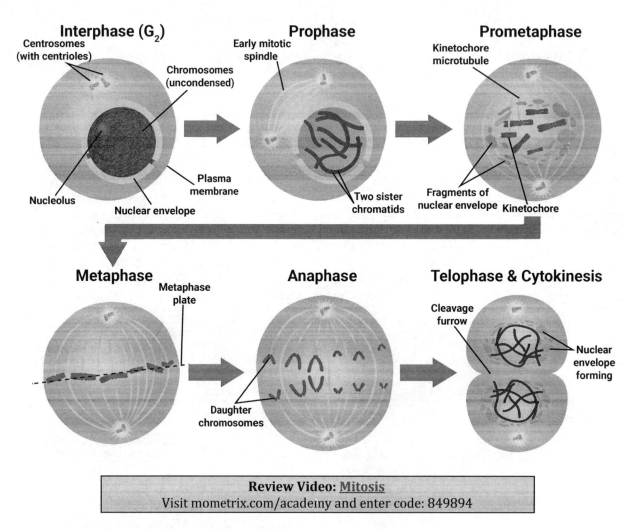

Review Video: Mitosis
Visit mometrix.com/academy and enter code: 849894

Cytokinesis

Cytokinesis is the dividing of the cytoplasm and cell membrane by the pinching of a cell into two new daughter cells at the end of mitosis. This occurs at the end of telophase when the actin filaments in the cytoskeleton form a contractile ring that narrows and divides the cell. In plant cells, a cell plate forms across the phragmoplast, which is the center of the spindle apparatus. In animal cells, as the contractile ring narrows, the cleavage furrow forms. Eventually, the contractile ring narrows down to the spindle apparatus joining the two cells and the cells eventually divide. Photos of the cell plate of a plant cell by

Copyright © Mometrix Media. You have been licensed one copy of this document for personal use only. Any other reproduction or redistribution is strictly prohibited. All rights reserved.

transmission electron microscopy (TEM) and the cleavage furrow of an animal cell by scanning electron microscopy (SEM) are shown below.

Animal cell

Contractile ring

Cleavage furrow

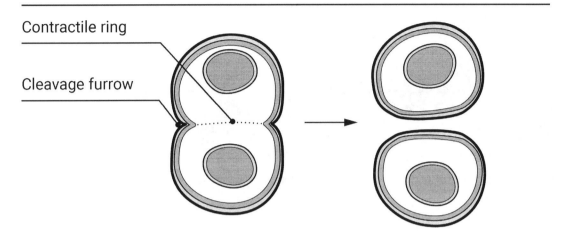

Plant cell

Golgi vesicles

Cell plate

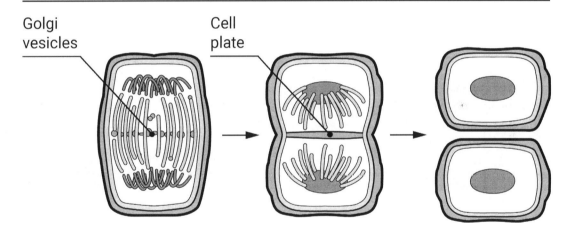

Meiosis

Meiosis is a type of cell division in which the number of chromosomes is reduced by half. Meiosis produces gametes, or egg and sperm cells. Meiosis occurs in two successive stages, which consist of a first mitotic division followed by a second mitotic division. During meiosis I, or the first meiotic division, the cell replicates its DNA in interphase and then continues through prophase I, metaphase I, anaphase I, and telophase I. At the end of meiosis I, there are two daughter cells that have the same number of chromosomes as the parent cell. During meiosis II, the cell enters a brief interphase but does not replicate its DNA. Then, the cell continues through prophase II, metaphase II, anaphase II, and telophase

99

Copyright © Mometrix Media. You have been licensed one copy of this document for personal use only. Any other reproduction or redistribution is strictly prohibited. All rights reserved.

II. During prophase II, the unduplicated chromosomes split. At the end of telophase II, there are four daughter cells that have half the number of chromosomes as the parent cell.

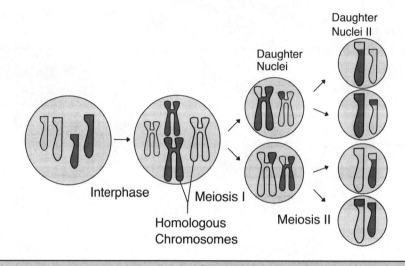

Review Video: Meiosis
Visit mometrix.com/academy and enter code: 247334

Cell Cycle Checkpoints

During the cell cycle, the cell goes through three checkpoints to ensure that the cell is dividing properly at each phase, that it is the appropriate time for division, and that the cell has not been damaged. The first checkpoint is at the end of the G1 phase just before the cell undergoes the S phase, or synthesis. At this checkpoint, a cell may continue with cell division, delay the division, or rest. This resting phase is called G0. In animal cells, the G1 checkpoint is called restriction. Proteins called cyclin D and cyclin E, which are dependent on enzymes cyclin-dependent kinase 4 and cyclin-dependent kinase 2 (CDK4 and CDK2), respectively, largely control this first checkpoint. The second checkpoint is at the end of the G2 phase just before the cell begins prophase during mitosis. The protein cyclin A, which is dependent on the enzyme CDK2, largely controls this checkpoint. During mitosis, the third checkpoint occurs at

Copyright © Mometrix Media. You have been licensed one copy of this document for personal use only. Any other reproduction or redistribution is strictly prohibited. All rights reserved.

metaphase to check that the chromosomes are lined up along the equatorial plane. This checkpoint is largely controlled by cyclin B, which is dependent upon the enzyme CDK1.

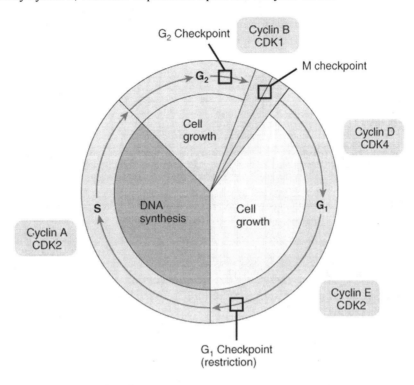

Chemical Bonding Properties of Carbon

Carbon is considered to be the central atom of organic compounds. Carbon atoms each have four valence electrons and require four more electrons to have a stable outer shell. Due to the repulsion between the valence electrons, the bond sites are all equidistant from each other. This enables carbon to form longs chains and rings. Carbon atoms can form four single covalent bonds with other atoms. For example, methane (CH_4) consists of one carbon atom singly bonded to four separate hydrogen atoms. Carbon atoms can also form double or triple covalent bonds. For example, an oxygen atom can form a double bond with a carbon atom, and a nitrogen atom can form a triple bond with a carbon atom.

Organic and Inorganic Molecules

Organic molecules contain carbon and hydrogen. Because carbon can form four covalent bonds, organic molecules can be very complex structures. Organic molecules can have carbon backbones that form long chains, branched chains, or even rings. Organic compounds tend to be less soluble in water than inorganic compounds. Organic compounds include four classes: carbohydrates, lipids, proteins, and nucleic acids. Specific examples of organic compounds include sucrose, cholesterol, insulin, and DNA. Inorganic molecules do not contain carbon and hydrogen. Inorganic compounds include salts and metals. Specific examples of inorganic molecules include sodium chloride, oxygen, and carbon dioxide.

Chemical Bonds

Chemical bonds are the attractive forces that bind atoms together to form molecules. Chemical bonds include covalent bonds, ionic bonds, and metallic bonds. Covalent bonds are formed from the sharing of electron pairs between two atoms in a molecule. In organic molecules, carbon atoms form single, double,

Copyright © Mometrix Media. You have been licensed one copy of this document for personal use only. Any other reproduction or redistribution is strictly prohibited. All rights reserved.

or triple covalent bonds. Organic compounds including proteins, carbohydrates, lipids, and nucleic acids are molecular compounds formed by covalent bonds.

Review Video: Basics of Organic Acids
Visit mometrix.com/academy and enter code: 238132

Review Video: Basics of Organic Compound Groups
Visit mometrix.com/academy and enter code: 889859

Intermolecular Forces

Intermolecular forces are the attractive forces between molecules. Intermolecular forces include hydrogen bonds, London or dispersion forces, and dipole-dipole forces. Hydrogen bonds are the attractive forces between molecules containing hydrogen atoms covalently bonded to oxygen, fluorine, or nitrogen. Hydrogen bonds bind the two strands of a DNA molecule to each other. Two hydrogen bonds join each adenosine and thymine, and three hydrogen bonds join each cytosine and guanine.

ATP

Adenosine triphosphate (ATP) is the energy source for most cellular functions. Each ATP molecule is a nucleotide consisting of a central ribose sugar flanked by a purine base and a chain of three phosphate groups. The purine base is adenine, and when adenine is joined to ribose, an adenosine is formed, explaining the name adenosine triphosphate. If one phosphate is removed from the end of the molecule, adenosine diphosphate (ADP) is formed.

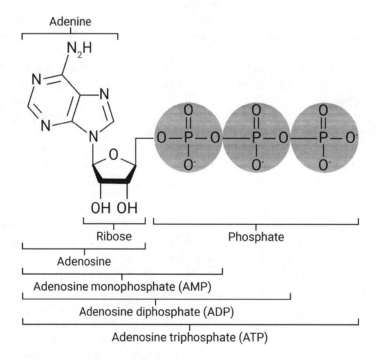

Properties of Water

Water exhibits numerous properties. Water has a high surface tension due to the cohesion between water molecules from the hydrogen bonds between the molecules. The capillary action of water is also due to this cohesion, and the adhesion of water is due to its polarity. Water is an excellent solvent due to its polarity and is considered the universal solvent. Water exists naturally as a solid, liquid, and gas. The density of water decreases as ice freezes and forms crystals in the solid phase. Water is most dense at

Copyright © Mometrix Media. You have been licensed one copy of this document for personal use only. Any other reproduction or redistribution is strictly prohibited. All rights reserved.

4°C. Water can act as an acid or base in chemical reactions. Pure water is an insulator because it has virtually no ions. Water has a high specific heat capacity due to its low molecular mass and bent molecular shape.

Biological Macromolecules

Macromolecules are large molecules made up of smaller organic molecules. Four classes of macromolecules include carbohydrates, nucleic acids, proteins, and lipids. Carbohydrates, proteins, and nucleic acids are polymers that are formed when the monomers are joined together in a dehydration process. In this dehydration process, the monomers are joined by a covalent bond and a water molecule is released. The monomers in carbohydrates are simple sugars such as glucose. Polysaccharides are polymers of carbohydrates. The monomers in proteins are amino acids. The amino acids form polypeptide chains, which are folded into proteins. The monomers in nucleic acids are nucleotides. Lipids are not actually considered to be polymers. Lipids typically are classified as fats, phospholipids, or steroids.

> **Review Video: Macromolecules**
> Visit mometrix.com/academy and enter code: 220156

Concentration Gradients

Concentration gradients, also called diffusion gradients, are differences in the concentration or the number of molecules of solutes in a solution between two regions. A gradient can also result from an unequal distribution of ions across a cell membrane. Solutes move along a concentration gradient by random motion from the region of high concentration toward the region of low concentration in a process called diffusion. Diffusion is the movement of molecules or ions down a concentration gradient. Diffusion is the method by which oxygen, carbon dioxide, and other nonpolar molecules cross a cell membrane. The steepness of the concentration gradient affects the rate of diffusion. Passive transport makes use of concentration gradients as well as electric gradients to move substances across the cell membrane. Active transport can move a substance against its concentration gradient.

Laws of Thermodynamics and Gibbs Free Energy

The first law of thermodynamics states that energy can neither be created nor destroyed. Energy may change forms, but the energy in a closed system is constant. The second law of thermodynamics states that systems tend toward a state of lower energy and greater disorder. This disorder is called entropy. According to the second law of thermodynamics, entropy is increasing. Gibbs free energy is the energy a system that is available or "free" to be released to perform work at a constant temperature. Organisms must be able to use energy to survive. Biological processes such as the chemical reactions involved in metabolism are governed by these laws.

Anabolic and Catabolic Reactions

Anabolism and catabolism are metabolic processes. Anabolism is essentially the synthesis of large molecules from monomers, whereas catabolism is the decomposition of large molecules into their component monomers. Anabolism uses energy, whereas catabolism produces energy. Anabolism typically builds and repair tissues, and catabolism typically burns stored food to produce energy. Protein synthesis, which is the polymerization of amino acids to form proteins, is an anabolic reaction. Mineralization of bones is also an anabolic process. An example of a catabolic reaction is hydrolysis, which is the decomposition of polymers into monomers that releases a water molecule and energy. Cellular respiration is a catabolic process in which typically glucose combines with oxygen to release energy in the form of adenosine triphosphate (ATP).

Copyright © Mometrix Media. You have been licensed one copy of this document for personal use only. Any other reproduction or redistribution is strictly prohibited. All rights reserved.

Oxidation-Reduction Reactions

Oxidation-reduction reactions, or redox reactions, involve the transfer of electrons from one substance to another. Reduction occurs in the substance that gains the electrons. Oxidation occurs in the substance that loses the electrons. Cellular respiration and photosynthesis are redox reactions. Cells use the energy stored in food during the redox reaction of cellular respiration. During cellular respiration, glucose molecules are oxidized and oxygen molecules are reduced. Because electrons lose energy when being transferred to oxygen, the electrons are usually first transferred to the coenzyme NAD^+, which is reduced to NADH. The NADH then releases the energy in steps to the oxygen. During photosynthesis, water molecules are split and oxidized and carbon dioxide molecules are reduced. During photosynthesis, when the water molecules are split, electrons are transferred with the hydrogen ions to the carbon dioxide molecules.

Active Site Structure and Substrate Binding

Each enzyme has a complex three-dimensional shape that is specifically designed to fit to a particular reactant, which is called the substrate. The enzyme and the substrate join temporarily forming the enzyme-substrate complex. This complex is unstable, and the chemical bonds are likely to be altered to produce a new molecule or molecules. Each enzyme can only combine with specific substrates because of this "lock-and-key" fit. Each enzyme has a designated binding site on the surface that binds to the substrate. Often, the binding site and the active site are at the same location. The enzyme and the substrate are specifically designed for each other, and they are both flexible and can bend and fold to fit into each other as they come together. This concept is referred to as the *induced fit hypothesis*.

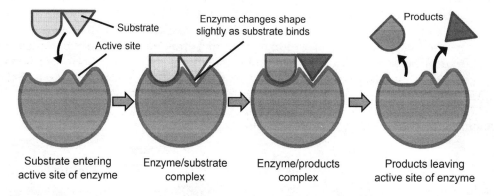

| Substrate entering active site of enzyme | Enzyme/substrate complex | Enzyme/products complex | Products leaving active site of enzyme |

Effects of Temperature, pH, and Inhibitors on Enzyme Activity

The rate of an enzyme-controlled reaction is affected by factors such as temperature, pH, and inhibitors. According to kinetic-molecular theory, increasing the temperature increases the rate of molecular motion. Typically, increasing the temperature increases the rate of these reactions. The optimum temperature is the temperature at which the rate is the fastest and the most product is formed. Increasing the temperature above the optimum temperature actually decreases the reaction rate due to changes on the enzyme's structure that affect substrate binding. The pH also affects enzyme activity due to hydrogen ions binding to the enzyme's surface and changing the enzyme's surface shape. Because enzymes must have a specific shape for their specific substrate, enzymes have a certain pH range in which they can function. Inhibitors are molecules that attach to the enzymes and interfere with substrate binding, thus they decreasing or even halting enzyme-controlled reactions.

Regulation of Enzymes by Feedback Inhibition

Enzyme-controlled reactions can be regulated by feedback inhibition, or negative feedback. Feedback inhibition can be illustrated by a furnace and thermostat. The inhibitor in this system is the heat. When the furnace runs, the temperature increases. When the temperature reaches a specific level, the

Copyright © Mometrix Media. You have been licensed one copy of this document for personal use only. Any other reproduction or redistribution is strictly prohibited. All rights reserved.

thermostat switches the furnace off. When the temperature decreases below a specific level, the thermostat switches the furnace back on, and the cycle begins again. In enzyme-controlled reactions, the end products of a metabolic pathway bind to the enzymes that initiate the metabolic pathway. This causes the reaction rate to decrease. The more product there is, the less product is produced. The less product there is, the more product is produced. This process of feedback inhibition enables a stable range of concentrations that are necessary for homeostasis.

> **Review Video: Enzymes**
> Visit mometrix.com/academy and enter code: 656995

Biochemical Pathways

Autotrophs that use light to produce energy use photosynthesis as a biochemical pathway. In eukaryotic autotrophs photosynthesis takes place in chloroplasts. Prokaryotic autotrophs that use inorganic chemical reactions to produce energy use chemosynthesis as a biochemical pathway. Heterotrophs require food and use cellular respiration to release energy from chemical bonds in the food. All organisms use cellular respiration to release energy from stored food. Cellular respiration can be aerobic or anaerobic. Most eukaryotes use cellular respiration that takes place in the mitochondria.

Photosynthesis

Photosynthesis is a food-making process that occurs in three processes: light-capturing events, light-dependent reactions, and light-independent reactions. In light-capturing events, the thylakoids of the chloroplasts, which contain chlorophyll and accessory pigments, absorb light energy and produce excited electrons. Thylakoids also contain enzymes and electron-transport molecules. Molecules involved in this process are arranged in groups called photosystems. In light-dependent reactions, the excited electrons from the light-capturing events are moved by electron transport in a series of steps in which they are used to split water into hydrogen and oxygen ions. The oxygen is released, and the $NADP^+$ bonds with the hydrogen atoms and forms NADPH. ATP is produced from the excited electrons. The light-independent reactions use this ATP, NADPH, and carbon dioxide to produce sugars.

C3 and C4 Photosynthesis

Three types of photosynthesis are C3, C4, and crassulacean acid metabolism (CAM). C3 and C4 photosynthesis are named for the type of carbon molecule (three-carbon or four-carbon) that is made during the first step of the reaction. The first step of C3 photosynthesis is the formation of two three-carbon molecules (3-phosphoglycerate) from a reaction between carbon dioxide and a five-carbon molecule (ribulose 1,5-bisphosphate). The first step of C4 photosynthesis is the formation of a four-carbon molecule (oxaloacetate) from a reaction between carbon dioxide and a three-carbon molecule (phosphoenolpyruvate). More than 95% of plants perform C3 photosynthesis. C4 photosynthesis can be used by plants in sunlight-intense regions because it helps conserve water.

Crassulacean Acid Metabolism

Crassulacean acid metabolism (CAM) is a form of photosynthesis adapted to dry environments. During nighttime, pores of the plant leaves (stomata) open to receive carbon dioxide, which combines with phosphoenolpyruvate (three-carbon molecule) to form malate (four-carbon molecule). Malate is stored in vacuoles. During the daytime, the stomata are closed and the malate is transported to chloroplasts, where malate is broken down into pyruvate (three-carbon molecule) and carbon dioxide. The carbon dioxide released from malate is used in photosynthesis during the daytime. One advantage of the CAM cycle is that it minimizes loss of water through the stomata during the daytime. A second advantage is that concentrating carbon dioxide in the chloroplasts in this manner increases the efficiency of the

Copyright © Mometrix Media. You have been licensed one copy of this document for personal use only. Any other reproduction or redistribution is strictly prohibited. All rights reserved.

enzyme that converts carbon dioxide and ribulose 1,5-bisphosphate into two 3-phosphoglycerate molecules.

Review Video: Photosynthesis in Biology
Visit mometrix.com/academy and enter code: 402602

Aerobic Respiration

Aerobic cellular respiration is a series of enzyme-controlled chemical reactions in which oxygen reacts with glucose to produce carbon dioxide and water, releasing energy in the form of adenosine triphosphate (ATP). Cellular respiration occurs in a series of three processes: glycolysis, the Krebs cycle, and the electron-transport system.

Review Video: Aerobic Respiration
Visit mometrix.com/academy and enter code: 770290

Glycolysis

Glycolysis is a series of enzyme-controlled chemical reactions that occur in the cell's cytoplasm. Each glucose molecule is split in half to produce two pyruvic acid molecules and four ATP molecules and two NADH molecules. Because two ATP molecules are used to split the glucose molecule, glycolysis nets two ATP molecules.

Krebs Cycle

The Krebs cycle, also known as the citric acid cycle, is a series of enzyme-controlled chemical reactions that occur in the cell's mitochondria. The Krebs cycle breaks down the pyruvic acid from glycolysis and releases carbon dioxide and ATP. It also releases electrons, which are collected by NAD^+ and other molecules. These electrons are delivered to the electron-transport system.

Electron-Transport System

The electron-transport system is a series of enzyme-controlled chemical reactions that occurs in the cell's mitochondria. Through a series of reactions in which oxygen atoms are reduced by accepting the electrons from the Krebs cycle, a large amount of ATP is produced. The oxygen ions join with hydrogen ions to produce water. Most of the ATP produced during cellular respiration occurs in the electron-transport system.

Chemosynthesis

Chemosynthesis is the food-making process of chemoautotrophs in extreme environments such as deep-sea-vents. In general, chemosynthesis involves the oxidation of inorganic substances. Chemosynthesis is unlike photosynthesis in that chemosynthesis does not require light. Sulfur bacteria live near or in deep-sea vents. Some actually live in other organisms such as huge tube worms near the vents. Hydrogen sulfide is released from deep-sea vents. Instead of sunlight, chemosynthesis uses the energy stored in the chemical bonds of chemicals such as hydrogen sulfide. Carbon is obtained from molecules such as carbon dioxide. During chemosynthesis, the electrons that are removed from the inorganic molecules are combined with carbon possibly from the dissolved carbon dioxide in the seawater or from methane from deep-sea vents to form organic molecules in the form of carbohydrates. Some bacteria use metal ions such as iron and magnesium to obtain the needed electrons. Methanobacteria such as those found in human intestines combine carbon dioxide and hydrogen gas and release methane as a waste product. Nitrogen bacteria such as nitrogen-fixing bacteria in the nodules of legumes convert atmospheric nitrogen into nitrates.

Copyright © Mometrix Media. You have been licensed one copy of this document for personal use only. Any other reproduction or redistribution is strictly prohibited. All rights reserved.

Importance and Structural Organization of Cells

Cells are the basic structural units of all organisms. All organisms have a highly organized cellular structure. In single-celled organisms, that single cell contains all of the components necessary for life. In multicellular organisms, cells can become specialized. Different types of cells can have different functions. Life begins as a single cell whether by asexual or sexual reproduction. All cells contain DNA and RNA and can synthesize proteins. Each cell consists of nucleic acids, cytoplasm, and a cell membrane. Specialized organelles such as mitochondria and chloroplasts have specific functions within the cell.

Energy

All cells must obtain and use energy in order to grow, make repairs, and reproduce. Cells use energy to take in food, process that food, and eliminate wastes from this process. Cells obtain the energy they need by the breaking of bonds of molecules. Organisms differ in how they obtain food. Plants and other autotrophs produce energy through photosynthesis or chemosynthesis. Animals and other heterotrophs obtain their energy from consuming autotrophs or other heterotrophs. Cellular respiration is the process of converting nutrient molecules into energy.

Growth and Reproduction

All organisms must be capable of growth and reproduction. Growth is necessary for multicellular organisms to develop and mature. Growth allows cells to be replaced or repaired. All cells eventually die. Without growth from cell division, tissues could not be maintained or repaired. Through mitosis, most cells routinely replace themselves with identical daughter cells. All organisms eventually die. Reproduction is necessary to increase the number of individuals in a population. Reproduction is either sexual by the joining of gametes or asexual by binary fission or some other related method. Not all organisms reproduce, but all must grow or they will die. Even single-celled organisms grow a small amount.

Adaptation to Environment

Organisms must be able to adapt to their environment in order to thrive or survive. Individual organisms must be able to recognize stimuli in their surroundings and adapt quickly. For example, an individual euglena can sense light and respond by moving toward the light. Individual organisms must also be able to adapt to changes in the environment on a larger scale. For example, plants must be able to respond to the change in the length of the day to flower at the correct time. Populations must also be able to adapt to a changing environment. Evolution by natural selection is the process by which populations change over many generations. For example, wooly mammoths were unable to adapt to a warming climate and are now extinct, but many species of deer did adapt and are abundant today.

Structure, Organization, Modes of Nutrition, and Reproduction of Animals

Animals are multicellular organism with eukaryotic cells that do not have cell walls surrounding their plasma membranes. Animals have several possible structural body forms. Animals can be relatively simple in structure such as sponges, which do not have a nervous system. Other animals are more complex with cells organized into tissues, and tissues organized into organs, and organs even further organized into systems. Invertebrates such as arthropods, nematodes, and annelids have complex body systems. Vertebrates including fish, amphibians, reptiles, birds, and mammals are the most complex with detailed systems such as those with gills, air sacs, or lungs designed to exchange respiratory gases. All animals are heterotrophs and obtain their nutrition by consuming autotrophs or other heterotrophs. Most animals are motile, but some animals move their environment to bring food to them. All animals

107

Copyright © Mometrix Media. You have been licensed one copy of this document for personal use only. Any other reproduction or redistribution is strictly prohibited. All rights reserved.

reproduce sexually at some point in their life cycle. Typically, this involves the union of a sperm and egg to produce a zygote.

Review Video: Arthropoda
Visit mometrix.com/academy and enter code: 523466

Characteristics of the Major Animal Phyla

Body Planes

Animals can exhibit bilateral symmetry, radial symmetry, or asymmetry. With bilateral symmetry, the organism can be cut in half along only one plane to produce two identical halves. Most animals, including all vertebrates such as mammals, birds, reptiles, amphibians, and fish, exhibit bilateral symmetry. Many invertebrates including arthropods and crustaceans also exhibit bilateral symmetry. With radial symmetry, the organism can be cut in half along several planes to produce two identical halves. Starfish, sea urchins, and jellyfish exhibit radial symmetry. With asymmetry, the organism exhibits no symmetry. Very few organisms in the animal phyla exhibit asymmetry, but a few species of sponges are asymmetrical.

Body Cavities

Animals can be grouped based on their types of body cavities. A coelom is a fluid-filled body cavity between the alimentary canal and the body wall. The three body plans based on the formation of the coelom are acoelomates, pseudocoelomates, and coelomates. Acoelomates do not have body cavities. Pseudocoelomates have a body cavity called a pseudocoelom. Pseudocoeloms are not considered true coeloms. Pseudocoeloms are located between mesoderm and endoderm instead of actually in the mesoderm as in a true coelom. Coelomates have a true coelom located within the mesoderm. Simple or primitive animals such as sponges, jellyfish, sea anemones, hydras, flatworms, and ribbon worms are acoelomates. Pseudocoelomates include roundworms and rotifers. Most animals including arthropods, mollusks, annelids, echinoderms, and chordates are coelomates.

Modes of Reproduction

Animals can reproduce sexually or asexually. Most animals reproduce sexually. In sexual reproduction, males and females have different reproductive organs that produce gametes. Males have testes that produce sperm, and females have ovaries that produce eggs. During fertilization, a sperm cell unites with an egg cell, forming a zygote. Fertilization can occur internally such as in most mammals and birds or externally such as aquatic animals such as fish and frogs. The zygote undergoes cell division, which develops into an embryo and eventually develops into an adult organism. Some embryos develop in eggs such as in fish, amphibians, reptiles, and birds. Some mammals are oviparous and lay eggs. Most mammals are viviparous and have a uterus in which the embryo develops. Some mammals are marsupials and give birth to an immature fetus that finishes developing in a pouch. Some animals reproduce asexually. For example, hydras reproduce by budding, and starfish and planarians can reproduce by fragmentation and regeneration. Some fish, frogs, and insects reproduce by parthenogenesis.

Modes of Temperature Regulation

Animals can be classified as either homeotherms or poikilotherms. Homeotherms, also called warm-blooded animals or endotherms, maintain a constant body temperature regardless of the temperature of the environment. Homeotherms such as mammals and birds have a high metabolic rate because much energy is needed to maintain the constant temperature. Poikilotherms, also called cold-blooded animals or ectotherms, do not maintain a constant body temperature. Their body temperature fluctuates with

Copyright © Mometrix Media. You have been licensed one copy of this document for personal use only. Any other reproduction or redistribution is strictly prohibited. All rights reserved.

the temperature of the environment. Poikilotherms such as arthropods, fish, amphibians, and reptiles have metabolic rates that fluctuate with their body temperature.

Review Video: <u>Basic Characteristics of Organisms</u>
Visit mometrix.com/academy and enter code: 314694

Cells

Cells are the basic structural units of all living things. Cells are composed of various molecules including proteins, carbohydrates, lipids, and nucleic acids. All animal cells are eukaryotic and have a nucleus, cytoplasm, and a cell membrane. Organelles include mitochondria, ribosomes, endoplasmic reticulum, Golgi apparatuses, and vacuoles. Specialized cells are numerous, including but not limited to various muscle cells, nerve cells, epithelial cells, bone cells, blood cells, and cartilage cells. Cells are grouped to together in tissues to perform specific functions.

Organizational Hierarchy within Multicellular Organisms

Cells are the smallest living units of organisms. Tissues are groups of cells that work together to perform a specific function. Organs are groups of tissues that work together to perform a specific function. Organ systems are groups of organs that work together to perform a specific function. An organism is an individual that contains several body systems.

Tissues

Tissues are groups of cells that work together to perform a specific function. Tissues can be grouped into four broad categories: muscle tissue, nerve tissue, epithelial tissue, and connective tissue. Muscle tissue is involved in body movement. Muscle tissues can be composed of skeletal muscle cells, cardiac muscle cells, or smooth muscle cells. Skeletal muscles include the muscles commonly called biceps, triceps, hamstrings, and quadriceps. Cardiac muscle tissue is found only in the heart. Smooth muscle tissue provides tension in the blood vessels, controls pupil dilation, and aids in peristalsis. Nerve tissue is located in the brain, spinal cord, and nerves. Epithelial tissue makes up the layers of the skin and various membranes. Connective tissues include bone tissue, cartilage, tendons, ligaments, fat, blood, and lymph. Tissues are grouped together as organs to perform specific functions.

Organs and Organ Systems

Organs are groups of tissues that work together to perform specific functions. Organ systems are groups of organs that work together to perform specific functions. Complex animals have several organs that are grouped together in multiple systems. In mammals, there are 11 major organ systems: integumentary system, respiratory system, cardiovascular system, endocrine system, nervous system, immune system, digestive system, excretory system, muscular system, skeletal system, and reproductive system.

Cardiovascular System

The main functions of the cardiovascular system are gas exchange, the delivery of nutrients and hormones, and waste removal. The cardiovascular system consists primarily of the heart, blood, and blood vessels. The heart is a pump that pushes blood through the arteries. Arteries are blood vessels that carry blood away from the heart, and veins are blood vessels that carry blood back to the heart. The exchange of materials between blood and cells occur in the capillaries, which are the smallest of the blood vessels. All vertebrates and a few invertebrates including annelids, squids, and octopuses have a closed circulatory system. Mammals, birds and crocodilians have a four-chambered heart. Most amphibians and reptiles have a three-chambered heart. Fish have only a two-chambered heart.

Copyright © Mometrix Media. You have been licensed one copy of this document for personal use only. Any other reproduction or redistribution is strictly prohibited. All rights reserved.

Arthropods and most mollusks have open circulatory systems. Many invertebrates do not have a cardiovascular system. For example, echinoderms have a water vascular system.

Respiratory System

The function of the respiratory system is to move air in and out of the body in order to facilitate the exchange of oxygen and carbon dioxide. The respiratory system consists of the nasal passages, pharynx, larynx, trachea, bronchial tubes, lungs, and diaphragm. Bronchial tubes branch into bronchioles, which end in clusters of alveoli. The alveoli are tiny sacs inside the lungs where gas exchange takes place. When the diaphragm contracts, the volume of the chest increases, which reduces the pressure in the lungs. Then, air is inhaled through the nose or mouth and passes through the pharynx, larynx, trachea, and bronchial tubes into the lungs. When the diaphragm relaxes, the volume in the chest cavity decreases, forcing the air out of the lungs.

> **Review Video: Respiratory System**
> Visit mometrix.com/academy and enter code: 783075

Reproductive System

The main function of the reproductive system is to propagate the species. Most animals reproduce sexually at some point in their life cycle. Typically, this involves the union of a sperm and egg to produce a zygote. In complex animals, the female reproductive system includes one or more ovaries, which produce the egg cell. The male reproductive system includes one or more testes, which produce the sperm.

Internal and External Fertilization

Eggs may be fertilized internally or externally. In internal fertilization in mammals, the sperm unites with the egg in the oviduct. In mammals, the zygote begins to divide, and the blastula implants in the uterus. In birds, after the egg is fertilized, albumen, membranes, and egg shell are added. Reptiles lay amniotic eggs covered by a leathery shell. Amphibians and most fish fertilize eggs externally. But some fish give birth to live young.

Invertebrates

Most invertebrates reproduce sexually. Invertebrates may have separate sexes or be hermaphroditic, in which the organisms produces sperm and eggs either at the same time or separately at some time in their life cycle. Many invertebrates such as insects also have complex reproductive systems. Some invertebrates reproduce asexually by budding, fragmentation, or parthenogenesis.

Digestive System

The main function of the digestive system is to process the food that is consumed by the animal. This includes mechanical and chemical processing. Depending on the animal, mechanical processes can happen in various ways. Mammals have teeth to chew their food. Saliva is secreted, which contains enzymes to begin the breakdown of starches. Many animals such as birds, earthworms, crocodilians, and crustaceans have a gizzard or gizzard-like organ that grinds the food. Many animals such as mammals, birds, reptiles, amphibians, and fish have a stomach that stores and absorbs food. Gastric juice containing enzymes and hydrochloric acid is mixed with the food. The intestine or intestines absorb nutrients and reabsorb water from the undigested material. Many animals have a liver, gallbladder, and pancreas, which aid in digestion of proteins and fats although not being part of the muscular tube through which the waste passes. Undigested wasted are eliminated from the body through an anus or cloaca.

110

Copyright © Mometrix Media. You have been licensed one copy of this document for personal use only. Any other reproduction or redistribution is strictly prohibited. All rights reserved.

Mometrix

Review Video: Gastrointestinal System
Visit mometrix.com/academy and enter code: 378740

Excretory System

All animals have some type of excretory system that has the main function of metabolizing food and eliminating metabolic wastes. In complex animals such as mammals, the excretory system consists of the kidneys, ureters, urinary bladder, and urethra. Urea and other toxic wastes must be eliminated from the body. The kidneys constantly filter the blood. The nephron is the working unit of the kidney. Each nephron functions like a tiny filter. Nephrons not only filter the blood, but they also facilitate reabsorption and secretion. Basically, the glomerulus filters the blood. Water and dissolved materials such as glucose and amino acids pass on into the Bowman's capsule. Depending on concentration gradients, water and dissolved materials can pass back into the blood primarily through the proximal convoluted tubule. Additional water can be removed at the loop of Henle. Antidiuretic hormone regulates the water that is lost or reabsorbed. Urine passes from the kidneys through the ureters to the urinary bladder where it is stored before it is expelled from the body through the urethra.

Kidneys

The kidneys are involved in blood filtration, pH balance, and the reabsorption of nutrients to maintain proper blood volume and ion balance. The nephron is the working unit of the kidney. The parts of the nephron include the glomerulus, Bowman's capsule, and loop of Henle. Filtration takes place in the nephron's glomerulus. Water and dissolved materials such as glucose and amino acids pass on into the Bowman's capsule. Depending on concentration gradients, water and dissolved materials can pass back into the blood primarily through the proximal convoluted tubule. Reabsorption and water removal occurs in the loop of Henle and the conducting duct. Urine and other nitrogenous wastes pass from the kidneys to the bladders and are expelled.

Nervous System

All animals except sponges have a nervous system. The main function of the nervous system is to coordinate the activities of the body. The nervous system consists of the brain, spinal cord, peripheral nerves, and sense organs. Sense organs such as the ears, eyes, nose, taste buds, and pressure receptors receive stimuli from the environment and relay that information through nerves and the spinal cord to the brain where the information is processed. The brain sends signals through the spinal cord and peripheral nerves to the organs and muscles. The autonomic nervous system controls all routine body functions by the sympathetic and parasympathetic divisions. Reflexes, which are also part of the nervous system, may involve only a few nerve cells and bypass the brain when an immediate response is necessary.

Endocrine System

The endocrine system consists of several ductless glands, which secrete hormones directly into the bloodstream. The pituitary gland is the master gland, which controls the functions of the other glands. The pituitary gland regulates skeletal growth and the development of the reproductive organs. The pineal gland regulates sleep cycles. The thyroid gland regulates metabolism and helps regulate the calcium level in the blood. The parathyroid glands also help regulate the blood calcium level. The adrenal glands secrete the emergency hormone epinephrine, stimulate body repairs, and regulate sodium and potassium levels in the blood. The islets of Langerhans located in the pancreas secrete insulin and glucagon to regulate the blood sugar level. In females, ovaries produce estrogen, which stimulates sexual development, and progesterone, which functions during pregnancy. In males, the testes secrete testosterone, which stimulates sexual development and sperm production.

111

Copyright © Mometrix Media. You have been licensed one copy of this document for personal use only. Any other reproduction or redistribution is strictly prohibited. All rights reserved.

Review Video: Endocrine System
Visit mometrix.com/academy and enter code: 678939

Immune System

The immune system in animals defends the body against infection and disease. The immune system can be divided into two broad categories: innate immunity and adaptive immunity. Innate immunity includes the skin and mucous membranes, which provide a physical barrier to prevent pathogens from entering the body. Special chemicals including enzymes and proteins in mucus, tears, sweat, and stomach juices destroy pathogens. Numerous white blood cells such as neutrophils and macrophages protect the body from invading pathogens. Adaptive immunity involves the body responding to a specific antigen. Typically, B-lymphocytes or B cells produce antibodies against a specific antigen, and T-lymphocytes or T-cells take special roles as helpers, regulators, or killers. Some T-cells function as memory cells.

Review Video: Immune System
Visit mometrix.com/academy and enter code: 622899

Maintenance of Homeostasis in Organisms

Role of Feedback Mechanisms

Feedback mechanisms play a major role in homeostasis in organisms. Each feedback mechanism consists of receptors, an integrator, and effectors. Receptors such as mechanoreceptors or thermoreceptors in the skin detect the stimuli. The integrator such as the brain or spinal cord receives the information concerning the stimuli and sends out signals to other parts of the body. The effectors such as muscles or glands respond to the stimulus. Basically, the receptors receive the stimuli and notify the integrator, which signals the effectors to respond. Feedback mechanisms can be negative or positive. Negative-feedback mechanisms are mechanisms that provide a decrease in response with an increase in stimulus that inhibits the stimulus, which in turn decreases the response. Positive-feedback mechanisms are mechanisms that provide an increase in response with an increase in stimulus, which actually increases the stimulus, which in turn increases the response.

Role of Hypothalamus

The hypothalamus plays a major role in the homoeostasis of vertebrates. Homeostasis is regulation of internal chemistry to maintain a constant internal environment. The hypothalamus is the central portion of the brain just above the brainstem, which is linked to the endocrine system through the pituitary gland. The hypothalamus releases special hormones that influence the secretion of pituitary hormones. The hypothalamus regulates the fundamental physiological state by controlling body temperature, hunger, thirst, sleep, behaviors related to attachment, sexual development, fight-or-flight stress response, and circadian rhythms.

Role of Endocrine System and Hormones

All vertebrates have an endocrine system that consists of numerous ductless glands that produce hormones that help coordinate many functions of the body. Hormones are signaling molecules that are received by receptors. Many hormones are secreted in response to signals from the pituitary gland and hypothalamus gland. Other hormones are secreted in response to signals from inside the body. Hormones can consist of amino acids, proteins, or lipid molecules such as steroid hormones. Hormones can affect target cells, which have the correct receptor that is able to bind to that particular hormone. Most cells have receptors for more than one type of hormone. Hormones are distributed to the target cells in the blood by the cardiovascular system. Hormones incorporate feedback mechanisms to help the body maintain homeostasis.

Copyright © Mometrix Media. You have been licensed one copy of this document for personal use only. Any other reproduction or redistribution is strictly prohibited. All rights reserved.

Role of Antidiuretic Hormone

Antidiuretic hormone (ADH) helps maintain homeostasis in vertebrates. ADH is produced by the posterior pituitary gland, and it regulates the reabsorption of water in the kidneys and concentrates the urine. The stimulus in this feedback mechanism is a drop in blood volume due to water loss. This signal is picked up by the hypothalamus, which signals the pituitary gland to secrete ADH. ADH is carried by the cardiovascular system to the nephrons in the kidneys signaling them to reabsorb more water and send less out as waste. As more water is reabsorbed, the blood volume increases, which is monitored by the hypothalamus. As the blood volume reaches the set point, the hypothalamus signals for a decrease in the secretion of ADH, and the cycle continues.

Role of Insulin and Glucagon

Insulin and glucagon are hormones that help maintain the glucose concentration in the blood. Insulin and glucagon are secreted by the clumps of endocrine cells called the pancreatic islets that are located in the pancreas. Insulin and glucagon work together to maintain the blood glucose level. Insulin stimulates cells to remove glucose from the blood. Glucagon stimulates the liver to convert glycogen to glucose. After eating, glucose levels increase in the blood. This stimulus signals the pancreas to stop the secretion of glucagon and to start secreting insulin. Cells respond to the insulin and remove glucose from the blood, lowering the level of glucose in the blood. Later, after eating, the level of glucose in the blood decreases further. This stimulus signals the pancreas to secrete glucagon and decrease the secretion of insulin. In response to the stimulus, the liver converts glycogen to glucose, and the level of glucose in the blood rises. When the individual eats, the cycle begins again.

Thermoregulation

Animals exhibit many adaptations that help them achieve homeostasis, or a stable internal environment. Some of these adaptions are behavioral. Most organisms exhibit some type of behavioral thermoregulation. Thermoregulation is the ability to keep the body temperature within certain boundaries. The type of behavioral thermoregulation depends on whether the animal is an endotherm or an ectotherm. Ectotherms are "cold-blooded," and their body temperature changes with their external environment. To regulate their temperature, ectotherms often move to an appropriate location. Fish move to warmer waters. Animals will climb to higher grounds. Diurnal ectotherms such as reptiles often bask in the sun to increase their body temperatures. Butterflies are heliotherms in that they derive nearly all of their heat from basking in the sun. Endotherms are "warm-blooded" and maintain a stable body temperature by internal means. However, many animals that live in hot environments have adapted to the nocturnal lifestyle. Desert animals are often nocturnal to escape high daytime temperatures. Other nocturnal animals sleep during the day in underground burrows or dens. Birds can spread their wings to capture heat from the sun.

Gamete Formation

Gametogenesis is the formation of gametes. Gametes are reproductive cells. Gametes are produced by meiosis. Meiosis is a special type of cell division that consists of two consecutive mitotic divisions referred to as meiosis I and meiosis II. Meiosis I is a reduction division in which a diploid cell is reduced to two haploid daughter cells that contain only one of each pair of homologous chromosomes. During meiosis II, those haploid cells are further divided to form four haploid cells. Spermatogenesis in males produces four viable sperm cells from each complete cycle of meiosis. Oogenesis produces four daughter cells, but only one is a viable egg and the other three are polar bodies.

Fertilization

Fertilization is the union of a sperm cell and an egg cell to produce a zygote. Many sperm may bind to an egg, but only one joins with the egg and injects its nuclei into the egg. Fertilization can be external or internal. External fertilization takes place outside of the female's body. For example, many fish, amphibians, crustaceans, mollusks, and corals reproduce externally by spawning or releasing gametes

113

Copyright © Mometrix Media. You have been licensed one copy of this document for personal use only. Any other reproduction or redistribution is strictly prohibited. All rights reserved.

into the water simultaneously or right after each other. Reptiles and birds reproduce by internal fertilization. All mammals except monotremes (e.g. platypus) reproduce by internal fertilization.

Embryonic Development

Embryonic development in animals is typically divided into four stages: cleavage, patterning, differentiation, and growth. Cleavage occurs immediately after fertilization when the large single-celled zygote immediately begins to divide into smaller and smaller cells without an increase in mass. A hollow ball of cells forms a blastula. Next, during patterning, gastrulation occurs. During gastrulation, the cells are organized into three primary germ layers: ectoderm, mesoderm, and endoderm. Then, the cells in these layers differentiate into special tissues and organs. For example, the nervous system develops from the ectoderm. The muscular system develops from the mesoderm. Much of the digestive system develops from the endoderm. The final stage of embryonic development is growth and further tissue specialization. The embryo continues to grow until ready for hatching or birth.

Postnatal Growth

Postnatal growth occurs from hatching or birth until death. The length of the postnatal growth depends on the species. Elephants can live 70 years, but mice only about 4 years. Right after animals are hatched or born, they go through a period of rapid growth and development. In vertebrates, bones lengthen, muscles grow in bulk, and fat is deposited. At maturity, bones stop growing in length, but bones can grow in width and repair themselves throughout the animal's lifetime, and muscle deposition slows down. Fat cells continue to increase and decrease in size throughout the animal's life. Growth is controlled by genetics but is also influenced by nutrition and disease. Most animals are sexually mature in less than two years and can produce offspring.

Viruses

Viruses are nonliving, infectious particles that act as parasites in living organisms. Viruses are acellular, which means that they lack cell structure. Viruses cannot reproduce outside of living cells. The structure of a virus is a core of a nucleic acid, which may be either DNA or RNA, surrounded by a protein coat or capsid. In some viruses, the capsid may be surrounded by a lipid membrane or envelope. Viruses can contain up to 500 genes. Viruses have various shapes and usually are too small to be seen without the aid of an electron microscope. Viruses can infect plants, animals, fungi, protists, and bacteria. Viruses can attack only specific types of cells that have specific receptors on their surfaces. Viruses do not divide or reproduce like living cells. Viruses are replicated by the machinery of the host cell. The nucleic acid of the virus takes control of the host cell's metabolic pathways to make copies of itself. The host cell usually bursts to release these copies.

Bacteria

Bacteria are small, prokaryotic, single-celled organisms. Bacteria have a circular loop of DNA (plasmid) that is not contained within a nuclear membrane. Bacterial ribosomes are not bound to endoplasmic reticulum, as in eukaryotes. A cell wall containing peptidoglycan surrounds the bacterial plasma membrane. Some bacteria such as pathogens are further encased in gel-like capsules. Bacteria can be autotrophs or heterotrophs. Some bacteria heterotrophs are saprophytes that function as decomposers in ecosystems, and some are pathogens. Many types of bacteria share commensal or mutualistic relationships with other organisms. Most bacteria reproduce asexually by binary fission. Two identical daughter cells are produced from one parent cell. Some bacteria can transfer genetic material to other bacteria through a process called conjugation. Some bacteria can incorporate DNA from the environment in a process called transformation.

Copyright © Mometrix Media. You have been licensed one copy of this document for personal use only. Any other reproduction or redistribution is strictly prohibited. All rights reserved.

Protists

Protists are small, eukaryotic, single-celled organisms. Although protists are small, they are much larger than prokaryotic bacteria. Protists have three general forms, which include plantlike protists, animal-like protists, and fungus-like protists. Plantlike protists are algae that contain chlorophyll and perform photosynthesis. Animal-like protists are protozoa with no cell walls that typically lack chlorophyll and are grouped by their method of locomotion. Fungus-like protists, which do not have chitin in their cell walls, are generally grouped as either slime molds or water molds. Protists may be autotrophic or heterotrophic. Autotrophic protists include many species of algae. Heterotrophic protists include parasitic, commensalistic, and mutualistic protozoa. Slime molds are heterotrophic fungus-like protists, which consume microorganisms. Some protists reproduce sexually, but most reproduce asexually by binary fission. Some reproduce asexually by spores. Some reproduce by alternation of generations and require two hosts in their life cycle.

Fungi

Fungi are nonmotile organisms with eukaryotic cells containing chitin in their cell walls. Most fungi are multicellular, but a few including yeast are unicellular. Fungi have multicellular filaments called hyphae that are grouped together in mycelia. Fungi do not perform photosynthesis. All fungi are heterotrophs. Fungi can be parasitic, mutalistic or free living. Free-living fungi include mushrooms and toadstools. Parasitic fungi include fungi responsible for ringworm and athlete's foot. Mycorrhizae are mutualistic fungi that live in or near plant roots increasing the roots' surface area of absorption. Almost all fungi reproduce asexually by spores, but most fungi also have a sexual phase in the production of spores. Some fungi reproduce by budding or fragmentation.

> **Review Video: Feeding Among Heterotrophs**
> Visit mometrix.com/academy and enter code: 836017
>
> **Review Video: Kingdom Fungi**
> Visit mometrix.com/academy and enter code: 315081

Plants

Plants are multicellular organisms with eukaryotic cells containing cellulose in their cell walls. Plant cells have chlorophyll and perform photosynthesis. Plants can be vascular or nonvascular. Vascular plants have true leaves, stems, and roots that contain xylem and phloem. Nonvascular plants lack true leaves, stems and roots and do not have any true vascular tissue but instead rely on diffusion and osmosis for most transport of materials. Almost all plants are autotrophic, relying on photosynthesis for food. A small number do not have chlorophyll and are parasitic, but these are extremely rare. Plants can reproduce sexually or asexually. Many plants reproduce by seeds produced in the fruits of the plants. Some plants reproduce by seeds on cones. Ferns reproduce by spores. Some plants can reproduce asexually by vegetative reproduction.

> **Review Video: Kingdom Plantae**
> Visit mometrix.com/academy and enter code: 710084

Vascular and Nonvascular Plants

Vascular plants, also referred to as tracheophytes, have dermal tissue, meristematic tissue, ground tissues, and vascular tissues. Nonvascular plants, also referred to a bryophytes, do not have the vascular tissue xylem and phloem. Vascular plants can grow very tall, whereas nonvascular plants are short and close to the ground. Vascular plants can be found in dry regions, but nonvascular plants typically grow near or in moist areas. Vascular plants have leaves, roots, and stems, but nonvascular plants have

115

Copyright © Mometrix Media. You have been licensed one copy of this document for personal use only. Any other reproduction or redistribution is strictly prohibited. All rights reserved.

leaflike, rootlike, and stemlike structures that do not have true vascular tissue. Vascular plants include angiosperms, gymnosperms, and ferns. Nonvascular plants include mosses and liverworts.

Flowering Versus Nonflowering Plants

Angiosperms and gymnosperms are both vascular plants. Angiosperms are flowering plants, and gymnosperms are nonflowering plants. Angiosperms reproduce by seeds that are enclosed in an ovary, usually in a fruit. Angiosperms can be further classified as either monocots or dicots. Gymnosperms reproduce by unenclosed or "naked" seeds on scales, leaves, or cones. Angiosperms include grasses, garden flowers, vegetables, and broadleaf trees such as maples, birches, elms, and oaks. Gymnosperms include conifers such as pines, spruces, cedars, and redwoods.

> **Review Video: Fruits in Flowering Plants**
> Visit mometrix.com/academy and enter code: 867090

Monocots and Dicots

Angiosperms can be classified as either monocots or dicots. The seeds of monocots have one cotyledon, and the seeds of dicots have two cotyledons. The flowers of monocots have petals in multiples of three, and the flowers of dicots have petals in multiples of four or five. The leaves of monocots are slender with parallel veins, and the leaves of dicots are broad and flat with branching veins. The vascular bundles in monocots are distributed throughout the stem. The vascular bundles in dicots are arranged in rings. Monocots have a fibrous root system, and dicots have a taproot system.

Plant Dermal Tissue

Plant dermal tissue consists of the epidermis and the dermis. The epidermis is usually a single layer of cells that covers younger plants. The epidermis protects the plant by secreting the cuticle, which is a waxy substance that helps prevent water loss and infections. The epidermis in leaves has tiny pores called stomata. Guard cells in the epidermis control the opening and closing of the stomata. The epidermis usually does not have chloroplasts. The epidermis may be replaced by periderm in older plants. The periderm is also referred to as bark. The layers of the periderm are cork cells or phellem, phelloderm, and cork cambium or phellogen. Cork is the outer layer of the periderm and consists of nonliving cells. The periderm protects the plant and provides insulation.

Plant Vascular Tissue

The two major types of plant vascular tissue are xylem and phloem. Xylem and phloem are bound together in vascular bundles. A meristem called vascular cambium is located between the xylem and phloem and produces new xylem and phloem. Xylem is made up of tracheids and vessel elements. All vascular plants contain tracheids, but only angiosperms contain vessel elements. Xylem provides support and conducts water and dissolved minerals from the root and upward throughout the plant by transpirational pull and root pressure. In woody plants, xylem is commonly referred to as wood. Phloem is made up of companion cells and sieve-tube cells. Phloem conducts nutrients including sucrose produced during photosynthesis and organic materials throughout the plant. By active transport, the companion vessels move glucose in and out of the sieve-tube cells.

Plant Ground Tissue

The three major types of ground tissue are parenchyma tissue, collenchyma tissue, and sclerenchyma tissue. Most ground tissue is made up of parenchyma. Parenchyma is formed by parenchyma cells, and it provides photosynthesis, food storage, and tissue repair. The soft "filler" tissues in plants are usually parenchyma. The mesophyll in leaves is parenchyma tissue. Collenchyma is made of collenchyma cells and provides support in roots, stems, and petioles. Sclerenchyma tissue is made of sclereid cells, which

Copyright © Mometrix Media. You have been licensed one copy of this document for personal use only. Any other reproduction or redistribution is strictly prohibited. All rights reserved.

are more rigid than the collenchyma cells, and provides rigid support and protection. Plant sclerenchyma tissue may contain cellulose or lignin. Fabrics such as jute, hemp, and flax are made of sclerenchyma tissue.

Plant Meristematic Tissue

Meristems or meristematic tissues are the regions of plant growth. The cells in meristems are undifferentiated and always remain totipotent, which means they can always develop into any type of special tissue. Meristem cells produce all the new cells in a plant and regenerate damaged parts. Cells of meristems reproduce asexually through mitosis or cell division that is regulated by hormones. The two types of meristems are lateral meristems and apical meristems. Primary growth occurs at apical meristems. Roots and shoots have meristem tissue at their tips and can grow in length. Primary meristems include the protoderm, which produces epidermis; the procambium, which produces cambium; xylem and phloem; and the ground meristem, which produces ground tissue including parenchyma. Secondary growth occurs at the lateral or secondary meristems. Secondary meristems include the vascular cambium and cork cambium. Secondary growth causes an increase in diameter.

Flowers

The primary function of flowers is to produce seeds for reproduction of the plant. Flowers have a pedicel or stalk with a receptacle or enlarged upper portion, which holds the developing seeds. Flowers also can have sepals and petals. Sepals are leaflike structures and protect the bud. Petals, which are collectively called the corolla, help to attract pollinators. Plants can have stamens, pistils, or both depending on the type of plant. The stamen consists of the anther and filament. The anther produces the pollen, which produces the sperm cells. The pistil consists of the stigma, style, and ovary. The ovary contains the ovules, which house the egg cells.

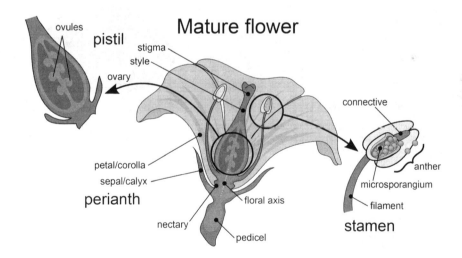

Stems

Plants can have either woody or nonwoody (herbaceous) stems. The stem is divided into nodes and internodes. Buds are located at the nodes and may develop into leaves, roots, flowers, cones, or more stems. Stems consist of dermal tissue, ground tissue, and vascular tissue. Dicot stems have vascular bundles distributed through the stem. Monocots have rings of vascular bundles. Stems have four main functions: (1) they provide support to leaves, flowers, and fruits; (2) they transport materials in the xylem and phloem; (3) they store food; and (4) they have meristems, which provide all of the new cells for the plant.

Copyright © Mometrix Media. You have been licensed one copy of this document for personal use only. Any other reproduction or redistribution is strictly prohibited. All rights reserved.

Leaves

The primary function of a leaf is to manufacture food through photosynthesis. The leaf consists of a flat portion called the blade and a stalk called the petiole. The edge of the leaf is called the margin and can be entire, toothed, or lobed. Veins transport food and water and make up the skeleton of the leaf. The large central vein is called the midrib. The blade has an upper and lower epidermis. The epidermis is covered by a protective cuticle. The lower epidermis contains many stomata, which are pores that allow air to enter and leave the leaf. Stomata also regulate transpiration. The middle portion of the leaf is called the mesophyll. The mesophyll consists of the palisade mesophyll and the spongy mesophyll. Most photosynthesis occurs in chloroplasts located in the palisade mesophyll.

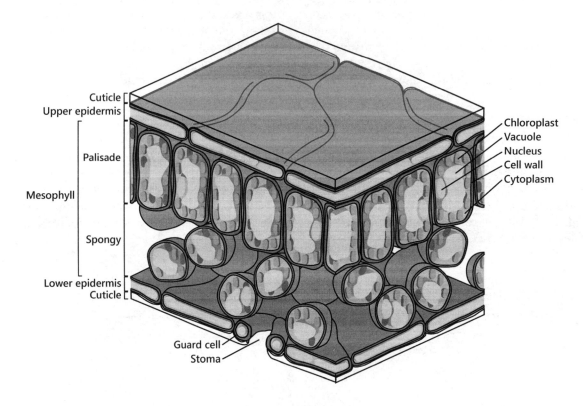

Roots

The primary functions of roots are to anchor the plant, absorb materials, and store food. The two basic types of root systems are taproot systems and fibrous root systems. Taproot systems have a primary root with many smaller secondary roots. Fibrous root systems, which lack a primary root, consist of a mass of many small secondary roots. The root has three main regions: the area of maturation, the area of elongation, and the area of cell division or the meristematic region. The root is covered by an epidermal cell, some of which develops into root hairs. Root hairs absorb water and minerals by osmosis, and capillary action helps move the water upward through the roots to the rest of the plant. The center of the root is the vascular cylinder, which contains the xylem and phloem. The vascular cylinder is surrounded by the cortex where the food is stored. Primary growth occurs at the root tip. Secondary growth occurs at the vascular cambium located between the xylem and phloem.

Pollination Strategies

Pollination is the transfer of pollen from the anther of the stamen to the stigma of the pistil on the same plant or on a different plant. Pollinators can be either abiotic (not derived from a living organism) or biotic (derived from a living organism). Abiotic pollinators include wind and water. Approximately 20%

Copyright © Mometrix Media. You have been licensed one copy of this document for personal use only. Any other reproduction or redistribution is strictly prohibited. All rights reserved.

of pollination occurs by abiotic pollinators. For example, grasses are typically pollinated by wind, and aquatic plants are typically pollinated by water. Biotic pollinators include insects, birds, mammals, and occasionally reptiles. Most biotic pollinators are insects. Many plants have colored petals and strong scents, which attract insects. Pollen rubs off on the insects and is transferred as they move from plant to plant.

Seed Dispersal Methods

Methods of seed dispersal can be abiotic or biotic. Methods of seed dispersal include gravity, wind, water, and animals. Some plants produce seeds in fruits that get eaten by animals and then are distributed to new locations in the animals' waste. Some seeds (e.g. dandelions) have structures to aid in dispersal by wind. Some seeds have barbs that get caught in animal hair or bird feathers and are then carried to new locations by the animals. Some animals bury seeds for food storage but do not return for the seeds. The seeds of aquatic plants can be dispersed by water. The seeds of plants near rivers, streams, lakes, and beaches (e.g. coconuts) are often dispersed by water. Some plants, in a method called mechanical dispersal, can propel or shoot their seeds away from them even up to several feet. Touch-me-nots and violets can reproduce by mechanical dispersal.

Alternation of Generations

Alternation of generations, also referred to as metagenesis, contains both a sexual phase and an asexual phase in the life cycle of the plant. Mosses and ferns reproduce by alternation of generations: the sexual phase is called the gametophyte, and the asexual phase is called the sporophyte. During the sexual phase, a sperm fertilizes an egg to form a zygote. By mitosis, the zygote develops into the sporophyte. The sporangia in the sori of the sporophyte produce the spores through meiosis. The spores germinate and by mitosis produce the gametophyte.

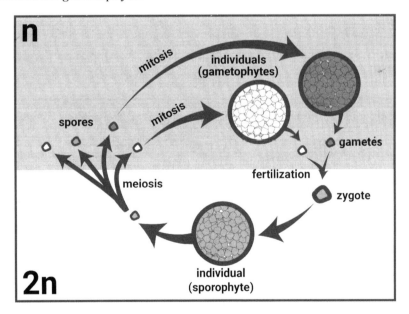

Obtaining and Transporting Water and Inorganic Nutrients

Inorganic nutrients (4) and water (5) enter plants through the root hair and travel to the xylem. Once the water, minerals, and salts have crossed the endodermis, they must be moved upward through the xylem by water uptake. Most of a plant's water is lost through the stomata (3) by transpiration. This loss is necessary to provide the tension needed to pull the water and nutrients up through the xylem. In order to maintain the remaining water that is necessary for the functioning of the plant, guard cells (2) control the stomata. Whether an individual stoma is closed or open is controlled by two guard cells.

Copyright © Mometrix Media. You have been licensed one copy of this document for personal use only. Any other reproduction or redistribution is strictly prohibited. All rights reserved.

When the guard cells lose water and become flaccid, they collapse together, closing the stoma. When the guard cells swell with water and become turgid, they move apart, opening the stoma.

Use of Roots

Plant roots have numerous root hairs that absorb water and inorganic nutrients such as minerals and salts. Root hairs are thin, hairlike outgrowths of the root's epidermal cells that exponentially increase the root's surface area. Water molecules cross the cell membranes of the root hairs by osmosis and then travel on to the vascular cylinder. Inorganic nutrients are transported across the cell membranes of the root endodermis by active transport. The endodermis is a single layer of cells that the water and nutrients must pass through by osmosis or active transport. Casparian strips, which are waxy waterproof deposits, line the channels between the cells of the endodermis to prevent crossing there. Water passes through by osmosis, but mineral uptake is controlled by transport proteins.

Use of Xylem

The xylem contains dead, water-conducting cells called tracheids and vessels. The movement of water upward through the tracheids and vessels is explained by the cohesion-tension theory. First, water is lost through evaporation of the plant's surface through transpiration. This can occur at any surface exposed to air but is mainly through the stomata in the epidermis. This transpiration puts the water inside the xylem in a state of tension. Because water is cohesive due to the strong hydrogen bonds between molecules, the water is pulled up the xylem as long as the water is transpiring.

Glucose Produced During Photosynthesis

Plants produce glucose during photosynthesis. That glucose then enters reactions to form sucrose, starch, and cellulose. Glucose is a simple carbohydrate or monosaccharide. Plants do not transport glucose molecules. Instead, the glucose is joined to a fructose to form a sucrose, which is transported in sap. Sucrose is a disaccharide. Glucose and sucrose are simple carbohydrates. Starches and cellulose are long chains of glucose molecules called polysaccharides. Plants store glucose as starch, and plants use cellulose for rigidity in their cell walls. Both starch and cellulose are complex carbohydrates.

Use of Phloem to Transport Products of Photosynthesis

The movement of sugars and other materials from the leaves to other tissues throughout the plants is called translocation. Nutrients are translocated from sources (areas with excess sugars) such as mature leaves to sinks (areas where sugars are needed) such as flowers, fruits, developing leaves, and roots. Phloem vessels are found in the vascular bundles along with the xylem. Phloem contains conducting cells called sieve elements, which are connected end to end in sieve tubes. Sieve tubes carry sap from sugar sources to sugar sinks. Phloem sap contains mostly sucrose dissolved in water. The sap can also contain proteins, amino acids, and hormones. Some plants transport sugar alcohols. Loading the sugar into the sieve tubes causes water to enter the tubes by osmosis, creating a higher hydrostatic pressure at the source end of the tube. Sugar is removed from the sieve tube at the sink end, and water again follows by osmosis lowering the pressure. This process is referred to as the pressure-flow mechanism.

Copyright © Mometrix Media. You have been licensed one copy of this document for personal use only. Any other reproduction or redistribution is strictly prohibited. All rights reserved.

Molecular Biology, Genetics, and Evolution

Mechanisms of Evolution

Natural and Artificial Selection

Natural selection and artificial selection are both mechanisms of evolution. Natural selection is a process of nature. Natural selection is the way in which a population can change over generations. Every population has variations in individual heritable traits. Not all individuals of a population reproduce. The organisms best suited for survival typically reproduce and pass on their genetic traits. Typically, the more advantageous a trait is, the more common that trait becomes in a population. Natural selection brings about evolutionary adaptations and is responsible for biological diversity. Artificial selection is another mechanism of evolution. Artificial selection is a process brought about by humans. Artificial selection is the selective breeding of domesticated animals and plants such as when farmers choose animals or plants with desirable traits to reproduce. Artificial selection has led to the evolution of farm stock and crops. For example, cauliflower, broccoli, and cabbage all evolved due to artificial selection of the wild mustard plant.

Sexual Selection

Sexual selection is a special case of natural selection in animal populations. Sexual selection occurs because some animals are more likely to find mates than other animals. The two main contributors to sexual selection are competition of males and mate selection by females. An example of male competition is in the mating practices of the redwing blackbird. Some males have huge territories and numerous mates that they defend. Other males have small territories, and some even have no mates. An example of mate selection by females is the mating practices of peacocks. Male peacocks display large, colorful tail feathers to attract females. Females are more likely to choose males with the larger, more colorful displays.

Coevolution

Coevolution describes a rare phenomenon in which two populations with a close ecological relationship undergo reciprocal adaptations simultaneously and evolve together, affecting each other's evolution. General examples of coevolution include predator and prey, or plant and pollinator, and parasites and their hosts. A specific example of coevolution is the yucca moths and the yucca plants. Yucca plants can only be pollinated by the yucca moths. The yucca moths lay their eggs in the yucca flowers, and their larvae grow inside the ovary.

Adaptive Radiation

Adaptive radiation is an evolutionary process in which a species branches out and adapts and fills numerous unoccupied ecological niches. The adaptations occur relatively quickly, driven by natural selection and resulting in new phenotypes and possibly new species eventually. An example of adaptive radiation is the finches that Darwin studied on the Galápagos Islands. Darwin recorded 13 different varieties of finches, which differed in the size and shape of their beaks. Through the process of natural selection, each type of finch adapted to the specific environment and specifically the food sources of the island to which it belonged. On newly formed islands with many unoccupied ecological niches, the adaptive radiation process occurred quickly due to the lack of competing species and predators.

Review Video: Organic Evolution
Visit mometrix.com/academy and enter code: 108959

Copyright © Mometrix Media. You have been licensed one copy of this document for personal use only. Any other reproduction or redistribution is strictly prohibited. All rights reserved.

Evidence Supporting Evolution

<u>Molecular Evidence</u>

Because all organisms are made up of cells, all organisms are alike on a fundamental level. Cells share similar components, which are made up of molecules. Specifically, all cells contain DNA and RNA. This should indicate that all species descended from a common ancestor. Humans and chimpanzees share approximately 98% of their genes in common, and humans and bacteria share approximately 7% of their genes in common. Humans and zebra fish share approximately 85% of their genes in common. Humans and mustard greens share approximately 15% of their genes in common. Biologists have been able to use DNA sequence comparisons of modern organisms to reconstruct the "root" of the tree of life. The fact that RNA can store information, replicate itself, and code for proteins suggests that RNA could have could have evolved first, followed by DNA.

<u>Homology</u>

Homology is the similarity of structures of different species based on a similar structure in a common evolutionary ancestor. The forelimbs of humans, dogs, birds, and whales all have the same basic pattern of the bones. Specifically, all of these organisms have a humerus, radius, and ulna. Tetrapods all have limbs with five digits at some stage in their development. For example, embryonic birds start with limbs with five digits, but adult bird wings have only three digits. They are all modifications of the same basic evolutionary structure from a common ancestor. Tetrapods resemble the fossils of extinct transitional animal called the *Eusthenopteron*. This would seem to indicate that evolution primarily modifies preexisting structures.

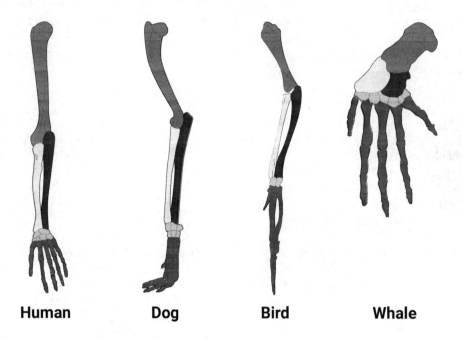

Human   **Dog**   **Bird**   **Whale**

<u>Embryology</u>

The stages of embryonic development reveal homologies between species. These homologies are evidence of a common ancestor. For example, in chicken embryos and mammalian embryos, both include a stage in which slits and arches appear in the embryo's neck region that are strikingly similar to gill slits and gill arches in fish embryos. Adult chickens and adult mammals do not have gills, but this embryonic homology indicates that birds and mammals share a common ancestor with fish. As another example, some species of toothless whales have embryos that initially develop teeth that are later absorbed, which indicates that these whales have an ancestor with teeth in the adult form. Finally, most tetrapods have five-digit limbs, but birds have three-digit limbs in their wings. However, embryonic

Copyright © Mometrix Media. You have been licensed one copy of this document for personal use only. Any other reproduction or redistribution is strictly prohibited. All rights reserved.

birds initially have five-digit limbs in their wings, which develop into a three-digit wing. Tetrapods such as reptiles, mammals, and birds all share a common ancestor with five-digit limbs.

Endosymbiosis Theory

The endosymbiosis theory is foundational to evolution. Endosymbiosis provides the path for prokaryotes to give rise to eukaryotes. Specifically, endosymbiosis explains the development of the organelles of mitochondria in animals and chloroplasts in plants. This theory states that some eukaryotic organelles such as mitochondria and chloroplasts originated as free living cells. According to this theory, primitive, heterotrophic eukaryotes engulfed smaller, autotrophic bacteria prokaryotes, but the bacteria were not digested. Instead, the eukaryotes and the bacteria formed a symbiotic relationship. Eventually, the bacteria transformed into mitochondrion or chloroplasts.

Supporting Evidence

Several facts support the endosymbiosis theory. Mitochondria and chloroplasts contain their own DNA and can both only arise from other preexisting mitochondria and chloroplasts. The genomes of mitochondria and chloroplasts consist of single, circular DNA molecules with no histones. This is similar to bacteria genomes, not eukaryote genomes. Also, the RNA, ribosomes, and protein synthesis of mitochondria and chloroplasts are remarkably similar to those of bacteria, and both use oxygen to produce ATP. These organelles have a double phospholipid layer that is typical of engulfed bacteria. This theory also involves a secondary endosymbiosis in which the original eukaryotic cells that have engulfed the bacteria are then engulfed themselves by another free-living eukaryote.

Convergent Evolution

Convergent evolution is the evolutionary process in which two or more unrelated species become increasingly similar in appearance. In convergent evolution, natural selection leads to adaptation in these unrelated species belonging to the same kind of environment. For example, the mammals shown

Copyright © Mometrix Media. You have been licensed one copy of this document for personal use only. Any other reproduction or redistribution is strictly prohibited. All rights reserved.

below, although found in different parts of the world, developed similar appearances due to their similar environments.

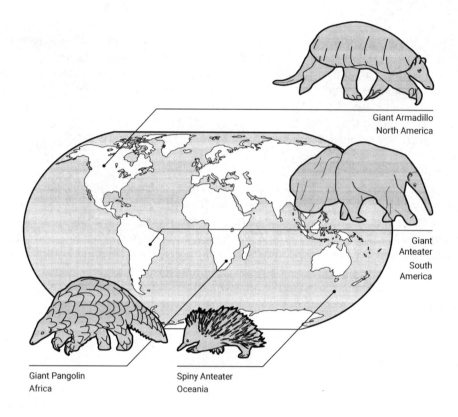

Giant Armadillo
North America

Giant Anteater
South America

Giant Pangolin
Africa

Spiny Anteater
Oceania

Divergent Evolution

Divergent evolution is the evolutionary process in which organisms of one species become increasingly dissimilar in appearance. As several small adaptations occur due to natural selection, the organisms will finally reach a point at which two new species are formed. Then, these two species will further diverge from each other as they continue to evolve. Adaptive radiation is an example of divergent evolution.

Copyright © Mometrix Media. You have been licensed one copy of this document for personal use only. Any other reproduction or redistribution is strictly prohibited. All rights reserved.

Another example is the divergent evolution of the wooly mammoth and the modern elephant from a common ancestor.

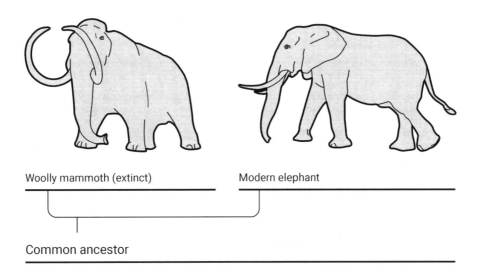

Woolly mammoth (extinct)   Modern elephant

Common ancestor

Fossil Record

The fossil record provides many types of support for evolution including comparisons from rock layers, transition fossils, and homologies with modern organisms. First, fossils from rock layers from all over the world have been compared, enabling scientists to develop a sequence of life from simple to complex. Based on the fossil record, the geologic timeline chronicles the history of all living things. For example, the fossil record clearly indicates that invertebrates developed before vertebrates and that fish developed before amphibians. Second, numerous transitional fossils have been found. Transitional fossils show an intermediate state between an ancestral form of an organism and the form of its descendants. These fossils show the path of evolutionary change. For example, many transition fossils documenting the evolutionary change from fish to amphibians have been discovered. In 2004, scientists discovered *Tiktaalik roseae*, or the "fishapod," which is a 375-million-year-old fossil that exhibits both fish and amphibian characteristics. For example, scientists have determined that *Pakicetus,* an extinct land mammal, is an early ancestor of modern whales and dolphins based on the specialized structures of the inner ear. Most fossils exhibit homologies with modern organisms. For example, extinct horses are similar to modern horses, indicating a common ancestor.

Cephalization

Two major evolutionary trends are cephalization and multicellularity. Cephalization is the evolutionary trend that can be summarized as "the evolution of the head." In most animals, nerve tissue has been concentrated into a brain at one end of an organism over many generations. Eventually, a head enclosing a brain and housing sensory organs was produced at one end of the organism. Many invertebrates, such as arthropods and annelids and all vertebrates, have undergone cephalization. However, some invertebrates, such as echinoderms and sponges, have not undergone cephalization, and these organisms literally do not have a head.

Multicellularity

Another evolutionary trend is multicellularity. Life has evolved from simple, single-celled organisms to complex, multicellular organisms. Over millions of years, single-celled organisms gave rise to biofilms,

Copyright © Mometrix Media. You have been licensed one copy of this document for personal use only. Any other reproduction or redistribution is strictly prohibited. All rights reserved.

which gave rise to multicellular organisms, which gave rise to all of the major phyla of multicellular organisms present today..

Speciation

Significance of Reproductive Isolation

Biological species are groups of organisms that can breed and produce viable offspring. New species may originate due to reproductive isolation between members of the same species. Prezygotic barriers occur before fertilization and stop or hinder species from mating. Postzygotic barriers occur after fertilization but prevent the hybrids from living or being fertile. If gene flow between two groups of a species is hindered or stopped completely, more significant genetic differences between the two groups can accumulate. In order for speciation to occur, differences between two incipient or emerging species must occur. For the two incipient species to completely split, one of two things must occur. Either mating between the incipient species cannot occur, or the offspring must be nonviable or sterile. These situations can occur in many ways. For example, a change in the mating location or a change in the mating rituals can keep mating from occurring. Changes dues to natural selection or genetic drift may affect mating or viability of offspring. Various modes of geographic and population isolation may occur, but the key to speciation in each type is still the reduced gene flow.

Modes

Speciation has various modes that bring about the reduced gene flow needed for incipient species to fully separate. Allopatric speciation occurs between two incipient species that become geographically isolated populations. Say, for some geographic reason, two or more groups within a species cannot mate with each other. This could be due to a volcanic eruption, a desert, or a river. Some may still mate, but the gene flow is greatly reduced. Peripatric speciation is a more specific type of allopatric speciation. Peripatric speciation occurs when an extremely small group is geographically isolated at the edge of the rest of the population. This small population size brings about genetic drift relatively quickly. Parapatric speciation occurs within a continuously distributed population. This occurs due to a geographic distance instead of a geographic barrier. Individuals in the population simply choose to mate with close neighbors, leading to a reduced gene flow. Natural selection in the range of those individuals brings about further differentiation among members of the species spread out across the population. Sympatric speciation occurs when a new species develops within a population with no geographic isolation. Sympatric speciation is uncommon but may occur when a species inhabits a new niche.

Models of Evolutionary Rates

Gradualism

Gradualism is a model of evolutionary rates that states that evolutionary changes occurred slowly or gradually by a divergence of lineages due largely to natural selection. These accumulated changes occurred over millions of years. Many transitional forms occurred between ancestors and modern descendants. Although not all of these transitional forms were preserved in the fossil record, the fossil record clearly supports gradualism. Many transition fossils show adaptations as organisms evolve. The geologic time scale describes this gradual change from simple to complex organisms over millions of years.

Punctuated Equilibrium

Punctuated equilibrium is a model of evolutionary rates that states that in some instances, evolutionary changes occurred in relatively short burst that "punctuate" long periods of equilibrium of little or no change. These "short" periods would still consist of hundreds of thousands of years. Most scientists believe that punctuated equilibrium occurred along with gradualism. The fossil record supports punctuated equilibrium for many organisms. Punctuated equilibrium provides an explanation for the

Copyright © Mometrix Media. You have been licensed one copy of this document for personal use only. Any other reproduction or redistribution is strictly prohibited. All rights reserved.

supposed numerous "missing links" in the fossil record. If punctuated equilibrium is validated, then there actually are no missing links.

Explanations for the Origin of Life on Earth

Panspermia

The word *panspermia* is a Greek work that means "seeds everywhere." Panspermia is one possible explanation for the origin of life on Earth that states that "seeds" of life exist throughout the universe and can be transferred from one location to another. Three types of panspermia based on the seed-dispersal method have been proposed. Lithopanspermia is described as rocks transferring microorganisms between solar systems. Ballistic panspermia is described as rocks transferring microorganisms within a solar system. Directed panspermia is described as intelligent extraterrestrials spreading the seeds to other planets and solar systems. The panspermia hypothesis only proposes the origin of life on Earth. It does not offer an explanation for the origin of life in the universe or explain the origin of the seeds themselves.

Abiotic Synthesis of Organic Compounds

Scientists have performed sophisticated experiments to determine how the first organic compounds appeared on Earth. First, scientists performed controlled experiments that closely resembled the conditions similar to an early Earth. In the classic Miller–Urey experiment (1953), the Earth's early atmosphere was simulated with water, methane, ammonia, and hydrogen that were stimulated by an electric discharge. The Miller–Urey experiment produced complex organic compounds including several amino acids, sugars, and hydrocarbons. Later experiments by other scientists produced nucleic acids. Recently, Jeffrey Bada, a former student of Miller, was able to produce amino acids in a simulation using the Earth's current atmospheric conditions with the addition of iron and carbonate to the simulation. This is significant because in previous studies using Earth's current atmosphere, the amino acids were destroyed by the nitrites produced by the nitrogen.

Atmospheric Composition

The early atmosphere of Earth had little or possibly no oxygen. Early rocks had high levels of iron at their surfaces. Without oxygen, the iron just entered into the early oceans as ions. In the same time frame, early photosynthetic algae were beginning to grow abundantly in the early ocean. During photosynthesis, the algae would produce oxygen gas, which oxidized the iron at the rocks' surfaces, forming an iron oxide. This process basically kept the algae in an oxygen-free environment. As the algae population grew much larger, it eventually produced such a large amount of oxygen that it could not be removed by the iron in the rocks. Because the algae at this time were intolerant to oxygen, the algae became extinct. Over time, a new iron-rich layer of sediments formed, and algae populations reformed, and the cycle began again. This cycle repeated itself for millions of years. Iron-rich layers of sediment alternated with iron-poor layers. Gradually, algae and other life forms evolved that were tolerant to oxygen, stabilizing the oxygen concentration in the atmosphere at levels similar to those of today.

Development of Self-Replication

Several theories for the origin of life involve the self-replication of molecules. In order for life to have originated on Earth, proteins and RNA must have been replicated. Theories that combine the replication of proteins and RNA seem promising. One such theory is called RNA world. RNA world explains how the pathway of DNA to RNA to protein may have originated by proposing the reverse process. In RNA world, RNA is the precursor to DNA. Scientists have shown that RNA can actually function both as a gene and as an enzyme. Also, RNA can be transcribed into DNA. In RNA world, RNA molecules self-replicated and evolved through recombination and mutations. RNA molecules developed the ability to act as enzymes.

Copyright © Mometrix Media. You have been licensed one copy of this document for personal use only. Any other reproduction or redistribution is strictly prohibited. All rights reserved.

Eventually, RNA began to synthesize proteins. Finally, DNA molecules were copied from the RNA in a process of reverse transcription.

Causes of Extinction of Species

Lack of Genetic Diversity

Genetic diversity provides a mechanism for populations to adapt to changing environments or even human impacts. With a diverse genome, individuals possessing genes making them better suited for the environment are more likely to exist. Without genetic diversity, populations cannot develop adaptations. Populations cannot resist diseases or adapt to changes in the habitat. As the populations of endangered species decrease, genetic diversity decreases even further. Normally, natural selection selects genes that resist diseases or help the organism to adapt to changes in the habitat, but if those genes have drifted out of the population, the population cannot evolve and may become extinct. A small gene pool does not provide much variety for selection. For example, tigers in India are now in danger of extinction. Studies show that more than 90% of the genome has been lost largely due to a period when tigers were heavily killed by British officials and Indian royalty. With fewer than 2,000 tigers in the world and these in small populations, the genetic diversity can continue to decrease, possibly leading to extinction if much effort is not made to preserve the remaining genetic diversity.

Environmental Pressures

A changing environment may lead to the extinction of a species. If an animal has a small tolerance range to food sources and habitat needs or if a population is small, it is less likely to adapt to changes in the environment. Climate change and global warming can affect an ecosystem. Some species may not be able to adapt even to seemingly minor temperature changes especially if their populations are small. Animals needing cooler climates may need to move to cooler habitats. Melting ice caps and glaciers and rising sea levels can seriously disrupt many ecosystems and affect numerous species. For example, the giant panda feeds almost exclusively on bamboo. Bamboo is being threatened by global warming. Due to the dwindling of their food source, giant pandas are less able to adapt to a changing environment. The polar bear may become extinct due to global warming as the polar bears' habitat is destroyed. Sea turtles may become extinct as the rising sea levels destroy the beaches needed for egg laying. Even if the beaches are not destroyed, increasing temperatures affect the incubation process and the number of offspring being produced.

Human Impacts

Humans are responsible for impacting the environment in such a way as to endanger or harm species that may even lead to extinction. Humans destroy habitats directly through deforestation and clearing land for agriculture, logging, mining, and urbanization. Humans also threaten or endanger species through overfishing and overhunting. Pollution can destroy a habitat, and if a species is unable to relocate, this can cause extinction. Introduction of an invasive species that introduces a new predator or competitor to the ecosystem can cause extinction. An example of human impacts leading to the extinction of a species is the case of the passenger pigeon. Millions of passenger pigeons were killed for meat from around 1850 to 1880. Because passenger pigeons only laid one egg at a time, huge flocks were destroyed. The last passenger pigeon died in 1914.

> **Review Video:** Genetic vs. Environmental Traits
> Visit mometrix.com/academy and enter code: 750684

Interspecific Competition

Interspecific competition is competition between individuals of different species for the same limited resources such as food, water, sunlight, and living space. This is especially threatening if the two species share a limiting resource and that resource is not in abundant supply. Interspecific competition can limit

Copyright © Mometrix Media. You have been licensed one copy of this document for personal use only. Any other reproduction or redistribution is strictly prohibited. All rights reserved.

the population size of a species. With reduced population size, there is less genetic variation. The species may not be able to adapt to environmental changes. For example, firs and spruces compete for resources in coniferous forests. Cheetahs and lions compete for prey in savannas.

Law of Segregation

The law of segregation states that the alleles for a trait separate when gametes are formed, which means that only one of the pair of alleles for a given trait is passed to the gamete. This can be shown in monohybrid crosses. A monohybrid cross is a genetic cross for a single trait that has two alleles. A monohybrid cross can be used to show which allele is dominant for a single trait. The first monohybrid cross typically occurs between two homozygous parents. Each parent is homozygous for a separate allele for a particular trait. For example, in pea plants, green pods (G) are dominant over yellow pods (g). In a genetic cross of two pea plants that are homozygous for pod color, the F_1 generation will be 100% heterozygous green pods.

	g	g
G	Gg	Gg
G	Gg	Gg

Review Video: Punnett Square
Visit mometrix.com/academy and enter code: 853855

Monohybrid Cross for a Cross Between Two Gg Parents

If the plants with the heterozygous green pods are crossed, the F_2 generation should be 50% heterozygous green, 25% homozygous green, and 25% homozygous yellow.

	G	g
G	GG	Gg
g	Gg	gg

Law of Independent Assortment

Mendel's law of independent assortment states that alleles of one characteristic separate independently of the alleles of another characteristic. This means that traits are transmitted independently of each other. This can be shown in dihybrid crosses.

Dihybrid Cross for the F2 Generation of a Cross between GGYY and Ggyy Parents

A dihybrid cross is a genetic cross for two traits that each have two alleles. For example, in pea plants, green pods (G) are dominant over yellow pods (g), and yellow seeds (Y) are dominant over green seeds (y). In a genetic cross of two pea plants that are homozygous for pod color and seed color, the F_1 generation will be 100% heterozygous green pods and yellow seeds (GgYy). If these F_1 plants are crossed, the resulting F_2 generation is shown below. There are nine genotypes for green-pod, yellow-seed plants: one GGYY, two GGYy, two GgYY, and four GgYy. There are three genotypes for green-pod, green-seed plants: one GGyy and two Ggyy. There are three genotypes for yellow-pod, yellow-seed

Copyright © Mometrix Media. You have been licensed one copy of this document for personal use only. Any other reproduction or redistribution is strictly prohibited. All rights reserved.

plants: one ggYY and two ggYy. There is only one genotype for yellow-pod, green-seed plants: ggyy. This cross has a 9:3:3:1 ratio.

	GY	Gy	gY	gy
GY	GGYY	GGYy	GgYY	GgYy
Gy	GGYy	GGyy	GgYy	Ggyy
gY	GgYY	GgYY	ggYY	ggYy
gy	GgYy	Ggyy	ggYy	ggyy

Pedigree

Pedigree analysis is a type of genetic analysis in which an inherited trait is studied and traced through several generations of a family to determine how that trait is inherited. A pedigree is a chart arranged as a type of family tree using symbols for people and lines to represent the relationships between those people. Squares usually represent males, and circles represent females. Horizontal lines represent a male and female mating, and the vertical lines beneath them represent their children. Usually, family members who possess the trait are fully shaded and those that are carriers only of the trait are half-shaded. Genotypes and phenotypes are determined for each individual if possible. The pedigree below shows the family tree of a family in which the first male who was red-green color blind mated with the first female who was unaffected. They had five children. The three sons were unaffected, and the two daughters were carriers.

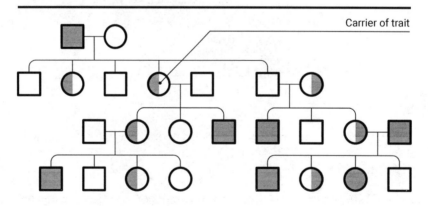

Inheritance of Red-Green Color Blindness: an X-linked Recessive Trait

Non-Mendelian Inheritance Concepts

Linkage

Linkage is an exception to Mendel's law of independent assortment. Linkage can occur when two genes are located on the same chromosome. Each chromosome has several genes, and those genes tend to be inherited together. Genes that are located on the same chromosome and tend to be inherited together are called linkage groups. Because the genes are on the same chromosome, they do not separate during meiosis. During meiosis, the genes in a linkage group always go into the same gamete together. Due to linkage, genes with different characteristics are inherited together more frequently than is predicted using the laws of probability. An example of a linkage group is found on chromosome number 4. This linkage group includes genes for Parkinson's disease, narcolepsy, and Huntington's disease.

Copyright © Mometrix Media. You have been licensed one copy of this document for personal use only. Any other reproduction or redistribution is strictly prohibited. All rights reserved.

Review Video: Mendelian & Non-Mendelian Concepts (Co-Dominance, Incomplete Dominance, Polygenic Inheritance, and Multiple Alleles)
Visit mometrix.com/academy and enter code: 113159

Sex-linked inheritance

Sex-linked inheritance is an exception to Mendel's law of independent assortment. In human genetics, females have two X chromosomes, and males have one X and one Y chromosome. Sex-linked traits are carried on the X chromosome. Because females have two X chromosomes, they have two copies of genes found on the X chromosome. Females may possess a recessive allele for various disorders on one X chromosome, but as long as they possess the dominant allele for normal functioning on the other X chromosome, they will not have the disorder. Females who are heterozygous for a trait such as color blindness or hemophilia are only carriers. Because males have only one X chromosome, if they possess the recessive allele for a disorder, it will be expressed. Examples of traits that are a result of sex linkage are color blindness, hemophilia, a form of muscular dystrophy, and some forms of anemia.

Multiple alleles

Multiple alleles result in a type of non-Mendelian inheritance. In Mendelian inheritance, only two alleles for each gene exist. For example, Mendel's pea plants were either tall or short. Mendel's pea plants had either yellow or green pods. Often, there are more than two possibilities for a particular trait. For example, in human genetics, blood type has many variations. Multiple allele inheritance occurs where there are more than two different alleles of a gene for a particular trait. Even though there may be several alleles for a particular trait, each individual can still only possess two of those possible alleles. For example, the three human blood alleles are I^A (blood contains type A antigens), I^B (blood contains type B antigens), and i (blood contains neither type A nor type B antigens).

Blood types and their possible genotypes are shown below.

Blood Type (Phenotype)	Genotype
A	I^AI^A, I^AI^O
B	I^BI^B, I^BI^O
AB	I^AI^B
O	ii

Incomplete dominance

Incomplete dominance is an exception to Mendel's law of dominance. In these situations, there is no dominant or recessive allele. Instead, both alleles of a heterozygote are expressed, and when they are, they blend or mix. For example, there are two alleles for petal color for snapdragons: red (C^R) and white (C^W). Crossing a red snapdragon with a white snapdragon yields an F_1 generation that is 100% heterozygous pink. Crossing two pink snapdragons yields an F_2 generation that is 50% heterozygous pink (C^RC^W), 25% homozygous white (C^WC^W), and 25% homozygous red (C^RC^R).

Laws of Dominance and Codominance

The law of dominance states that a dominant trait is always expressed. Codominance is an exception to the law of dominance. In codominance, a heterozygote simultaneously expresses both genes for a trait without blending. For example, in certain horses, the hair colors red (D^R) and white (D^W) are codominant. Horses with the genotype D^RD^W have coats composed of red hairs and white hairs, which when mixed together causes their coats to have a golden color.

131

Copyright © Mometrix Media. You have been licensed one copy of this document for personal use only. Any other reproduction or redistribution is strictly prohibited. All rights reserved.

Polygenic Inheritance

Polygenic inheritance occurs when a trait is determined by the interaction of many different genes. In Mendelian genetics, traits are determined by just one pair of genes with two alleles. For example, Mendel's pea plants had either red or white flowers, and his plants were either tall or short. An example of polygenic genetic inheritance in human genetics is skin color and height. Each is controlled by at least four pairs of genes. Skin color has many variations between very light and very dark. Height has many variations between very short and very tall. Eye color and intelligence are also polygenic.

Epistasis

Epistasis occurs when a gene at one locus inhibits the expression of a gene at another locus. For example, in mice, black hair (B) is dominant over brown hair (b). But a different gene at a different locus determines whether or not pigment is deposited (C for deposited and c for not deposited) on the mouse hair. A black mouse with genotypes BB or Bb will only have that color deposited if the pigment genotype is CC or Cc. A black mouse with genotype BBcc will be white. A brown mouse can have genotypes bbCC or bbCc, but a mouse with genotype bbcc will also be white.

Pleiotropy

In Mendelian inheritance, each gene can influence only one trait. Most genes can affect many traits or have multiple phenotypes. Pleiotropy is the situation in which one gene influences several seemingly unrelated traits. A gene that affects multiple traits is pleiotropic. Pleiotropy can be due to normal or mutated genes. Genes code for proteins. Because proteins are often used in more than one tissue or more than one area of the body, a missing protein can cause many complications. For example, the hormone insulin is a protein. If the insulin receptors are faulty, then the cells cannot recognize and use the insulin. Other examples of pleiotropy include inherited diseases such as cystic fibrosis, sickle-cell anemia, phenylketonuria (PKU), and albinism.

Mitochondrial Inheritance

Mitochondria are cellular organelles that produce energy for the cell. Mitochondria contain their own DNA consisting of 37 genes arranged in a circular structure. Mitochondrial DNA is transmitted maternally, which means that these mitochondrial genes are only inherited from the mother. The offspring's mitochondria only come from the oocyte (egg cell), not from the sperm. Sperm cells only contain mitochondria in their tails, which does not enter the egg during fertilization. Mitochondrial inheritance is not consistent with Mendelian inheritance in which the zygote derives half of the genetic material from the mother and half from the father. Most of these genes code for proteins related to muscular disorders.

Genetic Variation

Mutations

Mutations are one of the main sources of genetic variation. Mutations are changes in DNA. The changes can be gene mutations such as the point mutations of substitution, addition, or deletion, or the changes can be on the chromosomal level such as the chromosomal aberrations of translocations, deletions, inversions, and duplications. Mutations are random and can benefit, harm, or have no effect on the individual. Somatic mutations do not affect inheritance and therefore do not affect genetic variation with regard to evolution. Germline mutations that occur in gametes (eggs and sperm) can be passed to offspring and therefore are very important to genetic variation and evolution. Mutations introduce new genetic information into the genome.

Copyright © Mometrix Media. You have been licensed one copy of this document for personal use only. Any other reproduction or redistribution is strictly prohibited. All rights reserved.

Crossing over

Crossing over is a major source of genetic variation. Crossing over is the exchange of equivalent segments of DNA between homologous chromosomes. Crossing over occurs during meiosis in prophase I. During synapsis, a tetrad is formed when homologous chromosomes pair up. Also during synapsis, the chromatids are extremely close together and sometimes the chromatids swap genes. Because genes have more than one allele, this allows for an exchange of genetic information. Crossing over is that exchange of genes. Crossing over can occur several times along the length of the chromosomes. Although crossing over does not introduce new information, it does introduce new combinations of the information that is available. Without crossing over during meiosis, only two genetically different gametes can be formed. With just one instance of crossing over, four genetically different gametes can be formed. With crossing over, each gamete contains genes from both the father and the mother. Crossing over leads to variation in traits among gametes, which leads to variation in traits among offspring.

Independent assortment during sexual reproduction

Independent assortment during sexual reproduction is a source of genetic variation. Mutations originally brought about changes in DNA leading to alleles or different forms of the same gene. During sexual reproduction, these alleles are "shuffled" or "independently sorted," producing individuals with unique combinations of traits. Gametes are produced during meiosis, which consists of two cell divisions: meiosis I and meiosis II. Meiosis I is a reduction division in which the diploid parent cell divides into two haploid daughter cells. During the metaphase of meiosis I, the homologous pairs (one from the mother and one from the father) align on the equatorial plane. The orientation of the homologous pairs is random, and each placement is independent of another's placement. The number of possible arrangements increases exponentially as the number of chromosomes increases. The independent assortment of chromosomes during metaphase in meiosis I provides a variety of gametes with tremendous differences in their combinations of chromosomes.

> **Review Video: Gene & Alleles**
> Visit mometrix.com/academy and enter code: 363997
>
> **Review Video: Gene Mutation**
> Visit mometrix.com/academy and enter code: 955485

Chromosomal Aberrations

Chromosomal aberrations are changes in DNA sequences on the chromosomal level. These mutations typically involve many genes and often result in miscarriages. Chromosomal aberrations include translocations, deletions, inversions, and duplications. Translocations occur when a piece of DNA breaks off of one chromosome and is joined to another chromosome. Deletions occur when a piece of DNA breaks off on a chromosome and is lost without reattaching. Inversions occur when a piece of DNA breaks off of one chromosome and becomes reattached to that same chromosome but with an inverted or flipped orientation. Duplications occur when a piece of DNA is replicated and attached to the original piece of DNA in sequence.

Chromosomal Changes that Lead to Down Syndrome

Down syndrome is a type of aneuploidy (abnormal number of chromosomes) in which an individual has three copies of chromosome 21, as shown in the karyotype below. When a gamete with an extra 21st chromosome unites with a normal gamete, the result is a group of three chromosomes instead of a

Copyright © Mometrix Media. You have been licensed one copy of this document for personal use only. Any other reproduction or redistribution is strictly prohibited. All rights reserved.

diploid set. A trisomy can occur as a result of nondisjunction, which occurs when a pair of chromosomes fails to separate during meiosis in the formation of an egg or sperm cell.

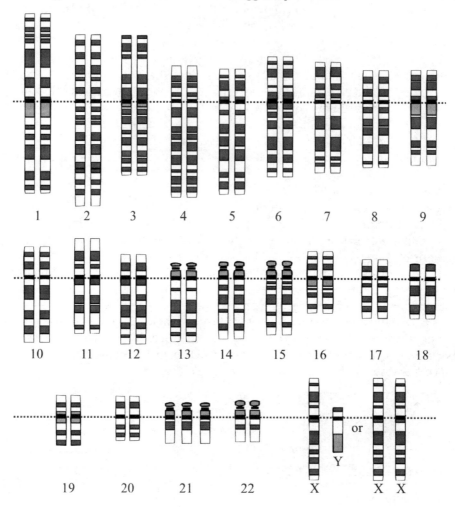

Genetics of Sickle-Cell Anemia

Sickle cell anemia is a genetic disorder that is the result of a gene mutation. Specifically, sickle cell anemia is the result of the point mutation in which adenine is substituted for thymine. This results in a defective form of hemoglobin. Sickle-cell anemia occurs when a person is homozygous for the defective gene. Sickle-cell trait occurs when a person is heterozygous for the defective gene, and this person is a carrier but usually suffers no ill effects. Sickle cell anemia is an example of pleiotropy, in which a change in one gene affects multiple aspects of a person's health. These health problems are due to the abnormally sickle-shaped red blood cells that block the flow of blood, damaging tissues and organs. The sickle-shaped cells tend to rupture, leading to anemia.

Sources of Genetic Exchange

Genetic exchange, or the transfer of DNA from one organism to another, is a source of genetic variation. Three general types of genetic exchange are transduction, transformation, and conjugation. Transduction occurs when genetic material is transferred from one bacterium to another by a bacteriophage. A bacteriophage is a virus that infects a bacterium. As the new bacteriophages are replicated, some of the host bacteria DNA can be added to the virus particles. Transformation occurs when a cell obtains new genetic information from its environment or surroundings. Many bacteria take up DNA fragments such as plasmids from their surroundings to obtain new genes. Conjugation occurs

Copyright © Mometrix Media. You have been licensed one copy of this document for personal use only. Any other reproduction or redistribution is strictly prohibited. All rights reserved.

when bacteria or single-celled organisms are in direct contact with each other. Genes can be transferred from one into the other while the two cells are joined.

Genetic Drift

Genetic drift is a microevolutionary process that causes random changes in allele frequencies that are not the result of natural selection. Genetic drift can result in a loss of genetic diversity. Genetic drift greatly impacts small populations. Two special forms of genetic drift are the genetic bottleneck and the founder effect. A genetic bottleneck occurs when there is a drastic reduction in population due to some change such as overhunting, disease, or habitat loss. When a population is greatly reduced in size, many alleles can be lost. Even if the population size greatly increases again, the lost alleles represent lost genetic diversity. The founder effect occurs when one individual or a few individuals populate a new area such as an island. This new population is limited to the alleles of the founder(s) unless mutations occur or new individuals immigrate to the region.

Gene Flow

Gene flow is a microevolutionary process in which alleles enter a population by immigration and leave a population by emigration. Gene flow helps counter genetic drift. When individuals from one genetically distinct population immigrate to a different genetically distinct population, alleles and their genetic information are added to the new population. The added alleles will change the gene frequencies within the population. This increases genetic diversity. If individuals with rare alleles emigrate from a population, the genetic diversity is decreased. Gene flow reduces the genetic differences between populations.

HW Equilibrium

Hardy–Weinberg (HW) equilibrium is a theoretical concept that uses a mathematical relationship to study gene frequencies. According to HW, if specific conditions are met, the proportions of genotypes in a population can be described by the equation: $p^2 + 2pq + q^2 = 1$, in which p is the frequency of the dominant allele and q is the frequency of the recessive allele. Also, p^2 is the frequency of the homozygous dominant genotype, $2pq$ is the frequency of the heterozygous genotype, and q^2 is the frequency of the homozygous recessive genotype. In addition, the sum of p and q must be equal to one. If the frequencies on the left side of the equation have a sum of one, then the population is in equilibrium, and evolution is not taking place. If the frequencies on the left side of the equation do not have a sum of one, then evolution is taking place. Therefore, the HW equation is only true for populations that are in equilibrium. The HW equilibrium requires the following five conditions to be met: 1) The population must be very large; 2) Mating is random; 3) There are no mutations; 4) No immigration or emigration can occur; and 5) All individuals of the population have an equal chance to survive and reproduce. According to this concept, if all five conditions are met, the gene frequencies will remain constant. In reality, these five conditions are rarely met except in a laboratory situation.

Calculation of Allele Frequency

> Explain how to calculate allele frequencies of a simple genetic locus at which there are two alleles (A and a) in a population of 1,000 individuals given that the population consists of 120 individuals homozygous for the dominant allele (AA), 480 heterozygous individuals (Aa), and 400 individuals homozygous for the recessive allele (aa).

To calculate the frequency of an allele, divide the total number of those alleles in the population by the total number of alleles in the population for that locus as shown in the following equation:

$$\text{allele frequency} = \frac{\text{total \# of allelles in population}}{\text{total \# of alleles in the population for that locus}}.$$

135

Copyright © Mometrix Media. You have been licensed one copy of this document for personal use only. Any other reproduction or redistribution is strictly prohibited. All rights reserved.

First, find the total number of each type of allele. The 120 *AA* individuals produce 240 *A* alleles. The 480 heterozygous individuals produce 480 *A* alleles and 480 *a* alleles. The 400 *aa* individuals produce 800 *a* alleles. Therefore, there is a total of 720 *A* alleles and 1280 *a* alleles. Adding the 720 and 1,280 yields a total of 2,000 alleles in the population for that locus. The allele frequency for $A = \frac{720}{2,000}$ or 0.36. The allele frequency for $a = \frac{1,280}{2,000}$ or 0.64.

Nucleotide Structure

A nucleotide, whether DNA or RNA, contains three components: a phosphate group, a ringed, five-carbon sugar (deoxyribose in DNA, ribose in RNA), and a nitrogen-containing base. The phosphate group binds to one side of the ringed, five-carbon sugar. The nitrogen-containing base binds to the opposite side of the ringed, five-carbon sugar. A nucleotide strand is formed by covalently linking the phosphate groups of the nucleotides into a linear sequence.

DNA and RNA

Structural similarities

Structural similarities between DNA and RNA:

- DNA and RNA are both nucleic acids composed of nucleotides made up of a sugar, a base, and a phosphate molecule.
- DNA and RNA have three of their four bases in common: guanine, cytosine, and adenine.

Structural differences, location, and function

Structural differences between DNA and RNA:

- DNA contains the base thymine, but RNA replaces thymine with uracil.
- DNA contains the sugar deoxyribose, but RNA contains the sugar ribose.
- DNA is double stranded, but RNA is single stranded.

Location – DNA is located in the nucleus and mitochondria. RNA is found in the nucleus, ribosomes, and cytoplasm.

Function – DNA contains the genetic blueprint and instructions for the cell. RNA carries out those instructions.

Copyright © Mometrix Media. You have been licensed one copy of this document for personal use only. Any other reproduction or redistribution is strictly prohibited. All rights reserved.

Types and functions of RNA

Types of RNA include ribosomal RNA (rRNA), transfer RNA (tRNA), and messenger RNA (mRNA).

- rRNA: forms the RNA component of the ribosome. It is evolutionarily conserved, which means it can be used to study relationships in organisms.
- mRNA: used by the ribosome to generate proteins (translation). The mRNA contains three-nucleotide "codons" that code for specific amino acids in a protein sequence.
- tRNA: functions in translation by carrying an amino acid to the corresponding codon on the mRNA strand.

Review Video: DNA
Visit mometrix.com/academy and enter code: 639552

Review Video: DNA Mutations
Visit mometrix.com/academy and enter code: 822061

Review Video: DNA Replication
Visit mometrix.com/academy and enter code: 128118

Complementary Base Pairing

According to Chargaff's rule, DNA always has a 1:1 ratio of purine to pyrimidine. The amount of adenine always equals the amount of thymine, and the amount of guanine always equals the amount of cytosine. DNA contains the bases guanine, cytosine, thymine, and adenine. RNA also contains guanine, cytosine, and adenine, but thymine is replaced with uracil. In DNA, adenine always pairs with thymine, and guanine always pairs with cytosine. In RNA, adenine always pairs with uracil, and guanine always pairs with cytosine. The pairs are bonded together with hydrogen bonds.

Double helix structure of DNA

Double-stranded DNA consists of two complimentary strands that adopt the shape of a double helix, which resembles a twisted ladder. The "sides" of the ladder are the phosphate backbones of the complimentary strands. The "rungs" of the ladder are the sugar-base components, which are held together (base paired) by hydrogen bonds between the nitrogenous bases in opposite strands. In DNA, adenine (A) base pairs with thymine (T) and guanine (G) base pairs with cytosine (C).

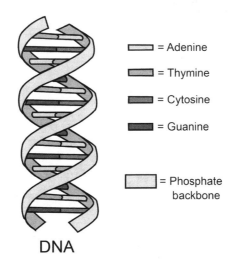

= Adenine

= Thymine

= Cytosine

= Guanine

= Phosphate backbone

DNA

Copyright © Mometrix Media. You have been licensed one copy of this document for personal use only. Any other reproduction or redistribution is strictly prohibited. All rights reserved.

Organization of Prokaryotic DNA

Prokaryotes lack distinct a nucleus with DNA. Prokaryotic DNA is organized primarily into a central loop contained in the cytoplasm. Prokaryotes may also contain smaller loops of DNA known as plasmids that contain other genes. Most prokaryotes lack histones. Archae are an example of prokaryotes that do contain histones.

Organization of Eukaryotic DNA

Eukaryotes have a nucleus with multiple chromosomes, each containing a tightly-compacted, double-helix DNA molecule. The structural sub-components of chromosomes include histones, nucleosomes, and chromatin.

- Histones are positively-charged, DNA-binding proteins.
- A nucleosome is composed of eight histone proteins around which approximately 146 base pairs of DNA are wrapped. The nucleosome is often called a "beads on a string" structure.
- Chromatin is made up of compacted nucleosomes.
- Chromosomes are made up of compacted chromatin.

RNA is also thought to play a role in chromatin structure.

Telomeres

Eukaryotic chromosomes have telomeres located at their tips. Telomeres are repetitive sequences of DNA that maintain the ends of the linear chromosomes and keep those ends from deteriorating.

DNA Replication

DNA replication begins when the double strands of the parent DNA molecule are unwound and unzipped. The enzyme helicase separates the two strands by breaking the hydrogen bonds between the base pairs that make up the rungs of the twisted ladder. These two single strands of DNA are called the replication fork. Each separate DNA strand provides a template for the complementary DNA bases, G with C and A with T. The opposite ends of DNA are called the 5' and 3' ends. After the DNA is separated, the enzyme RNA primase lays down an RNA primer that the enzyme DNA polymerase binds to initiate replication. DNA polymerase replicates DNA from the 3' end towards the 5' end. Of the two strands open during replication, the strand with the 3' end will be replicated as a single, continuous leading strand. The strand with the 5' end will be replicated into shorter, unlinked segments known as Okizaki fragments. The enzyme RNAse removes the RNA primers used to initiate replication of the two strands.

Copyright © Mometrix Media. You have been licensed one copy of this document for personal use only. Any other reproduction or redistribution is strictly prohibited. All rights reserved.

A separate DNA polymerase fills in gaps after the RNA primer is removed. The Okizaki fragments are joined by the enzyme DNA ligase.

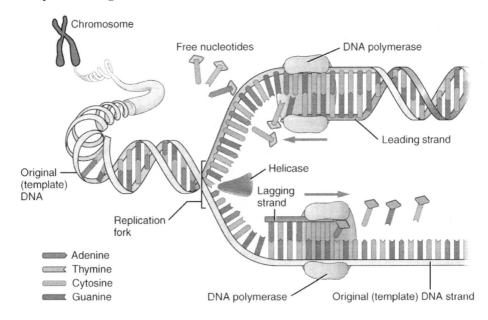

Transcription

Transcription is the process by which a segment of DNA is copied onto a working blueprint called RNA. Each gene has a special region called a promoter that guides the beginning of the transcription process. RNA polymerase unwinds the DNA at the promoter region and makes an RNA copy of the DNA gene by adding the complementary nucleotides, G with C , C with G, T with A, and A with U. This forms a single strand of messenger RNA or mRNA.

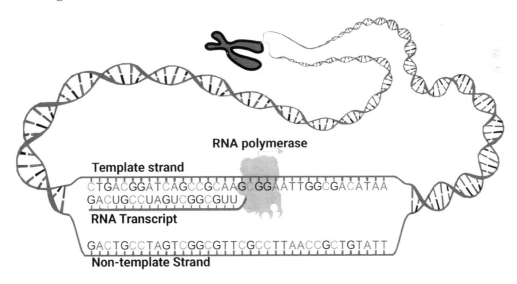

Processing Mrna

In addition to being transcribed, the mRNA must also be processed. First, a 5' cap (modified guanine nucleotide) is added, which helps promote ribosome recognition and preventing mRNA degradation. Second, a string of adenosine ribonucleotides are added to the 3' end of the mRNA, forming a structure known as a poly(A) tail. The poly(A) tail helps prevent mRNA degradation. The mRNA transcript may

139

Copyright © Mometrix Media. You have been licensed one copy of this document for personal use only. Any other reproduction or redistribution is strictly prohibited. All rights reserved.

contain regions that do not code for protein, called introns. The regions that do code for protein are called exons. If introns are present, they will be removed in a process called splicing by a structure known as the spliceosome. After addition of the 5' cap, addition of the poly(A) tail, and splicing, the mRNA is ready for translation.

Translation

Ribosomes synthesize proteins from mRNA in a process called translation. The ribosome has three tRNA binding sites—A, P, and E. Translation initiates when the "A site" becomes occupied by the tRNA molecule corresponding to the mRNA start codon. The ribosome then moves the first tRNA from the "A site" to the "P site." The "A site" is then occupied by the tRNA molecule corresponding to the second mRNA codon. The ribosome then transfers the amino acid on the "P site" tRNA to the amino acid on the "A site" tRNA. The first tRNA, which now has no amino acid, is moved from the "P site" the "E site." The second tRNA, complexed to a chain of two amino acids, is moved from the "A site" to the "P site." The "A site" is then occupied by the tRNA corresponding to the third mRNA codon. The "P site" amino acid chain is transferred to the amino acid bound to the "A site" tRNA. The first tRNA then exits from the "E site" and the second and third tRNA molecules shift, opening the "A site" for the next tRNA. The growing amino acid chain continues to be transferred from the "P site" to the "A site" until translation is complete.

Regulation of Gene Expression

Role of promoters

Promoters are DNA sequences located upstream of the gene needed for transcription. Promoters signal the beginning of transcription. Special proteins called transcription factors, which bind to promoters, subsequently provide binding sites for the RNA polymerase, which is the enzyme that transcribes the RNA. Promoters in the Archaea and Eukaryota domains often contain a nucleotide sequence TATA, which is called a TATA box. The TATA box is usually 25 nucleotides upstream of the transcription start site, and it is the location at which the DNA is unwound.

Role of enhancers

Enhancers are DNA sequences that regulate gene expression by providing a binding site for proteins that regulate RNA polymerase in transcribing proteins. Enhancers can greatly increase the expression of genes in their range. They can be hundreds or thousands of base pairs upstream or downstream from the genes they control. Some enhancers are located within the gene they control. Enhancers are functional over large distances. Most genes are controlled by two or three enhancers, but some may be controlled by more. Enhancers provide binding sites for regulatory proteins that either promote or inhibit RNA polymerase activity. Enhancers are more common in eukaryotes than prokaryotes.

> **Review Video: Regulation of Gene Expression**
> Visit mometrix.com/academy and enter code: 651793

Role of transcription factors

Transcription factors are DNA-binding proteins that help regulate gene expression in eukaryotes and prokaryotes. In eukaryotes that have promoter or enhancer regions, transcription factors bind near these regions and increase the ability of the RNA polymerase to start transcription. In eukaryotes, because genes are typically turned "off," transcription factors typically work to turn genes "on." The opposite is often true in bacteria, and transcription factors often work to turn genes off.

Role of operons

Operons are segments of DNA or groups of genes that are controlled by one promoter. Operons consist of an operator, a promoter, and structural gene(s). The operator provides a binding side for a repressor

Copyright © Mometrix Media. You have been licensed one copy of this document for personal use only. Any other reproduction or redistribution is strictly prohibited. All rights reserved.

that inhibits the binding of RNA polymerase. The promoter provides the binding site for the RNA polymerase. The structural genes provide the sequence that codes for a protein. Operons are transcribed as single units and code for a single mRNA molecule, which produces proteins with related functions. Operons have been found in prokaryotes, eukaryotes, and viruses. For example, the lac (lactose) operon in certain bacteria controls the production of the enzymes needed to digest lactose. If lactose is already available in the cell, the lactose binds to the repressor protein to prevent the repressor protein from binding to the operator. The gene is transcribed, and the enzymes necessary for the digestion of the lactose are produced. If there is no lactose that needs to be digested, the repressor protein binds to the operator. The gene is not transcribed, and the enzyme is not produced. This allows the cell to only code for proteins as needed by the cell.

Role of epigenetics

Epigenetics studies factors or mechanisms that determine if genes are active (switched on) or dormant (switched off). These mechanisms can alter gene function or gene expression without altering the sequences of the DNA itself. An example is the addition of a methyl group (methylation) to the histones. Acetylation, the addition of an acetyl group, and phosphorylation, the addition of a phosphoryl group, are also modifications to the proteins associated with DNA that can switch genes on or off or affect their activity level.

Differential Gene Expression

Differential gene expression is the expression of different sets of gene by cells with identical DNA molecules. The unused genes in a differentiated cell remain in the cell but are not expressed. Actually, only a few genes are expressed in each cell. For example, during mammalian embryonic development, the undifferentiated zygote undergoes cell division through mitosis. As the number of cells increases, selected cells undergo differentiation to become specialized components in the developing tissues of the embryo.

Stem Cells

Stem cells are undifferentiated cells that can divide without limit and that can differentiate to produce the specialized cells that each organism needs. Embryonic stem cells are harvested from the embryo at the blastocyst stage or from the developing gonads of the embryo. Stem cells can be pluripotent or multipotent depending on their source. Early embryonic stem cells are pluripotent. This means they have not undergone any differentiation and have the ability to become any special type of cell. After embryonic stem cells begin to differentiate, they may be limited to specializing into a specific tissue type. These stem cells are considered to be multipotent because they can only develop into a few different types of cells. Adult stem cells, also called somatic stem cells, are harvested from organs and tissues and can differentiate into those types of cells in that particular organ or tissue. Umbilical cord blood stem cells can be harvested from the umbilical cord of a newborn baby. Adult stem cells and umbilical cord blood stem cells are multipotent. Induced pluripotent cells (iPS) are somatic cells that have been manipulated to act like pluripotent cells. Experiments have shown that iPS may be useful in treating diseases.

Copyright © Mometrix Media. You have been licensed one copy of this document for personal use only. Any other reproduction or redistribution is strictly prohibited. All rights reserved.

Mutations

Missense mutatinos, silent mutations, and nonsense mutations

Mutations are changes in DNA sequences. Point mutations are changes in a single nucleotide in a DNA sequence. Three types of point mutations are missense, silent, and nonsense.

- Missense mutations result in a codon for a different amino acid. An example is mutating TGT (Cysteine codon) to TGG (Tryptophan codon).
- Silent mutations result in a codon for the same amino acid as the original sequence. An example is mutating TGT (Cysteine codon) to TGC (a different Cysteine codon).
- Nonsense mutations insert a premature stop codon, typically resulting in a non-functional protein. An example is mutating TGT (Cysteine codon) to TGA (STOP codon).

> **Review Video: Codons**
> Visit mometrix.com/academy and enter code: 978172

Frameshift mutations and inversion mutations

Deletions and insertions can result in the addition of amino acids, the removal of amino acids, or cause a frameshift mutation. A frameshift mutation changes the reading frame of the mRNA (a new group of codons will be read), resulting in the formation of a new protein product. Mutations can also occur on the chromosomal level. For example, an inversion is when a piece of the chromosome inverts or flips its orientation.

Germline mutations and somatic mutations

Mutations can occur in somatic (body) cells and germ cells (egg and sperm). Somatic mutations develop after conception and occur in an organism's body cells such as bone cells, liver cells, or brain cells. Somatic mutations cannot be passed on from parent to offspring. The mutation is limited to the specific descendent of the cell in which the mutation occurred. The mutation is not in the other body cells unless they are descendants of the originally mutated cell. Somatic mutations may cause cancer or diseases. Some somatic mutations are silent. Germline mutations are present at conception and occur in an organism's germ cells, which are only egg and sperms cells. Germline mutations may be passed on from parent to offspring. Germline mutations will be present in every cell of an offspring that inherits a germline mutation. Germline mutations may cause diseases. Some germline mutations are silent.

Mutagens

Mutagens are physical and chemical agents that cause changes or errors in DNA replication. Mutagens are external factors to an organism. Examples include ionizing radiation such as ultraviolet radiation, x-rays, and gamma radiation. Viruses and microorganisms that integrate their DNA into host chromosomes are also mutagens. Mutagens include environmental poisons such as asbestos, coal tars, tobacco, and benzene. Alcohol and diets high in fat have been shown to be mutagenic. Not all mutations are caused by mutagens. Spontaneous mutations can occur in DNA due to molecular decay.

PCR

The polymerase chain reaction (PCR) is a laboratory technique used to rapidly copy selected segments of DNA. PCR can be performed on the DNA from a single cell. PCR is a hot-and-cold cycled reaction that uses a special heat-tolerant polymerase. The DNA sample is combined with this special DNA polymerase, primers, and free nucleotides. Primers are synthetic strands of DNA containing just a few bases. The first step is a high-temperature denaturation step (90–95°C) that causes the DNA strands to unwind. The second step is a low-temperature annealing step (~60°C) in which the primers anneal to the single-stranded DNA. The final step is an activation step that matches the activation temperature for the heat-resistant DNA polymerase (~70°C, depending on the enzyme). This final step results in the

Copyright © Mometrix Media. You have been licensed one copy of this document for personal use only. Any other reproduction or redistribution is strictly prohibited. All rights reserved.

formation of newly-synthesized, double-stranded DNA. These steps will be repeated on the same sample for multiple cycles, typically ~30. The number of DNA copies generated is 2^N, where N is the number of cycles.

DNA Sequencing

DNA sequencing is a laboratory technique used to determine the order or linear sequence of nucleotides of DNA fragments. A polymerase chain reaction (PCR) is used to isolate the needed DNA segment or DNA template. During PCR, some of each of the nucleotides containing the four bases, G, C, A, and T, is chemically altered and fluorescently tagged with different colors of dye. Also, the chemically altered nucleotides have the dideoxyribose sugar, which contains one less oxygen atom than the usual deoxyribose. When synthesis begins, the polymerase randomly adds either a regular nucleotide or an altered nucleotide. If the polymerase adds an altered nucleotide, synthesis stops. This way, each DNA fragment of the same length is tagged with the same color. Then, electrophoresis is used to separate DNA fragments according to length. The DNA sequence can be read by reading the tags of the shortest fragments to the tags of the longest fragments.

Human Genome Project

In 1990, the Human Genome Project (HGP), which involved scientists from 16 laboratories located in at least 6 different countries, was launched to map the human genome. The project was completed in 2003. The human genome consists of approximately 3.12 billion paired nucleotides. The genomes of several plants, animal, fungi, protists, bacteria, viruses, and even cell organelles have also been studied and mapped. Interesting comparisons can be made between these genomes. For example, the number of genes in an organism's genome does not indicate the complexity of that organism. Humans have approximately 21,000 genes, but the simpler roundworms have approximately 26,000 genes.

Gene Therapy

Gene therapy is an experimental but promising technique that introduces new genes into an organism to correct a specific disease caused by a defective gene. In gene therapy, the defective gene is replaced by a properly functioning gene. Gene therapy is most promising for diseases that are caused by a single defective gene. For example, gene therapy was first successfully used to treat severe combined immunodeficiency (SCID). One type of SCID is caused by a single defective gene on the X chromosome. Doctors removed some bone marrow from the test subjects, injected a retrovirus that was carrying the gene, and then re-implanted the bone marrow. The bone marrow cells then have the correct DNA sequence for the production of proteins for much-needed enzymes. Unfortunately, some of the first recipients developed leukemia, and the trials were halted. Later, researchers discovered that the leukemia was related to the location of the insertion of the retroviral vectors.

Cloning

Clones are exact biological copies of genes, cells, or multicellular organisms. There are natural clones and artificial clones. Many clones are produced in nature. Animals that can reproduce asexually by fragmentation or budding produce natural clones. Some plants such as strawberries can reproduce by stolons. Typically, in biology, cloning refers to gene cloning or the cloning of organisms. Gene cloning is the process of splicing genes that are needed to code for a specific protein and introducing them into a new cell with a DNA vector. Gene cloning has been used with bacteria in the production of human insulin and a human growth hormone replacement.

Cloning can also occur with an entire organism. This type of cloning is called a somatic cell nuclear transfer. The first mammal clone was Dolly the sheep. In this procedure, a nucleus of a somatic cell from the sheep to be cloned was transferred or injected into a denucleated egg cell of the surrogate mother sheep. The egg was stimulated to divide by electric shock, and then the embryo was implanted into the

Copyright © Mometrix Media. You have been licensed one copy of this document for personal use only. Any other reproduction or redistribution is strictly prohibited. All rights reserved.

uterus of the surrogate mother. Dolly was born identical to the egg nucleus donor, not the surrogate mother. Dolly and other cloned mammals typically have serious health problems. Dolly aged prematurely possibly due to the shortened telomeres from the adult somatic cell nucleus.

Review Video: Cloning
Visit mometrix.com/academy and enter code: 289634

Genetic Engineering and Genetically Engineered Cells

Genetic engineering is the manipulation of DNA outside of normal reproduction. This modified DNA is called recombinant DNA. Genetic engineering is prevalent in gene cloning, which is used in the production of genetically modified (GM) organisms and the production of GM food. Gene cloning involves cloning a specific gene that is needed for a specific purpose. Genes can be inserted into cells of an entirely different species. Genetically engineered cells are also called transgenic cells. GM organisms such plants or crops contain recombinant DNA. Many types of organisms such as plants, animals, fungi, and bacteria have been genetically modified. GM crops such as corn and soybeans can be engineered to be herbicide resistant to ensure that herbicides kill the weeds but not the crop plants. Crops can also be modified to be pest resistant in order to kill the insects that might damage the crops. Also, several foods can be genetically modified to increase nutritional value.

Review Video: Genetic Engineering and Genetically Engineered Cells
Visit mometrix.com/academy and enter code: 548687

Copyright © Mometrix Media. You have been licensed one copy of this document for personal use only. Any other reproduction or redistribution is strictly prohibited. All rights reserved.

Ecology and the Unity and Diversity of Life

Biosphere

Components

The biosphere is the region of the earth inhabited by living things. The components of the biosphere from smallest to largest are organisms, populations, communities, ecosystems, and biomes. Organisms of the same species make up a population. All of the populations in an area make up the community. The community combined with the physical environment for a region forms an ecosystem. Several ecosystems are grouped together to form large geographic regions called biomes.

Population

A population is a group of all the individuals of one species in a specific area or region at a certain time. A species is a group of organisms that can breed and produce fertile offspring. There may be many populations of a specific species in a large geographic region. Ecologists study the size, density, and growth rate of populations to determine their stability. The population density is the number of individuals per unit of area. Growth rates may be exponential or logistic. Population size continuously changes with births, deaths, and migrations. Ecologists also study how the individuals are dispersed within a population. Some species form clusters. Others are evenly or randomly spaced. Every population has limiting factors. Changes in the environment can reduce population size. Geography can limit population size. The individuals of a population react with each other and with other organisms in the community. Competition and predation affect population size.

Community Interactions

A community is all of the populations of different species that live in an area and interact with each other. Community interaction can be intraspecific or interspecific. Intraspecific interactions occur between members of the same species. Interspecific interactions occur between members of different species. Different types of interactions include competition, predation, and symbiosis. Communities with high diversity are more complex and more stable than communities with low diversity. The level of diversity can be seen in a food web of the community, which shows all the feeding relationships within the community.

Ecosystems

An ecosystem is the basic unit of ecology. An ecosystem is the sum of all the biotic and abiotic factors in an area. Biotic factors are all living things such as plants, animals, fungi, and microorganisms. Abiotic factors include the light, water, air, temperature, and soil in an area. Ecosystems obtain the energy they need from sunlight. Ecosystems contain biogeochemical cycles such as the hydrologic cycle and the nitrogen cycle. Ecosystems are generally classified as either terrestrial or aquatic. All of the living things within an ecosystem are called its community. The number and variety of living things within a community describes the ecosystem's biodiversity. Each ecosystem can only support a limited number of organisms known as the carrying capacity.

Biotic and Abiotic Factors in an Ecosystem

Every ecosystem consists of multiple abiotic and biotic factors. Abiotic factors are the nonbiological physical and chemical factors that affect the ecosystem. Abiotic factors include soil type, atmospheric conditions, sunlight, water, wind, chemical elements, and natural disturbances. In aquatic ecosystems, abiotic factors include salinity, turbidity, water depth, current, temperature, and light. Biotic factors are all of the living organisms in the ecosystem. Biotic factors include plants, algae, fungi, bacteria, archaea, animals, and protozoa.

Copyright © Mometrix Media. You have been licensed one copy of this document for personal use only. Any other reproduction or redistribution is strictly prohibited. All rights reserved.

Biomes

The biosphere consists of numerous biomes. A biome is a large region that supports a specific community. Each biome has a characteristic climate and geography. Differences in latitude, altitude, and worldwide patterns affect temperature, precipitation, and humidity. Biomes can be classified as terrestrial or aquatic biomes. Terrestrial biomes include ecosystems with land environments, such as tundra, coniferous forest, temperate broadleaf forest, temperate grassland, chaparral, desert, savannas, and tropical forests. Terrestrial biomes tend to grade into each other in regions called ecotones. Aquatic biomes are water-dwelling ecosystems. Aquatic biomes include lakes, coral reefs, rivers, oceanic pelagic zone, estuaries, intertidal zone, and the abyssal zone.

Aquatic Biomes

Aquatic biomes are characterized by multiple factors including the temperature of the water, the amount of dissolved solids in the water, the availability of light, the depth of the water, and the material at the bottom of the biome. Aquatic biomes are classified as marine regions or freshwater biomes based on the amount of dissolved salt in the water. Marine biomes include the pelagic zone, the benthic zone, coral reefs, and estuaries. Marine biomes have a salinity of at least 35 parts per thousand. Freshwater biomes include lakes, ponds, rivers, and streams. Freshwater biomes have a salinity that is less than 0.5 parts per thousand. Lakes and ponds, which are relatively stationary, consist of two zones: the littoral zone and the limnetic zone. The littoral zone is closest to the shore and is home to many plants (floating and rooted), invertebrates, crustaceans, amphibians, and fish. The limnetic zone is further from the shore and has no rooted plants. Rivers and streams typically originate in the mountains and make their way to the oceans. Because this water is running and colder, it contains different plants and animals than lakes and ponds. Salmon, trout, crayfish, plants, and algae are found in rivers and streams.

Marine Regions

Marine regions are located in three broad areas: the ocean, estuaries, and coral reefs. The ocean consists of two general regions—the pelagic zone and the benthic zone. The pelagic zone is in the open ocean. Organisms in the pelagic zone include phytoplankton such as algae and bacteria; zooplankton such as protozoa and crustaceans; and larger animals such as squid, sharks, and whales. The benthic zone consists of the floor and the ocean floor. Organisms in the benthic zone can include sponges, clams, oysters, starfish, sea anemones, sea urchins, worms, and fish. The deepest part of the benthic zone is called the abyssal plain. This is the deep ocean floor, which is home to numerous scavengers, many of which have light-generating capability. Estuaries are somewhat-enclosed coastal regions where water from rivers and streams is mixed with seawater. Coral reefs are located in warm, shallow water. Corals are small colonial animals that share a mutualistic relationship with algae.

Terrestrial Biomes

Terrestrial biomes are classified predominantly by their vegetation, which is primarily determined by precipitation and temperature. Tropical rainforests experience the highest annual precipitation and relatively high temperatures. The dominant vegetation in tropical forests is tall evergreen trees. Temperate deciduous forests experience moderate precipitation and temperatures. The dominant vegetation is deciduous trees. Boreal forests experience moderate precipitation and lower temperatures. The dominant vegetation is coniferous trees. The tundra experiences lower precipitation and cold temperatures. The dominant vegetation is shrubs. The savanna experiences lower precipitation

Copyright © Mometrix Media. You have been licensed one copy of this document for personal use only. Any other reproduction or redistribution is strictly prohibited. All rights reserved.

and high temperatures. The dominant vegetation is grasses. Deserts experience the lowest precipitation and the hottest temperatures. The dominant vegetation is scattered thorny plants.

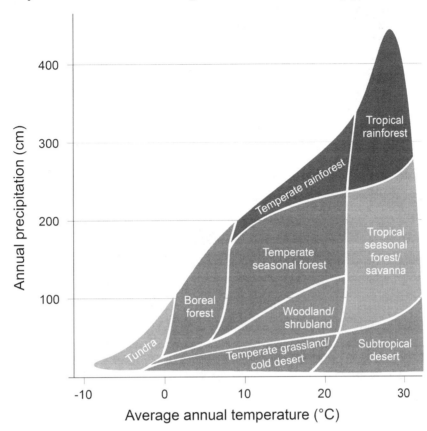

Influence of Resource Availability and Abiotic Factors on Population Size

Population size is affected by resource availability and abiotic factors. As the population density increases, intraspecific competition for available resources intensifies. If the availability of resources decreases, death rates may increase and birth rates may decrease. For example, territoriality for mating or nesting may limit available resources for individuals in a population and limit the population size. Abiotic factors such as temperature, rainfall, wind, and light intensity all influence the population size. For example, temperatures near a species' tolerance limit may decrease the population. Natural disasters such as fire or flood can destroy resources and greatly decrease a population's size. In general, any abiotic factor that reduces or limits resources will also reduce or limit population size.

Significance of Habitat and Niche to Populations

The habitat of an organism is the type of place where an organism usually lives. A habitat is a piece of an environmental area. A habitat may be a geographic area or even the body of another organism. The habitat describes an organism's natural living environment. A habitat includes biotic and abiotic factors such as temperature, light, food resources, and predators. Whereas a habitat describes an organism's "home," a niche can be thought of as an organism's "occupation." A niche describes an organism's functional role in the community and how the organism uses its habitat. A niche can be quite complex because it should include the impacts that the organism has on the biotic and abiotic surroundings. Niches can be broad or narrow.

Copyright © Mometrix Media. You have been licensed one copy of this document for personal use only. Any other reproduction or redistribution is strictly prohibited. All rights reserved.

Influence of Competition and Predation on Population Size

Feeding relationships between organisms can affect population size. Competition and predation both tend to limit population size. Competition occurs when two individuals need the same resource. Predation occurs when one individual is the resource for another individual. Competition occurs when individuals share a resource in the habitat. This competition can be intraspecific, which is between members of the same species, or interspecific, which is between members of different species. Intraspecific competition reduces resources as that species' own population increases. This limits population growth. Interspecific competition reduces resources as a different species uses those same resources. Predation occurs when one species is a food resource for another species. Predator and prey populations can cycle over a range of years. If prey resources increase, predator numbers increase. An example of the predator-prey population cycle is the Canadian lynx and snowshoe hare.

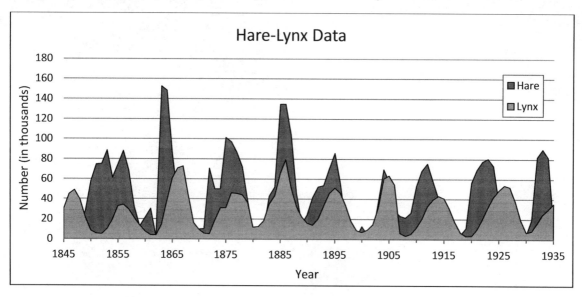

Logistic Population Growth Model

Populations vary over time due to deaths, births, immigration, and emigration. In most situations, resources such as food, water, and shelter are limited. Each environment or habitat can only support a limited number of individuals. This is known as the carrying capacity. Population growth models that factor in the carrying capacity are called logistic growth models. With logistic population growth models, the rate of population growth decreases as the population size increases. Logistic growth graphs as an S-shaped curve. Comparing logistic growth and exponential growth shows that the graph for exponential growth continues to become steeper, but the graph for logistics growth levels off once the population reaches the carrying capacity. As the population increases, fewer resources are available per individual. This limits the number of individuals that can occupy that environment or habitat.

Exponential Population Growth Model

Populations change over time due to births, deaths, and migrations. Sometimes, conditions are near ideal and populations can increase at their maximum rate exhibiting exponential growth. Exponential growth is growth in which the rate of change is proportional to the increasing size in an exponential progression. Exponential growth graphs as a J-shaped curve. Exponential growth is often observed in single-celled organisms such as bacteria or protozoa in which the population or number of cells increases by a factor of two per unit of time. One cell divides into two cells, which divide into four cells, and so forth. The exponential growth model describes population growth under ideal conditions. It does not take limiting factors or carrying capacity into account. Realistically, exponential growth cannot occur indefinitely, but it may occur for a period of time. It does show a species' capacity for increase and may

Copyright © Mometrix Media. You have been licensed one copy of this document for personal use only. Any other reproduction or redistribution is strictly prohibited. All rights reserved.

be helpful when studying a particular species or ecosystem. For example, if a species with no natural predator is introduced into a new habitat, that species may experience exponential growth. If this growth is allowed to go unchecked, the population may overshoot the carrying capacity and then starve. Efforts may need to be taken to reduce the population before this occurs.

Advantages and Disadvantages of Asexual Reproduction in Animals

Very few species of animals reproduce by asexual reproduction, and nearly all of those species also have the ability to reproduce sexually. While not common, asexual reproduction is useful for animals that tend to stay in one place and may not find mates. Asexual reproduction takes considerably less effort and energy than sexual reproduction. In asexual reproduction, all of the offspring are genetically identical to the parent. This can be a disadvantage because of the lack of genetic variation. Although asexual reproduction is advantageous in a stable environment, if the environment changes, the organisms may lack the genetic variability to survive or selectively adapt.

Life Histories

The life history of a species describes the typical organism's life cycle from birth through reproduction to death. Life histories can typically be classified as opportunistic life histories or equilibrial life histories. Species exhibiting opportunistic life histories are typically small, short-lived organisms that have a high reproductive capacity but invest little time and care into their offspring. Their population sizes tend to oscillate significantly over periods of several years. Species exhibiting equilibrial life histories are typically large, long-lived organisms that have a low reproductive capacity but invest much time and care into their offspring. Their populations tend to fluctuate within a smaller range. A general observation is that species that tend to produce numerous offspring typically tend to invest little care into that offspring, resulting in a high mortality rate of that offspring. Organisms of species that tend to produce few offspring typically invest much more care into that offspring, resulting in a lower mortality rate.

Symbiosis

Many species share a special nutritional relationship with another species, called symbiosis. The term symbiosis means "living together." In symbiosis, two organisms share a close physical relationship that can be helpful, harmful, or neutral for each organism. Three forms of symbiosis are parasitism, commensalism, and mutualism. Parasitism is a relationship between two organisms in which one organism is the parasite, and the other organism is the host. The parasite benefits from the relationship because the parasite obtains its nutrition from the host. The host is harmed from the relationship because the parasite is using the host's energy and giving nothing in return. For example, a tick and a dog share a parasitic relationship in which the tick is the parasite, and the dog is the host. Commensalism is a relationship between two organisms in which one benefits, and the other is not affected. For example, a small fish called a remora can attach to the belly of a shark and ride along. The remora is safe under the shark, and the shark is not affected. Mutualism is a relationship between two organisms in which both organisms benefit. For example, a rhinoceros usually can be seen with a few tick birds perched on its back. The tick birds are helped by the easy food source of ticks, and the rhino benefits from the tick removal.

Predation

Predation is a special nutritional relationship in which one organism is the predator, and the other organism is the prey. The predator benefits from the relationship, but the prey is harmed. The predator hunts and kills the prey for food. The predator is specially adapted to hunt its prey, and the prey is specially adapted to escape its predator. While predators harm (kill) their individual prey, predation usually helps the prey species. Predation keeps the population of the prey species under control and prevents them from overshooting the carrying capacity, which often leads to starvation. Also, predation

149

Copyright © Mometrix Media. You have been licensed one copy of this document for personal use only. Any other reproduction or redistribution is strictly prohibited. All rights reserved.

usually helps to remove weak or slow members of the prey species leaving the healthier, stronger, and better adapted individuals to reproduce. Examples of predator-prey relationships include lions and zebras, snakes and rats, and hawks and rabbits.

Competition and Territoriality

Competition is a relationship between two organisms in which the organisms compete for the same vital resource that is in short supply. Typically, both organisms are harmed, but one is usually harmed more than the other. They could be competing for resources such as food, water, mates, and space. Interspecific competition is between members of different species. Intraspecific competition is between members of the same species. Competition provides an avenue for natural selection. Territoriality can be considered to be a type of interspecific competition for space. Many animals including mammals, birds, reptiles, fish, spiders, and insects have exhibited territorial behavior. Once territories are established, there are fewer conflicts between organisms. For example, a male redwing blackbird can establish a large territory. By singing and flashing his red patches, he is able to warn other males to avoid his territory, and they can avoid fighting.

Altruistic Behaviors Between Animals

Altruism is a self-sacrificing behavior in which an individual animal may serve or protect another animal. For example, in a honey bee colony, there is one queen, many workers (females), and drones (males) only during the mating seasons. Adult workers do all the work of the hive and will die defending it. Another example of altruism is seen in a naked mole rat colony. Each colony has one queen that mates with a few males, and the rest of the colony is nonbreeding and lives to service the queen, her mates, and her offspring.

> **Review Video: Mutualism, Commensalism, and Parasitism**
> Visit mometrix.com/academy and enter code: 757249

Changes During Primary and Secondary Succession

Ecological succession is the process by which climax communities come into existence or are replaced by new climax communities when they are greatly changed or destroyed. The two types of ecological succession are primary succession and secondary succession. Primary succession occurs in a region where there is no soil and that has never been populated such as a new volcanic island or a region where a glacier has retreated. During the pioneer stage, the progression of species is typically lichen and algae, followed by small annual plants, then perennial herbs and grasses. During the intermediate stage, shrubs, grasses, and shade-intolerant trees are dominant. Finally, after hundreds of years, a climax community is reached with shade-tolerant trees. Secondary succession occurs when a climax community is destroyed or nearly destroyed such as after a forest fire or in an abandoned field. With secondary succession, the area starts with soil and seeds from the original climax community. Typically, in the first two years, weeds and annuals are dominant. This is followed by grasses and biennials. In a few years, shrubs and perennials are dominant followed by pine trees, which are eventually replaced by deciduous trees. Secondary succession takes place in less than 100 years.

Energy Flow in the Environment

Using Trophic Levels with an Energy Pyramid

Energy flow through an ecosystem can be tracked through an energy pyramid. An energy pyramid shows how energy is transferred from one trophic level to another. Producers always form the base of an energy pyramid, and the consumers form successive levels above the producers. Producers only store about 1% of the solar energy they receive. Then, each successive level only uses about 10% of the energy of the previous level. That means that primary consumers use about 10% of the energy used by

Copyright © Mometrix Media. You have been licensed one copy of this document for personal use only. Any other reproduction or redistribution is strictly prohibited. All rights reserved.

primary producers, such as grasses and trees. Next, secondary consumers use 10% of primary consumers' 10%, or 1% overall. This continues up for as many trophic levels as exist in a particular ecosystem.

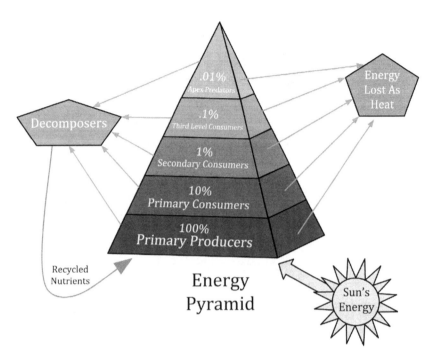

Copyright © Mometrix Media. You have been licensed one copy of this document for personal use only. Any other reproduction or redistribution is strictly prohibited. All rights reserved.

Food Web

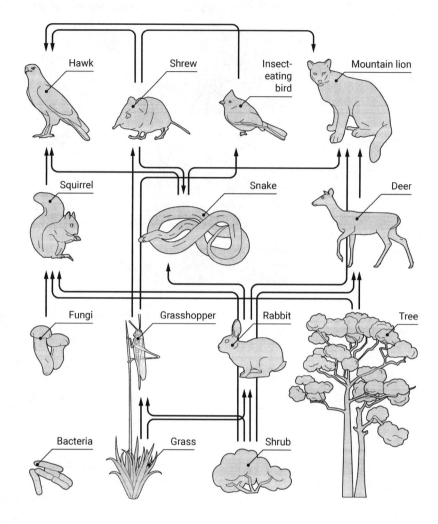

Energy flow through an ecosystem can be illustrated by a food web. Energy moves through the food web in the direction of the arrows. In the food web, producers such as grass, trees, and shrubs use energy from the sun to produce food through photosynthesis. Herbivores or primary consumers such as squirrels, grasshoppers, and rabbits obtain energy by eating the producers. Secondary consumers, which are carnivores such as snakes and shrews, obtain energy by eating the primary consumers. Tertiary consumers, which are carnivores such as hawks and mountain lions, obtain energy by eating the secondary consumers. Note that the hawk and the mountain lion can also be considered quaternary consumers in this food web if a different food chain within the web is followed.

> **Review Video: Food Webs**
> Visit mometrix.com/academy and enter code: 853254

Water Cycle

The water cycle, also referred to as the hydrologic cycle, is a biogeochemical cycle that describes the continuous movement of the Earth's water. Water in the form of precipitation such as rain or snow moves from the atmosphere to the ground. The water is collected in oceans, lakes, rivers, and other bodies of water. Heat from the sun causes water to evaporate from oceans, lakes, rivers, and other bodies of water. As plants transpire, this water also undergoes evaporation. This water vapor collects in

152

Copyright © Mometrix Media. You have been licensed one copy of this document for personal use only. Any other reproduction or redistribution is strictly prohibited. All rights reserved.

the sky and forms clouds. As the water vapor in the clouds cools, the water vapor condenses or sublimes depending on the conditions. Then, water moves back to the ground in the form of precipitation.

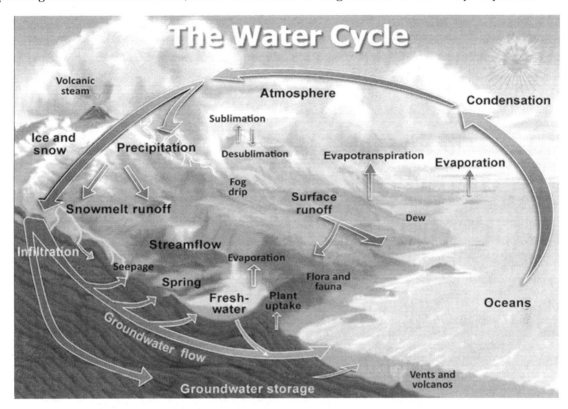

Carbon Cycle

The carbon cycle is a biogeochemical cycle that describes the continuous movement of the Earth's carbon. Carbon is in the atmosphere, the soil, living organisms, fossil fuels, oceans, and freshwater systems. These areas are referred to as carbon reservoirs. Carbon flows between these reservoirs in an exchange called the carbon cycle. In the atmosphere, carbon is in the form of carbon dioxide. Carbon moves from the atmosphere to plants through the process of photosynthesis. Carbon moves from plants to animals through food chains. Carbon moves from living organisms to the soil when these organisms die. Carbon moves from living organisms to the atmosphere through cellular respiration. Carbon moves

Copyright © Mometrix Media. You have been licensed one copy of this document for personal use only. Any other reproduction or redistribution is strictly prohibited. All rights reserved.

from fossil fuels to the atmosphere when fossil fuels are burned. Carbon moves from the atmosphere to the oceans and freshwater systems through absorption.

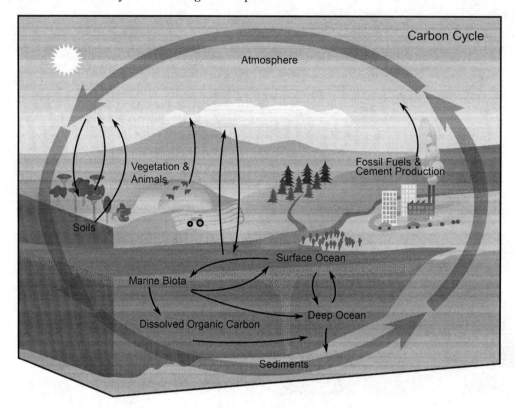

Nitrogen Cycle

The nitrogen cycle is a biogeochemical cycle that describes the continuous movement of the Earth's nitrogen. Approximately 78% of the Earth's atmosphere consists of nitrogen in its elemental form N_2. Nitrogen is essential to the formation of proteins, but most organisms cannot use nitrogen in this form and require the nitrogen to be converted into some form of nitrates. Lightning can cause nitrates to form in the atmosphere, which can be carried to the soil by rain to be used by plants. Legumes have nitrogen-fixing bacteria in their roots, which can convert the N_2 to ammonia (NH_3). Nitrifying bacteria in the soil can also convert ammonia into nitrates. Plants absorb nitrates from the soil, and animals can consume

Copyright © Mometrix Media. You have been licensed one copy of this document for personal use only. Any other reproduction or redistribution is strictly prohibited. All rights reserved.

the plants and other animals for protein. Denitrifying bacteria can convert unused nitrates back to nitrogen to be returned to the atmosphere.

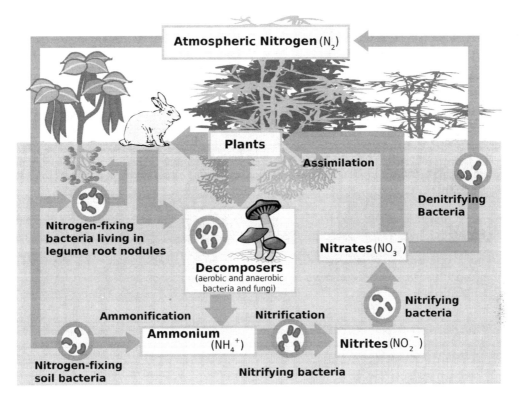

Phosphorus Cycle

The phosphorus cycle is a biogeochemical cycle that describes the continuous movement of the Earth's phosphorus. Phosphorus is found in rocks. When these rocks weather and erode, the phosphorus moves into the soil. The phosphorus found in the soil and rocks is in the form of phosphates or compounds with the PO_4^{3-} ion. When it rains, phosphates can be dissolved into the water. Plants are able to use phosphates from the soil. Plants need phosphorus for growth and development. Phosphorus is also a component of DNA, RNA, ATP, cell membranes, and bones. Plants and algae can absorb phosphate ions from the water and convert them into many organic compounds. Animals can get phosphorus by eating

Copyright © Mometrix Media. You have been licensed one copy of this document for personal use only. Any other reproduction or redistribution is strictly prohibited. All rights reserved.

food or drinking water. When organisms die, the phosphorus is returned to the soil. This is the slowest of all biogeochemical cycles.

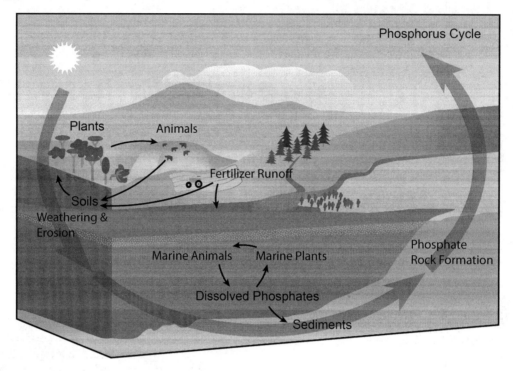

Natural Disturbances That Affect Ecosystems

A natural disturbance is an event caused by nature, not human activity. Natural disturbances can be brought on by weather such as fires from lightning, droughts, storms, wind, and freezing. Other natural disturbances include earthquakes, volcanic eruptions, and diseases. Natural disturbances can disrupt or disturb the ecosystem in many ways such as altering resources or removing individuals from the community. Natural disturbances can cover small regions, or they can affect an entire ecosystem. The effect may be long lasting and take several years to recover, or the effect may be minor and take only a few months to recover.

Effect of Fragmentation of Ecosystems on Biodiversity

Habitats can become fragmented due to natural disturbances such as fire, volcanic activity, and climate change. Some of the original habitat is destroyed during fragmentation, reducing the total area of the habitat. As a result, there may be insufficient food or other resources to support a species. The resulting habitats may also be reproductively isolated from each other, thus limiting genetic variation and biodiversity. Small fluctuations in resources or climate can be catastrophic in small populations. Larger populations may be able to overcome these fluctuations in variation.

Effects of Human Population on Ecological Systems and Biodiversity

Human population has been increasing at a near-exponential rate for the past 50 years. As the human population increases, the demand for resources such as food, water, land, and energy also increases. As the human population increases, the number of species decreases due to habitat destruction, introduced species, and overhunting. The increased greenhouse gases and resulting climate changes have also significantly affected many ecosystems as temperatures rise and habitats are slowly changed or even destroyed. Increasing human population means increasing pollution, which harms habitats. Many

Copyright © Mometrix Media. You have been licensed one copy of this document for personal use only. Any other reproduction or redistribution is strictly prohibited. All rights reserved.

animals have become extinct due to the effects of an exponentially increasing human population. High rates of extinction greatly reduce biodiversity.

Effects of Habitat Destruction by Humans on Ecological Systems and Biodiversity

Many habitats have been altered or destroyed by humans. In fact, habitat destruction brought about by human endeavors has been the most significant cause of species extinctions resulting in the decrease in biodiversity throughout the world. As the human population has increased exponentially, the extinction rate has also increased exponentially. This is largely due to habitat destruction by humans. Humans use many resources in their various enterprises including agriculture, industry, mining, logging, and recreation. Humans have cleared much land for agriculture and urban development. As habitats are destroyed, species are either destroyed or displaced. Often, habitats are fragmented into smaller areas, which only allow for small populations that are under threat by predators, diseases, weather, and limited resources. Especially hard hit are areas near the coastline, estuaries, and coral reefs. Nearly half of all mangrove ecosystems have been destroyed by human activity. Coral reefs have nearly been decimated from pollution such as oil spills and exploitation from the aquarium fish market and coral market.

Effects of Introduced Species on Ecological Systems and Biodiversity

Introduced species are species that are moved into new geographic regions by humans. They are also called invasive or nonnative species. Introduction can be intentional, such as the introduction of livestock, or unintentional, such as the introduction of Dutch elm disease. Introduced species can disrupt their new communities by using limited resources and preying on other members of the community. Introduced species are often free from predators and can reproduce exponentially. This typically causes a decrease in biodiversity. Introduced species are contributors or even responsible for numerous extinctions. For example, zebra mussels, which are native to the Black Sea and the Caspian Sea, were accidentally introduced to the Great Lakes. The zebra mussels greatly reduced the amount of plankton available for the native mussel species, many of which are now endangered.

Impact of Nonpoint Sources of Pollution on the Environment

Nonpoint-source pollution is the leading cause of water pollution in the United States. Nonpoint-source pollution is pollution that does not flow through a pipe, channel, or container. Most nonpoint-source pollution is due to agricultural runoff. Urban runoff from lawns, streets, and parking lots is also treated as nonpoint-source pollution because much of that storm water does not go into a storm drain before entering streams, rivers, lakes, or other bodies of water. Urban runoff contains chemicals such as lawn fertilizers, motor oils, grease, pesticides, soaps, and detergents, each of which is harmful to the environment.

Effects of Remediation on Ecological Systems and Biodiversity

In remediation, or land rehabilitation, environmental damages is reversed or stopped by attempting to restore land to its prior condition. Examples of remediation are reforestation and mine reclamation. Mining reclamation includes the backfilling of open-pit mines and covering ores containing sulfides to prevent rain from mixing with them to produce sulfuric acid. Reforestation is the restocking of forests and wetlands. This can at least partially offset the damaging effects brought about by the deforestation. Reforestation can help reduce global warming due to an increase in the absorption of light by the trees. Restoration can also help to restore the carbon cycle and counter erosion. Reforestation can help maintain or preserve the biodiversity of the region and possibly increase biodiversity if new organisms immigrate into the region.

Copyright © Mometrix Media. You have been licensed one copy of this document for personal use only. Any other reproduction or redistribution is strictly prohibited. All rights reserved.

Pollution Mitigation and the Clean Air Act

Pollution mitigation has greatly reduced pollution and its effects during the past 40 years. The Clean Air Act has reduced pollution by requiring that new industrial sites contain pollution-control technology. These technologies avoid or minimize the negative effects on the environment. For example, new coal-fired power plants are fitted with pollution-control devices that greatly reduce and nearly eliminate sulfur dioxide and nitrogen oxide emissions. This greatly reduces acid rain, improves water quality, and improves the overall health of ecosystems. Reducing acid rain improves soil quality, which in turn improves the health of producers, which consequently improves the health of consumers, essentially strengthening the entire ecosystem. Reduced greenhouse gas emissions have lessened the impact of global warming such as rising sea levels due to melting glaciers and the resulting loss of habitats and biodiversity. Reduced smog and haze improves the intensity of sunlight required for photosynthesis.

Resource Management

Resource management such as waste management and recycling greatly impacts the environment. Waste management is the monitoring, collection, transportation, and recycling of waste products. Well-managed landfills include using clay or another lining material to prevent liquid leachate and layers of soil on top to reduce odors and vermin. Wastes can be incinerated to reduce waste volume. Hazardous biomedical waste can be incinerated. However, incineration does emit pollutants and greenhouse gases. Proper waste management always includes recycling. Recycling is a method to recover resources. Recycled materials can be reprocessed into new products. Metals such as aluminum, copper, and steel are recycled. Plastics, glass, and paper products can be recycled. Organic materials such as plant materials and food scraps can be composted. The current trend is to shift from waste management to resource recovery. Wastes should be minimized and reduced to minimize the need for disposal. Unavoidable nonrecyclable wastes should be converted to energy by combustion if at all possible.

Impact of Global Warming, Rising Sea Levels, and Flooding on Society

Global warming caused largely by greenhouse gas emission will greatly affect society in the next several years. The increase in global temperature leads to more extreme weather events such hurricanes, tornadoes, floods, and droughts. Rising temperatures mean warmer summers. Warmer temperatures may shift tourism and improve agriculture, but global mortality rates may rise due to hotter heat waves. Rising temperatures cause weather patterns to shift, leading to more floods and droughts. Rising temperatures mean a decrease in glaciers, sea ice, ice sheets, and snow cover, which all contribute to rising sea levels. Rising sea levels lead to habitat change or loss, which greatly affects numerous species. Some motile species are already moving north to cooler climates. Earlier snowmelt and runoff may overwhelm water management systems. Diseases such as malaria that are spread by mosquitoes could spread further, possibly even to temperate regions. Rising sea levels mean higher storm surges and related issues.

Endangered Species Act

The Endangered Species Act (ESA) of 1973 has had a positive impact on many species. The law was designed to protect "imperiled species" from extinction due to factors such as loss of habitat, overhunting, and lack of conservation. The ESA also protects the species' ecosystems and removes threats to those ecosystems. If an animal is placed on the endangered or threatened list, it is prohibited to "harass, harm, pursue, hunt, shoot, wound, kill, trap, capture, or collect, or to attempt to engage in any such conduct" with the endangered animal. The populations of many species have increased significantly, including the whooping crane, the gray wolf, the red wolf, and the Hawaiian goose. Some species have even been removed from the endangered species list, including the bald eagle, the peregrine falcon, the gray whale, and the grizzly bear. The ESA has protected numerous species while balancing human economic needs and rights to private property.

Copyright © Mometrix Media. You have been licensed one copy of this document for personal use only. Any other reproduction or redistribution is strictly prohibited. All rights reserved.

National Park System

The purpose of the National Park System is to "conserve the scenery and the natural and historic objects and the wildlife therein and to provide for the enjoyment of the same in such manner and by such means as will leave them unimpaired for the enjoyment of future generations." The National Park System protects complete ecosystems and houses great biodiversity. National parks are an integral part of the survival of many species. National parks provide a home to hundreds of endangered or threatened species. Studies show that preserved habitats near national parks helps many species better survive. This will prevent fragmentation and further habitat loss. Nevertheless, National parks may be threatened by invasion species or pressure for use of land along park boundaries. Also, biodiversity is threatened even within national parks. Although many are vast, they still may not be large enough to support a species population.

Effects of Extraction of Minerals and Oil Drilling

The extraction of mineral and energy resources by mining and drilling has harmful effects on the environment including pollution and alterations to ecosystems. Mining requires large amounts of land, which harms habitats and affects biodiversity. Mining causes water pollution. Rainwater mixes with the heavy metals in mines and produces an acid runoff that harms aquatic life, birds, and mammals. The pollution is especially bad in countries without proper mining regulations. Open-pit mines and mountaintop removal techniques are especially harsh to the environment, and reclamation is often not regulated in developing countries. Mining often requires large-scale deforestation leading to a loss of habitat for many species. Toxic chemicals such as mercury and sulfuric acid are used in the mining process and are released into bodies of water, harming the aquatic life. If these toxic chemicals are leaked, the ground water is polluted. Oil drilling is controversial due to habitat disruption or loss. Oil spills are toxic to wildlife and difficult to clean up. Offshore drilling uses seismic waves to locate oil, which disturbs whales and dolphins and has been tied to hundreds of beached whales.

Sustainable Agriculture

The management of natural resources and the renewability or sustainability of those natural resources greatly impact society. Sustainable agriculture involves growing foods in economical ways that do not harm resources. If left unchecked, farming can deplete the soil of valuable nutrients. Crops grown in these depleted soils are less healthy and more susceptible to disease. Sustainable agriculture uses more effective pest control such as insect-resistant corn, which reduces runoff and water pollution in the surrounding area. Sustainable forestry involves replenishing trees as trees are being harvested, which maintains the environment.

Renewable and Nonrenewable Energy Resources

Energy sources such as wind, solar power, and biomass energy are all renewable. Wind power is clean with no pollution and no greenhouse gas emissions. Disadvantages of wind power include the use of land for wind farms, threats to birds, and the expense to build. Solar power has no greenhouse gas emissions, but some toxic metal wastes result in the production of photovoltaic cells, and solar power requires large areas of land. Biomass energy is sustainable, but its combustion produces greenhouse emissions. Farming biomass requires large areas of land. Fossil fuels, which are nonrenewable, cause substantially more air pollution and greenhouse gas emissions, contributing to habitat loss and global warming.

Copyright © Mometrix Media. You have been licensed one copy of this document for personal use only. Any other reproduction or redistribution is strictly prohibited. All rights reserved.

ILTS Practice Test

Molecular and Cellular Biology

1. The hydrogen bonds in a water molecule make water a good
   a. Solvent for lipids
   b. Participant in replacement reactions
   c. Surface for small particles and living organisms to move across
   d. Solvent for polysaccharides such as cellulose
   e. Example of an acid

2. The breakdown of a disaccharide releases energy which is stored as ATP. This is an example of a(n)
   a. Combination reaction
   b. Replacement reaction
   c. Endothermic reaction
   d. Exothermic reaction
   e. Thermodynamic reaction

3. Which of the following metabolic compounds is composed of only carbon, oxygen, and hydrogen?
   a. Phospholipids
   b. Glycogen
   c. Peptides
   d. RNA
   e. Vitamins

4. When an animal takes in more energy that it uses over an extended time, the extra chemical energy is stored as:
   a. Fat
   b. Starch
   c. Protein
   d. Enzymes
   e. Cholesterol

5. Which of the following molecules is thought to have acted as the first enzyme in early life on earth?
   a. Protein
   b. RNA
   c. DNA
   d. Triglycerides
   e. Phospholipids

6. Which of the following organelles is/are formed when the plasma membrane surrounds a particle outside of the cell?
   a. Golgi bodies
   b. Rough endoplasmic reticulum
   c. Lysosomes
   d. Secretory vesicles
   e. Endocytic vesicles

Copyright © Mometrix Media. You have been licensed one copy of this document for personal use only. Any other reproduction or redistribution is strictly prohibited. All rights reserved.

7. Which of the following plant organelles contain(s) pigment that give leaves their color?

    a. Centrioles
    b. Cell walls
    c. Chloroplasts
    d. Central vacuole
    e. Golgi apparatus

8. All but which of the following processes are ways of moving solutes across a plasma membrane?

    a. Osmosis
    b. Passive transport
    c. Active transport
    d. Facilitated diffusion
    e. Endocytosis

9. Prokaryotic and eukaryotic cells are similar in having which of the following?

    a. Membrane-bound organelles
    b. Protein-studded DNA
    c. Presence of a nucleus
    d. Integral membrane proteins in the plasma membrane
    e. Flagella composed of microtubules

10. Which of the following cell types has a peptidoglycan cell wall?

    a. Algae
    b. Bacteria
    c. Fungi
    d. Land plants
    e. Protists

11. Enzymes catalyze biochemical reactions by

    a. Lowering the potential energy of the products
    b. Separating inhibitors from products
    c. Forming a complex with the products
    d. Lowering the activation energy of the reaction
    e. Providing energy to the reaction

12. Which of the following is an example of a cofactor?

    a. Zinc
    b. Actin
    c. Cholesterol
    d. GTP
    e. Chlorophyll

13 Cyanide is a poison that binds to the active site of the enzyme cytochrome c and prevents its activity. Cyanide is a(n)

    a. Prosthetic group
    b. Cofactor
    c. Coenzyme
    d. Inhibitor
    e. Reverse regulator

Copyright © Mometrix Media. You have been licensed one copy of this document for personal use only. Any other reproduction or redistribution is strictly prohibited. All rights reserved.

14. The graph below shows the potential energy of molecules during the process of a chemical reaction. All of the following may be true EXCEPT

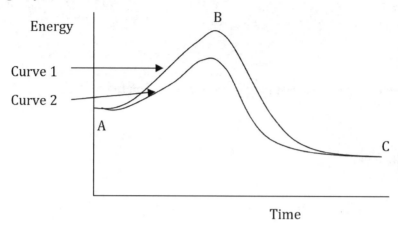

a. This is an endergonic reaction
b. The activation energy in curve 2 is less than the activation energy in curve 1
c. The energy of the products is less than the energy of the substrate
d. Curve 2 shows the reaction in the presence of an enzyme
e. The reaction required ATP

15. Which of the following is not a characteristic of enzymes?

a. They change shape when they bind their substrates
b. They can catalyze reactions in both forward and reverse directions
c. Their activity is sensitive to changes in temperature
d. They are always active on more than one kind of substrate
e. They may have more than one binding site

16. In a strenuously exercising muscle, NADH begins to accumulate in high concentration. Which of the following metabolic process will be activated to reduce the concentration of NADH?

a. Glycolysis
b. The Krebs cycle
c. Lactic acid fermentation
d. Oxidative phosphorylation
e. Acetyl CoA synthesis

17. Which of the following statements regarding chemiosmosis in mitochondria is not correct?

a. ATP synthase is powered by protons flowing through membrane channels
b. Energy from ATP is used to transport protons to the intermembrane space
c. Energy from the electron transport chain is used to transport protons to the intermembrane space
d. An electrical gradient and a pH gradient both exist across the inner membrane
e. The waste product of chemiosmosis is water

18. In photosynthesis, high-energy electrons move through electron transport chains to produce ATP and NADPH. Which of the following provides the energy to create high energy electrons?

a. NADH
b. NADP+
c. O2
d. Water
e. Light

Copyright © Mometrix Media. You have been licensed one copy of this document for personal use only. Any other reproduction or redistribution is strictly prohibited. All rights reserved.

19. Which of the following kinds of plants is most likely to perform CAM photosynthesis?

    a. Mosses
    b. Grasses
    c. Deciduous trees
    d. Cacti
    e. Legumes

20. The combination of DNA with histones is called

    a. A centromere
    b. Chromatin
    c. A chromatid
    d. Nucleoli
    e. A plasmid

21. How many chromosomes does a human cell have after meiosis I?

    a. 92
    b. 46
    c. 23
    d. 22
    e. 12

22. In plants and animals, genetic variation is introduced during

    a. Crossing over in mitosis
    b. Chromosome segregation in mitosis
    c. Cytokinesis of meiosis
    d. Anaphase I of meiosis
    e. Anaphase II of meiosis

23. DNA replication occurs during which of the following phases?

    a. Prophase I
    b. Prophase II
    c. Interphase I
    d. Interphase II
    e. Telophase I

24. The synaptonemal complex is present in which of the following phases of the cell cycle?

    a. Metaphase of mitosis
    b. Prophase of meiosis I
    c. Telophase of meiosis I
    d. Metaphase of meiosis II
    e. Telophase of meiosis II

25. A length of DNA coding for a particular protein is called a(n)

    a. Allele
    b. Genome
    c. Gene
    d. Transcript
    e. Codon

Copyright © Mometrix Media. You have been licensed one copy of this document for personal use only. Any other reproduction or redistribution is strictly prohibited. All rights reserved.

26. In DNA replication, which of the following enzymes is required for separating the DNA molecule into two strands?

    a. DNA polymerase
    b. Single strand binding protein
    c. DNA gyrase
    d. Helicase
    e. Primase

27. Which of the following chemical moieties forms the backbone of DNA?

    a. Nitrogenous bases
    b. Glycerol
    c. Amino groups
    d. Pentose and phosphate
    e. Glucose and phosphate

28. Which of the following is required for the activity of DNA polymerase?

    a. Okazaki fragments
    b. RNA primer
    c. Single-strand binding protein
    d. Leading strand
    e. Replication fork

29. Which of the following is the substrate for DNA ligase?

    a. Okazaki fragments
    b. RNA primer
    c. Single-strand binding protein
    d. Leading strand
    e. Replication fork

30. Which of the following is true of the enzyme telomerase?

    a. It is active on the leading strand during DNA synthesis
    b. It requires a chromosomal DNA template
    c. It acts in the $3' \rightarrow 5'$ direction
    d. It adds a repetitive DNA sequence to the end of chromosomes
    e. It takes the place of primase at the ends of chromosomes

31. Which enzyme in DNA replication is a potential source of new mutations?

    a. DNA ligase
    b. Primase
    c. DNA gyrase
    d. DNA polymerase
    e. Topoisomerase

32. Which of the following mutations is most likely to have a dramatic effect on the sequence of a protein?

    a. A point mutation
    b. A missense mutation
    c. A deletion
    d. A silent mutation
    e. A proofreading mutation

Copyright © Mometrix Media. You have been licensed one copy of this document for personal use only. Any other reproduction or redistribution is strictly prohibited. All rights reserved.

33. Which of the following could be an end product of transcription?

    a. rRNA
    b. DNA
    c. Protein
    d. snRNP
    e. Amino acids

34. The *lac* operon controls

    a. Conjugation between bacteria
    b. Chromatin organization
    c. Gene transcription
    d. Excision repair
    e. Termination of translation

35. All of the following are examples ways of controlling eukaryotic gene expression EXCEPT

    a. Regulatory proteins
    b. Nucleosome packing
    c. Methylation of DNA
    d. RNA interference
    e. Operons

36. Transfer of DNA between bacteria using a narrow tube called a pilus is called

    a. Transformation
    b. Transduction
    c. Operation
    d. Conjugation
    e. Conformation

37. A virus that has incorporated into the DNA of its host

    a. Lysogenic cycle
    b. Lytic cycle
    c. Retrovirus
    d. Provirus
    e. Bacteriophage

38. A virus in this stage is actively replicating DNA

    a. Lysogenic cycle
    b. Lytic cycle
    c. Retrovirus
    d. Provirus
    e. Bacteriophage

39. A bacterial mini-chromosome used in recombinant DNA technology is called a

    a. Centromere
    b. Telomere
    c. Plasmid
    d. Transposon
    e. cDNA

Copyright © Mometrix Media. You have been licensed one copy of this document for personal use only. Any other reproduction or redistribution is strictly prohibited. All rights reserved.

Organismal Biology

40. Which of the following parts of an angiosperm give rise to the fruit?
    a. Pedicel
    b. Filament
    c. Sepal
    d. Ovary
    e. Meristem

41. Which of the following structures is NOT present in gymnosperms?
    a. Leaves
    b. Pollen
    c. Flowers
    d. Stomata
    e. Roots

42. Which of the following plant structures allows for gas exchange?
    a. Xylem
    b. Phloem
    c. Cuticle
    d. Meristem
    e. Stomata

43. Which type of plant has leaves with parallel veins?
    a. Monocots
    b. Dicots
    c. Angiosperms
    d. Gymnosperms
    e. Nonvascular plants

44. Which type of plant does not produce fruits
    a. Monocots
    b. Dicots
    c. Angiosperms
    d. Gymnosperms
    e. Nonvascular plants

45. Which type of plant produces seeds that are housed inside a fruit
    a. Monocots
    b. Dicots
    c. Angiosperms
    d. Gymnosperms
    e. Nonvascular plants

Copyright © Mometrix Media. You have been licensed one copy of this document for personal use only. Any other reproduction or redistribution is strictly prohibited. All rights reserved.

Questions 46 and 47 pertain to the following diagram representing a cross section of a tree trunk.

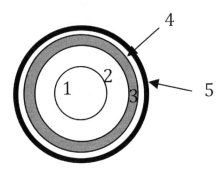

46. Which structure contains tissue that is dead at maturity?

    a. 1
    b. 2
    c. 3
    d. 4
    e. 5

47. Which structure transports carbohydrates to the roots?

    a. 1
    b. 2
    c. 3
    d. 4
    e. 5

48. In ferns, the joining of egg and sperm produces a zygote, which will grow into the

    a. Gametophyte
    b. Sporophyte
    c. Spore
    d. Sporangium
    e. Seedling

49. Which of the following is an example of the alternation of generations life cycle?

    a. Asexual reproduction of strawberries by runners
    b. Annual plants that live through a single growing season
    c. Ferns that have a large diploid and a diminutive haploid stage
    d. Insects that have distinct larval and adult stages
    e. Reptiles that have long periods of dormancy and metabolic inactivity

Copyright © Mometrix Media. You have been licensed one copy of this document for personal use only. Any other reproduction or redistribution is strictly prohibited. All rights reserved.

Questions 50 and 51 pertain to the following diagram of a complete, perfect flower.

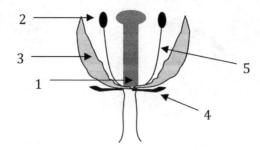

50. The structure in which microspores are produced.
    a. 1
    b. 2
    c. 3
    d. 4
    e. 5

51. The structures composed solely of diploid cells
    a. 1, 2, and 3
    b. 2, 3, and 4
    c. 3, 4, and 5
    d. 1, 4, and 5
    e. 1, 2, and 4

52. Auxins are plant hormones that are involved in all but which of the following processes?
    a. Fruit ripening
    b. Gravitropism
    c. Growth
    d. Phototropism
    e. Seed germination

53. Which of the following plant hormones is most likely to delay aging when sprayed on cut flowers and fruit?
    a. Ethylene
    b. Gibberellins
    c. Cytokinins
    d. Abscisic acid
    e. Jasmonic acid

54. Which of the following would most likely be disruptive to the flowering time of a day-neutral plant?
    a. Daylight interrupted by a brief dark period
    b. Daylight interrupted by a long dark period
    c. High daytime temperatures
    d. Night interrupted by a brief exposure to red light
    e. Night interrupted by a long exposure to red light

Copyright © Mometrix Media. You have been licensed one copy of this document for personal use only. Any other reproduction or redistribution is strictly prohibited. All rights reserved.

55. Animals exchange gases with the environment in all of the following ways EXCEPT

    a. Direct exchange through the skin
    b. Exchange through gills
    c. Stomata
    d. Tracheae
    e. Lungs

56. Which of the following blood components is involved in blood clotting?

    a. Red blood cells
    b. Platelets
    c. White blood cells
    d. Leukocytes
    e. Plasma

57. Which section of the digestive system is responsible for water reabsorption?

    a. The large intestine
    b. The duodenum
    c. The small intestine
    d. The gallbladder
    e. The stomach

58. When Ca^{2+} channels open in a presynaptic cell (doesn't the cell also depolarize?)

    a. The cell depolarizes
    b. The cell hyperpolarizes
    c. An action potential is propagated
    d. Synaptic vesicles release neurotransmitter
    e. The nerve signal is propagated by salutatory conduction

59. Which of the following processes is an example of positive feedback?

    a. High $CO2$ blood levels stimulate respiration which decreases blood $CO2$ levels
    b. High blood glucose levels stimulate insulin release, which makes muscle and liver cells take in glucose
    c. Increased nursing stimulates increased milk production in mammary glands
    d. Low blood oxygen levels stimulate erythropoietin production which increases red blood cell production by bone marrow
    e. Low blood calcium levels stimulate parathyroid hormone release from the parathyroid gland. Parathyroid hormone stimulates calcium release from bones.

60. Which of the following would be the most likely means of thermoregulation for a mammal in a cold environment?

    a. Adjusting body surface area
    b. Sweating
    c. Countercurrent exchange
    d. Muscle contractions
    e. Increased blood flow to extremities

61. Which hormone is *not* secreted by a gland in the brain?

    a. Human chorionic gonadotropin (HCG)
    b. Gonadotropin releasing hormone (GnRH)
    c. Luteinizing hormone (LH)
    d. Follicle stimulating hormone (FSH)
    e. None of these

Copyright © Mometrix Media. You have been licensed one copy of this document for personal use only. Any other reproduction or redistribution is strictly prohibited. All rights reserved.

62. Which hormone is secreted by the placenta throughout pregnancy?

    a. Human chorionic gonadotropin (HCG)
    b. Gonadotropin releasing hormone (GnRH)
    c. Luteinizing hormone (LH)
    d. Follicle stimulating hormone (FSH)
    e. None of these

63. Polar bodies are a by-product of

    a. Meiosis I
    b. Meiosis II
    c. Both meiosis I and II
    d. Zygote formation
    e. Mitosis of the morula

64. Which of the following hormones triggers ovulation in females?

    a. Estrogen
    b. Progesterone
    c. Serotonin
    d. Luteinizing hormone
    e. Testosterone

65. Spermatogenesis occurs in the

    a. Prostate gland
    b. Vas deferens
    c. Seminal vesicles
    d. Penis
    e. Seminiferous tubules

66. In which of the following stages of embryo development are the three primary germ layers first present?

    a. Zygote
    b. Gastrula
    c. Morula
    c. Blastula
    e. Coelomate

67. Which of the following extraembryonic membranes is an important source of nutrition in many non-human animal species but NOT in humans?

    a. Amnion
    b. Allantois
    c. Yolk sac
    d. Chorion
    e. Placenta

68. Which of the following is not a mechanism that contributes to cell differentiation and development in embryos?

    a. Asymmetrical cell division
    b. Asymmetrical cytoplasm distribution
    c. Organizer cells
    d. Location of cells on the lineage map
    e. Homeotic genes

Copyright © Mometrix Media. You have been licensed one copy of this document for personal use only. Any other reproduction or redistribution is strictly prohibited. All rights reserved.

69. Which of the following is true of the gastrula?

    a. It is a solid ball of cells
    b. It has three germ layers
    c. It is an extraembryonic membrane
    d. It gives rise to the blastula
    e. It derives from the zona pellucida

70. In birds, gastrulation occurs along the

    a. Dorsal lip of the embryo
    b. Embryonic disc
    c. Primitive streak
    d. Circular blastopore
    e. Inner cell mass

71. In snapdragons, the red (R) allele is incompletely dominant to the white (r) allele. If you saw a pink snapdragon, you would know

    a. Its phenotypes for both parents
    b. Its genotypes for both parents
    c. Its genotype for one parent
    d. Its genotype
    e. Its phenotype but not its genotype

72. In peas, purple flower color (P) is dominant to white (p) and tall stature (T) is dominant to dwarf (t). If the genes are unlinked, how many tall plants will be purple in the progeny of a $PpTt$ x $PpTT$ cross?

    a. 0
    b. ¼
    c. ½
    d. ¾
    e. 1

73. Which of the following does not obey the law of independent assortment?

    a. Two genes on opposite ends of a chromosome
    b. Flower color and height in snapdragons
    c. Two genes on separate chromosomes
    d. Seed color and flower color in peas
    e. Two genes next to each other on a chromosome

74. In a dihybrid cross between bean plants with red (R) wrinkled (w) seeds and white (r) smooth (W) seeds, the F1 progeny is all red and smooth. If the F1 plants are selfed, what proportion of the F2 will also be red and smooth if the genes are linked?

    a. All of them
    b. ¼
    c. 1/2
    d. 9/16
    e. None of them

Copyright © Mometrix Media. You have been licensed one copy of this document for personal use only. Any other reproduction or redistribution is strictly prohibited. All rights reserved.

75. Red-green color blindness is an X-linked trait. What is the probability that a mother that is heterozygous for this trait and a father with this trait will have affected children?

    a. 0
    b. ¼
    c. ½
    d. ¾
    e. 1

76. An individual with an AB blood type needs a blood transfusion. Which of the following types could NOT be a donor?

    a. O
    b. AB
    c. A
    d. B
    e. All of the above types can be donors

77. In humans, more than one gene contributes to the trait of hair color. This is an example of

    a. Pleiotropy
    b. Polygenic inheritance
    c. Codominance
    d. Linkage
    e. Epistasis

78. A child is born with type A blood and his mother has type A. Which of the following is NOT a possible combination of genotypes for the mother and father?

    a. IAIB and ii
    b. IAi and ii
    c. IA i and IB i
    d. IAi and IBIB
    e. IAIB and IBi

Copyright © Mometrix Media. You have been licensed one copy of this document for personal use only. Any other reproduction or redistribution is strictly prohibited. All rights reserved.

Population Biology

79. On a standard biomass pyramid, level 3 corresponds to which trophic level?

a. Producers
b. Decomposers
c. Primary consumers
d. Primary carnivores
e. Secondary carnivores

80. In the food chain below, vultures represent

grass → cow → wolf → vulture

a. Scavengers
b. Detritivores
c. Primary carnivores
d. Herbivores
e. Secondary consumers

81. Which of the following is the major way in which carbon is released into the environment?

a. Transpiration
b. Respiration
c. Fixation
d. Sedimentation
e. Absorption

82. What is the largest reservoir of nitrogen on the planet?

a. The ocean
b. Plants
c. Soil
d. The atmosphere
e. Sediments, including fossil fuels

83. The diagram below represents the three types of survivorship curves, describing how mortality varies as species age. Which of the following species is most likely to exhibit Type I survivorship?

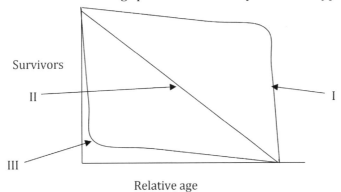

a. Frogs
b. Oysters
c. Salmon
d. Dolphins
e. Shrimp

Copyright © Mometrix Media. You have been licensed one copy of this document for personal use only. Any other reproduction or redistribution is strictly prohibited. All rights reserved.

84. A population of 1000 individuals has 110 births and 10 deaths in a year. Its growth rate (r) is equal to

    a. 0.01 per year
    b. 0.1 per year
    c. 0.09 per year
    d. 0.11 per year
    e. 0.009 per year

85. During primary succession, which species would most likely be a pioneer species?

    a. Lichens
    b. Fir trees
    c. Mosquitoes
    d. Dragonflies
    e. Mushrooms

86. Which of the following habitats would provide an opportunity for secondary succession?

    a. A retreating glacier
    b. Burned cropland
    c. A newly formed volcanic island
    d. A 500 year old forest
    e. A sand dune

87. Which biome is most likely to support the growth of epiphytes?

    a. Deserts
    b. Tropical rain forests
    c. Temperate deciduous forests
    d. Taigas
    e. Savannas

88. Which of the following is NOT a natural dispersal process that would lead to species colonization on an island?

    a. Mussels carried into a lake on the hull of a ship
    b. Drought connecting an island to other land
    c. Floating seeds
    d. Animals swimming long distances
    e. Birds adapted to flying long distances

89. When a population reaches its carrying capacity

    a. Other populations will be forced out of the habitat
    b. Density-dependent factors no longer play a role
    c. Density-independent factors no longer play a role
    d. The population growth rate approaches zero
    e. The population size begins to decrease

90. Which of the following is an example of a density-dependent limiting factor?

    a. Air pollution by a factory
    b. The toxic effect of waste products
    c. Nearby volcanic eruptions
    d. Frosts
    e. Fires

Copyright © Mometrix Media. You have been licensed one copy of this document for personal use only. Any other reproduction or redistribution is strictly prohibited. All rights reserved.

91. Two species of finches are able to utilize the same food supply, but their beaks are different. They are able to coexist on an island because of
   a. Niche overlap
   b. Character displacement
   c. Resource partitioning
   d. Competitive exclusion
   e. Realized niches

92. Lichens consist of fungi and algae. The algae supply sugars through performing photosynthesis while the fungi provide minerals and a place to attach. This is an example of
   a. Mutualism
   b. Commensalism
   c. Parasitism
   d. Coevolution
   e. Resource partitioning

93. Which of the following of Lamarck's evolutionary ideas turned out to be true?
   a. Natural selection
   b. Organisms naturally transform into increasingly complex organisms
   c. Inheritance of acquired characters
   d. Body parts develop with increased usage and weaken with disuse
   e. Genes are the basic units of inheritance

94. The weight of adult wolves is within a fairly narrow range, even if they are well-fed in zoos. This is an example of
   a. Stabilizing selection
   b. Directional selection
   c. Disruptive selection
   d. Sexual selection
   e. Artificial selection

95. Which of the following is a trait that results from disruptive selection?
   a. Insecticide resistance
   b. Male peacocks have colorful plumage while females do not
   c. Within the same species, some birds have large bills, while others have small bills.
   d. Human height
   e. Different varieties of wheat

96. Which of the following conditions would promote evolutionary change?
   a. Neutral selection
   b. Random mating
   c. A large population
   d. An isolated population
   e. Gene flow

97. Which of the following would create the greatest amount of genetic variation for a diploid species in a single generation?
   a. Crossing over
   b. Mutation
   c. Hybridization
   d. Independent assortment of homologs
   e. Random joining of gametes

175

Copyright © Mometrix Media. You have been licensed one copy of this document for personal use only. Any other reproduction or redistribution is strictly prohibited. All rights reserved.

98. A population of pea plants has 25% dwarf plants and 75% tall plants. The tall allele, T is dominant to the dwarf allele, t. What is the frequency of the T allele?

a. 0.75
b. 0.67
c. 0.5
d. 0.25
e. 0.16

99. Darwin's idea that evolution occurs by the gradual accumulation of small changes can be summarized as

a. Punctuated equilibrium
b. Phyletic gradualism
c. Convergent evolution
d. Adaptive radiation
e. Sympatric speciation

100. Which of the following processes of speciation would most likely occur if a species of bird were introduced into a group of islands that were previously uninhabited by animals?

a. Allopatric speciation
b. Adaptive radiation
c. Sympatric speciation
d. Artificial speciation
e. Hybridizing speciation

101. Hummingbirds drink nectar from *Ipomopsis* flowers. *Ipomopsis* are trumpet-shaped, and hummingbirds have long narrow beaks to access the nectar. These adaptations could best be described as

a. Divergent evolution
b. Convergent evolution
c. Parallel evolution
d. Coevolution
e. Macroevolution

102. All of the following are homologous structures EXCEPT

a. Bird feathers
b. Elephant eyelashes
c. Human fingernails
d. Dog fur
e. Insect exoskeleton

103. Human predation has cause the population of cheetahs to decline dramatically. Changes in allele frequencies in the remaining population of cheetahs would most likely be due to

a. Mutation
b. The bottleneck effect
c. The founder effect
d. Gene flow
e. Natural selection

Copyright © Mometrix Media. You have been licensed one copy of this document for personal use only. Any other reproduction or redistribution is strictly prohibited. All rights reserved.

104. The first living cells on earth were most likely

   a. Heterotrophs
   b. Autotrophs
   c. Aerobic
   d. Eukaryotes
   e. Photosynthetic

105. Evidence that humans share a common ancestor with other primates includes all of the following EXCEPT

   a. DNA sequence
   b. Fossil evidence of intermediate species
   c. Analogous structures
   d. Homologous structures
   e. Radiometric dating of fossils

For questions 106 – 108, match the sentence(s) with the choice below that most closely matches it. Each lettered choice may be used more than once or not at all.

   a. Associative learning
   b. Imprinting
   c. Habituation
   d. Chemical communication
   e. Territoriality

106. Sea anemones pull food into their mouths by withdrawing their tentacles. If the tentacles are stimulated with a non-food item, they will ignore the stimulus after a few futile attempts to capture the food.

107. Queen bees secrete pheromones that are eaten by workers and prevent the workers from being able to reproduce.

108. Salmon hatch in freshwater streams and then migrate to the ocean to mature. When they are mature, they swim upstream to their birthplace to spawn.

109. The species *Homo sapiens* first appeared in the fossil record approximately

   a. 10 million years ago
   b. 1 million years ago
   c. 100,000 years ago
   d. 10,000 years ago
   e. 6,000 years ago

110. Which of the following demographic changes would lead to a population with an older age composition?

   a. Increased birth rate
   b. Environmental pollution
   c. Increased availability of food
   d. Medical advancements that increase life expectancy
   e. Introduction of contraceptives

Copyright © Mometrix Media. You have been licensed one copy of this document for personal use only. Any other reproduction or redistribution is strictly prohibited. All rights reserved.

111. Which of the following factors has the greatest impact on birth rate in humans?

    a. The carrying capacity of the earth
    b. Age at reproductive maturity
    c. Reproductive lifetime
    d. Survivorship of offspring to reproductive maturity
    e. Socioeconomic factors

112. Which of the following organisms would be most likely to have mercury in their bodies?

    a. Mosquitoes
    b. Carnivorous insects
    c. Frogs
    d. Filter-feeding fish
    e. Fish-eating birds

113. Clear-cutting of rain forests leads to all of the following consequences EXCEPT

    a. Climate change
    b. Erosion
    c. Reduction in species diversity
    d. Air pollution
    e. Desertification

114. Burning fossil fuels releases sulfur dioxide and nitrogen dioxide. These pollutants lead to which environmental problem?

    a. Denitrification
    b. Acid rain
    c. Global climate change
    d. Ozone depletion
    e. Eutrophication

115. Genetic engineering

    a. Is a form of human reproduction
    b. Involves introducing new proteins to a cell
    c. Involves transient expression of genes
    d. Can have no environmental affects
    e. Requires using restriction enzymes to cut DNA

Copyright © Mometrix Media. You have been licensed one copy of this document for personal use only. Any other reproduction or redistribution is strictly prohibited. All rights reserved.

Answer Key and Explanations

Molecular and Cellular Biology

1. C: The hydrogen bonds between water molecules cause water molecules to attract each other (negative pole to positive pole). and "stick" together. This gives water a high surface tension, which allows small living organisms, such as water striders, to move across its surface. Since water is a polar molecule, it readily dissolves other polar and ionic molecules such as carbohydrates and amino acids. Polarity alone is not sufficient to make something soluble in water, however; for example, cellulose is polar but its molecular weight is so large that it is not soluble in water.

2. D: An exothermic reaction releases energy, whereas an endothermic reaction requires energy. The breakdown of a chemical compound is an example of a decomposition reaction (AB → A + B). A combination reaction (A + B →AB) is the reverse of a decomposition reaction, and a replacement (displacement) reaction is one where compound breaks apart and forms a new compound plus a free reactant (AB + C →AC + B or AB + CD → AD + CB).

3. B: Glycogen is a polysaccharide, a molecule composed of many bonded glucose molecules. Glucose is a carbohydrate, and all carbohydrates are composed of only carbon, oxygen, and hydrogen. Most other metabolic compounds contain other atoms, particularly nitrogen, phosphorous, and sulfur.

4. A: Long term energy storage in animals takes the form of fat. Animals also store energy as glycogen, and plants store energy as starch, but these substances are for shorter-term use. Fats are a good storage form for chemical energy because fatty acids bond to glycerol in a condensation reaction to form fats (triglycerides). This reaction, which releases water, allows for the compacting of high-energy fatty acids in a concentrated form.

5. B: Some RNA molecules in extant organisms have enzymatic activity; for example, the formation of peptide bonds on ribosomes is catalyzed by an RNA molecule. This and other information have led scientists to believe that the most likely molecules to first demonstrate enzymatic activity were RNA molecules.

6. E: Endocytosis is a process by which cells absorb larger molecules or even tiny organisms, such as bacteria, than would be able to pass through the plasma membrane. Endocytic vesicles containing molecules from the extracellular environment often undergo further processing once they enter the cell.

7. C: Chloroplasts contain the light-absorbing compound chlorophyll, which is essential in photosynthesis. This gives leaves their green color. Chloroplasts also contain yellow and red carotenoid pigments, which give leaves red and yellow colors in the fall as chloroplasts lose their chlorophyll.

8. A: Osmosis is the movement of water molecules (not solutes) across a semi-permeable membrane. Water moves from a region of higher concentration to a region of lower concentration. Osmosis occurs when the concentrations of a solute differ on either side of a semi-permeable membrane. For example, a cell (containing a higher concentration of water) in a salty solution (containing a lower concentration of water) will lose water as water leaves the cell. This continues until the solution outside the cell has the same salt concentration as the cytoplasm.

9. D: Both prokaryotes and eukaryotes interact with the extracellular environment and use membrane-bound or membrane-associated proteins to achieve this. They both use diffusion and active transport to move materials in and out of their cells. Prokaryotes have very few proteins associated with their DNA, whereas eukaryotes' DNA is richly studded with proteins. Both types of living things can have flagella, although with different structural characteristics in the two groups. The most important differences

Copyright © Mometrix Media. You have been licensed one copy of this document for personal use only. Any other reproduction or redistribution is strictly prohibited. All rights reserved.

between prokaryotes and eukaryotes are the lack of a nucleus and membrane-bound organelles in prokaryotes.

10. B: Bacteria and cyanobacteria have cell walls constructed from peptidoglycans – a polysaccharide and protein molecule. Other types of organisms with cell walls, for instance, plants and fungi, have cell walls composed of different polysaccharides. Plant cell walls are composed of cellulose, and fungal cell walls are composed of chitin.

11. D: Enzymes act as catalysts for biochemical reactions. A catalyst is not consumed in a reaction, but, rather, lowers the activation energy for that reaction. The potential energy of the substrate and the product remain the same, but the activation energy—the energy needed to make the reaction progress—can be lowered with the help of an enzyme.

12. A: A cofactor is an inorganic substance that is required for an enzymatic reaction to occur. Cofactors bind to the active site of the enzyme and enable the substrate to fit properly. Many cofactors are metal ions, such as zinc, iron, and copper.

13. D: Enzyme inhibitors attach to an enzyme and block substrates from entering the active site, thereby preventing enzyme activity. As stated in the question, cyanide is a poison that irreversibly binds to an enzyme and blocks its active site, thus fitting the definition of an enzyme inhibitor.

14. A: Because the energy of the products is less than the energy of the substrate, the reaction releases energy and is an exergonic reaction.

15. D: Enzymes are substrate-specific. Most enzymes catalyze only one biochemical reaction. Their active sites are specific for a certain type of substrate and do not bind to other substrates and catalyze other reactions.

16. C: Lactic acid fermentation converts pyruvate into lactate using high-energy electrons from NADH. This process allows ATP production to continue in anaerobic conditions by providing NAD^+ so that ATP can be made in glycolysis.

17. B: Proteins in the inner membrane of the mitochondrion accept high-energy electrons from NAD and $FADH_2$, and in turn transport protons from the matrix to the intermembrane space. The high proton concentration in the intermembrane space creates a gradient which is harnessed by ATP synthase to produce ATP.

18. E: Electrons trapped by the chlorophyll P680 molecule in photosystem II are energized by light. They are then transferred to electron acceptors in an electron transport chain.

19. D: CAM photosynthesis occurs in plants that grow where water loss must be minimized, such as cacti. These plants open their stomata and fix CO_2 at night. During the day, stomata are closed, reducing water loss. Thus, photosynthesis can proceed without water loss.

20. B: DNA wrapped around histone proteins is called chromatin. In a eukaryotic cell, DNA is always associated with protein; it is not "naked" as with prokaryotic cells.

21. C: The diploid chromosome number for humans is 46. After DNA duplication but before the first cell division of meiosis, there are 92 chromatids (46 chromosomes). After meiosis I is completed, the chromosome number is halved and equals 23. Each daughter cell is haploid, but the chromosomes are still paired (sister chromatids). During meiosis II, the two sister chromatids of each chromosome separate, resulting in 23 haploid chromosomes per germ cell.

Copyright © Mometrix Media. You have been licensed one copy of this document for personal use only. Any other reproduction or redistribution is strictly prohibited. All rights reserved.

22. D: In anaphase I, homologous chromosome pairs segregate randomly into daughter cells. This means that each daughter cell contains a unique combination of chromosomes that is different from the mother cell and different from its cognate daughter cell.

23. C: Although there are two cell divisions in meiosis, DNA replication occurs only once. It occurs in interphase I, before M phase begins.

24. B: The synaptonemal complex is the point of contact between homologous chromatids. It is formed when nonsister chromatids exchange genetic material through crossing over. Once prophase of meiosis I has completed, crossovers have resolved and the synaptonemal complex no longer exists. Rather, sister chromatids are held together at their centromeres prior to separation in anaphase II.

25. C: Genes code for proteins, and genes are discrete lengths of DNA on chromosomes. An allele is a variant of a gene (different DNA sequence). In diploid organisms, there may be two versions of each gene.

26. D: The enzyme helicase unwinds DNA. It depends on several other proteins to make the unwinding run smoothly, however. Single-strand binding protein holds the single stranded DNA in place, and topoisomerase helps relieve tension at the replication fork.

27. D: DNA is composed of nucleotides joined together in long chains. Nucleotides are composed of a pentose sugar, a phosphate group, and a nitrogenous base. The bases form the "rungs" of the ladder at the core of the DNA helix and the pentose-phosphates are on its outside, or backbone.

28. B: DNA replication begins with a short segment of RNA (not DNA). DNA polymerase cannot begin adding nucleotides without an existing piece of DNA (a primer).

29. A: DNA synthesis on the lagging strand forms short segments called Okazaki fragments. Because DNA polymerase can only add nucleotides in the $5' \rightarrow 3'$ direction, lagging strand synthesis is discontinuous. The final product is formed when DNA ligase joins Okazaki fragments together.

30. D: Each time a cell divides; a few base pairs of DNA at the end of each chromosome are lost. Telomerase is an enzyme that uses a built-in template to add a short sequence of DNA over and over at the end of chromosomes—a sort of protective "cap". This prevents the loss of genetic material with each round of DNA replication.

31. D: DNA polymerase does not match base pairs with 100% fidelity. Some level of mismatching is present for all DNA polymerases, and this is a source of mutation in nature. Cells have mechanisms of correcting base pair mismatches, but they do not fix all of them.

32. C: Insertions and deletions cause frameshift mutations. These mutations cause all subsequent nucleotides to be displaced by one position, and thereby cause all the amino acids to be different than they would have been if the mutation had not occurred.

33. A: Transcription is the process of creating an RNA strand from a DNA template. All forms of RNA, for example mRNA, tRNA, and rRNA, are products of transcription.

34. C: The *lac* operon controls transcription of the gene that allows bacteria to metabolize lactose. It codes for both structural and regulatory proteins and includes promoter and operator sequences.

35. E: Operons are common to prokaryotes. They are units of DNA that control the transcription of DNA and code for their own regulatory proteins as well as structural proteins.

Copyright © Mometrix Media. You have been licensed one copy of this document for personal use only. Any other reproduction or redistribution is strictly prohibited. All rights reserved.

36. D: Conjugation is direct transfer of plasmid DNA between bacteria through a pilus. The F plasmid contains genes that enable bacteria to produce pili and is often the DNA that is transferred between bacteria.

37. D: In the lysogenic cycle, viral DNA gets incorporated into the DNA of the host. A virus in this dormant stage is called a provirus. Eventually, an external cue may trigger the virus to excise itself and begin the lytic cycle.

38. B: In the lytic cycle, viruses use host resources to produce viral DNA and proteins in order to create new viruses. They destroy the host cell in the process by lysing it. For this reason, actively replicating viruses are said to be in the lytic cycle.

39. C: Plasmids are small circular pieces of DNA found in bacteria that are widely used in recombinant DNA technology. They are cut with restriction enzymes and DNA of interest is ligated to them. They can then easily be used to transform bacteria.

Organismal Biology

40. D: The ovary houses the ovules in a flower. Pollen grains fertilize ovules to create seeds, and the ovary matures into a fruit.

41. C: Gymnosperms reproduce by producing pollen and ovules, but they do not have flowers. Instead, their reproductive structures are cones or cone-like structures.

42. E: Stomata are openings on leaves that allow for gas exchange, which is essential for photosynthesis. Stomata are formed by guard cells, which open and close based on their turgidity.

43. A: Monocots differ from dicots in that they have one cotyledon, or embryonic leaf in their embryos. They also have parallel veination, fibrous roots, petals in multiples of three, and a random arrangement of vascular bundles in their stems.

44. E: Nonvascular plants do not produce fruits like angiosperms and gymnosperms do. They generally reproduce sexually, but produce spores instead of seeds.

45. C: Angiosperms produce flowers, with ovules inside of ovaries. The ovaries become a fruit, with seeds inside. Gymnosperms have naked seeds that are produced in cones or cone like structures.

46. A: The central, supporting pillar of the tree is known as heartwood. Heartwood does not function in the transport of water, and even though it is dead it will not decay or lose strength as long as the outer layers remain intact.

47. D: The phloem is the pipeline through which carbohydrates are transported to the roots. It is located outside of the xylem and lives for only a short time before becoming part of the outer bark.

48. B: In ferns, the mature diploid plant is called a sporophyte. Sporophytes undergo meiosis to produce spores, which develop into gametophytes, which produce gametes.

49. C: Alternation of generations means the alternation between the diploid and haploid phases in plants.

50. B: Anthers produce microspores (the male gametophytes of flowering plants), which undergo meiosis to produce pollen grains.

Copyright © Mometrix Media. You have been licensed one copy of this document for personal use only. Any other reproduction or redistribution is strictly prohibited. All rights reserved.

51. C: In flowering plants, the anthers house the male gametophytes (which produce sperm) and the pistils house the female gametophytes (which produce eggs). Eggs and sperm are haploid. All other tissues are solely diploid.

52. A: The plant hormone ethylene is responsible for fruit ripening. Auxins are involved in a range of processes involving growth and development.

53. C: Cytokinins stimulate cell division (cytokinesis) and have been found to delay senescence (aging). They are often sprayed on cut flowers and fruit to prolong their shelf life.

54. C: Day-neutral plants are not affected by day length in their flowering times. Rather, they respond to other environmental cues like temperature and water.

55. C: Plants exchange gases with the environment through pores in their leaves called stomata. Animals exchange gases with the environment in many different ways: small animals like flatworms exchange gases through their skin; insects use tracheae; and many species use lungs.

56. B: Platelets are cell fragments that are involved in blood clotting. Platelets are the site for the blood coagulation cascade. Its final steps are the formation of fibrinogen which, when cleaved, forms fibrin, the "skeleton" of the blood clot.

57. A: The large intestine's main function is the reabsorption of water into the body to form solid waste. It also allows for the absorption of vitamin K produced by microbes living inside the large intestine.

58. D: When Ca^{2+} channels open, calcium enters the axon terminal and causes synaptic vesicles to release neurotransmitter into the synaptic cleft.

59. C: In a positive feedback loop, an action intensifies a chain of events that, in turn, intensify the conditions that caused the action beyond normal limits. Nursing stimulates lactation, which promotes nursing. Contractions during childbirth, psychological hysteria, and sexual orgasm are all examples of positive feedback.

60. D: Mammals often warm themselves by altering their metabolism. Shivering warms animals due to the heat generated by contractions in trunk muscles.

61. A: HCG is secreted by the trophoblast, part of the early embryo, following implantation in the uterus. GnRH (gonadotropin-releasing hormone) is secreted by the hypothalamus, while LH (luteinizing hormone) and FSH (follicle-stimulating hormone) are secreted by the pituitary gland. GnRH stimulates the production of LH and FSH. LH stimulates ovulation and the production of estrogen and progesterone by the ovary in females, and testosterone production in males. FSH stimulates maturation of the ovarian follicle and estrogen production in females and sperm production in males.

62. E: The placenta secretes progesterone and estrogen once a pregnancy is established. Early in pregnancy, the placenta secretes hCG.

63. C: In oogenesis, meiosis I produces a secondary oocyte and a polar body. Both the first polar body and the secondary oocyte undergo meiosis II. The secondary oocyte divides to produce the ovum and the second polar body.

64. D: Positive feedback from rising levels of estrogen in the menstrual cycle produces a sudden surge of luteinizing hormone (LH). This high level triggers ovulation.

65. E: The testes contain hundreds of seminiferous tubules for the production of sperm, or spermatogenesis. This requires 64-72 days. Leydig cells surround the seminiferous tubules and produce male sex hormones called androgens, the most important of which is testosterone. Semen is made in the

Copyright © Mometrix Media. You have been licensed one copy of this document for personal use only. Any other reproduction or redistribution is strictly prohibited. All rights reserved.

seminal vesicles, prostate gland, and other glands. Sperm are transferred to the penis via the epididymis, where they become motile, and thence through the vas deferens.

66. B: The gastrula is formed from the blastocyst, which contains a bilayered embryonic disc. One layer of this disc's inner cell mass further subdivides into the epiblast and the hypoblast, resulting in the three primary germ layers (endoderm, mesoderm, ectoderm).

67. C: In birds and reptiles, the yolk sac contains the yolk, the main source of nutrients for the embryo. In humans, the yolk sac is empty and embryos receive nutrition through the placenta. However, the yolk sac forms part of the digestive system and is where the earliest blood cells and blood vessels are formed.

68. D: A lineage map describes the fates of cells in the early embryo: in other words, it tells which germ layer different cells will occupy. In some small organisms such as the nematode *Caenorhabditis elegans*, all of the adult cells can be traced back to the egg. A lineage map is not a mechanism of embryo development, but rather a tool for describing it.

69. B: The gastrula is the first three-layered stage of the embryo, containing ectoderm, mesoderm, and endoderm

70. C: In birds, the invagination of gastrulation occurs along a line called a primitive streak. Cells migrate to the primitive streak, and the embryo becomes elongated.

71. D: You would know the snapdragon has an *Rr* genotype, but you would not know whether its parents had an *Rr* genotype or a combination of Rr and *rr* or *RR* and *rr*.

72. D: All the plants will be tall, and flower color will assort independently of stature. In a *Pp* x *Pp* cross, ¾ of the progeny will be purple.

73. E: Two genes next to, or within a specified close distance of, each other, are said to be linked. Linked genes do not follow the law of independent assortment because they are too close together to be segregated from each other in meiosis.

74. C: If the genes are linked, there would be only two kinds of alleles produced by the F1 plants: *Rw* and *rW*. A Punnet square with these alleles reveals that half the progeny will have both an *R* and a *W* allele.

75. C: Half of the boys will receive the color-blind allele from the mother, and the other half will receive the normal one. All the girls will receive the color-blind allele from the father; half of them will also get one from the mother, while the other half will get the normal one. Therefore, half the children will be colorblind.

76. E: An individual with AB blood is tolerant to both the A carbohydrate on red blood cells and the B carbohydrate as "self" and can therefore accept any of the 4 different blood types.

77. B: When more than one gene contributes to a trait, inheritance of that trait is said to be polygenic. This type of inheritance does not follow the rules of Mendelian genetics.

78. D: The parents in D could only have offspring with AB or B blood types, not the A blood type.

Population Biology

79. D: At the lowest trophic level are the producers, followed by primary consumers. Primary carnivores follow consumers, followed by secondary carnivores.

80. A: Vultures eat carrion, or dead animals, so they are considered scavengers. Detritivores are heterotrophs that eat decomposing organic matter such as leaf litter. They are usually small.

Copyright © Mometrix Media. You have been licensed one copy of this document for personal use only. Any other reproduction or redistribution is strictly prohibited. All rights reserved.

81. B: Carbon is released in the form of CO_2 through respiration, burning, and decomposition.

82. D: Most nitrogen is in the atmosphere in the form of N_2. In order for it to be used by living things, it must be fixed by nitrogen-fixing bacteria. These microorganisms convert N_2 to ammonia, which then forms NH_4^+ (ammonium).

83. D: Type I curves describe species in which most individuals survive to middle age, after which deaths increase. Dolphins have few offspring, provide extended care to the young, and live a long time.

84. B: The growth rate is equal to the difference between births and deaths divided by population size.

85. A: Pioneer species colonize vacant habitats, and the first such species in a habitat demonstrate primary succession. Succession on rock or lava often begins with lichens. Lichens need very little organic material and can erode rock into soil to provide a growth substrate for other organisms.

86. B: Secondary succession occurs when a habitat has been entirely or partially disturbed or destroyed by abandonment, burning, storms, etc.

87. B: Epiphytes are plants that grow in the canopy of trees, and the tropical rain forest has a rich canopy because of its density and extensive moisture.

88. A: Transportation by humans or human-associated means is not considered a natural dispersal process.

89. D: Within a habitat, there is a maximum number of individuals that can continue to thrive, known as the habitat's carrying capacity. When the population size approaches this number, population growth will stop.

90. B: Density-dependent limiting factors on population growth are factors that vary with population density. Pollution from a factory, volcanic eruptions, frosts, and fires do not vary as a function of population size. Waste products, however, increase with population density and could limit further population increases.

91. B: Character displacement means that, although similar, species in the same habitat have evolved characteristics that reduce competition between them. It occurs as a result of resource partitioning.

92. A: Because both species benefit, lichens constitute an example of mutualism.

93. D: Natural selection was Darwin's idea, not Lamarck's. Mendel discovered that genes are the basic units of inheritance. Lamarck's observation about use and disuse is true, although he did not connect it with the underlying mechanism of natural selection.

94. A: Stabilizing selection is a form of selection in which a particular trait, such as weight, becomes stable within a population. It results in reduced genetic variability, and the disappearance of alleles for extreme traits. Over time, the most common phenotypes survive.

95. C: Disruptive selection occurs when the environment favors alleles for extreme traits. In the example, seasonal changes can make different types of food available at different times of the year, favoring the large or short bills, respectively.

96. E: Options A-D all describe conditions that would lead to genetic equilibrium, where no evolution would occur. Gene flow, which is the introduction or removal of alleles from a population, would allow natural selection to work and could promote evolutionary change.

Copyright © Mometrix Media. You have been licensed one copy of this document for personal use only. Any other reproduction or redistribution is strictly prohibited. All rights reserved.

97. C: Hybridization between two different species would result in more genetic variation than sexual reproduction within a species.

98. C: According to Hardy-Weinberg equilibrium, $p + q = 1$ and $p^2 + 2pq + q^2 = 1$. In this scenario, $q^2 = 0.25$, so $q = 0.5$. p must also be 0.5.

99. B: Phyletic gradualism is the view that evolution occurs at a more or less constant rate. Contrary to this view, punctuated equilibrium holds that evolutionary history consists of long periods of stasis punctuated by geologically short periods of evolution. This theory predicts that there will be few fossils revealing intermediate stages of evolution, whereas phyletic gradualism views the lack of intermediate-stage fossils as a deficit in the fossil record that will resolve when enough specimens are collected.

100. B: Adaptive radiation is the evolution of several species from a single ancestor. It occurs when a species colonizes a new area and members diverge geographically as they adapt to somewhat different conditions.

101. D: In coevolution, one species responds to new adaptations in another. Coevolution occurs between predator and prey, pathogens and the immune systems of animals, and plants and their pollinators.

102. E: Structures are homologous because they derive from a common ancestor. Insects do not share a common ancestor with birds and mammals. Birds and mammals share a reptile ancestor.

103. B: The bottleneck effect occurs when populations undergo a dramatic decrease in size. It could be due to natural or artificial causes.

104. A: The first living organisms probably had not yet evolved the ability to synthesize their own organic molecules for food. They were probably heterotrophs that consumed nutrition from the "organic soup."

105. C: Analogous structures do not reveal anything about common ancestors between species. They are simply features that arise due to adapting to similar ecological conditions.

106. C: Habituation is a learned behavior that teaches an animal to ignore meaningless or neutral stimuli.

107. D: Pheromones are chemicals used by animals for communication. They are released by certain individuals and elicit behavioral changes in other individuals.

108. B: Imprinting is a program for acquiring a behavior if an appropriate stimulus is given during a critical time period early in life. Salmon are imprinted with the odors of their birthplace after hatching.

109. C: *Homo sapiens* are thought to have evolved in Africa approximately 100,000 years ago.

110. D: Prolonging the life of individuals in a current population will lead to an older age composition. An increased birth rate will cause population growth, but a greater proportion will be younger, not older.

111. E: With many species, factors like food, space, and predation have large effects on reproduction. Humans are able to control or at least affect many of these challenges, as well as the reproductive process itself, so other factors like education, religion, wealth, and access to health care are more significant factors in birth rates.

112. E: Mercury is a fat-soluble pollutant and can be stored in body tissues. Animals higher up the food chain that eat other animals are most likely to accumulate mercury in their bodies.

Copyright © Mometrix Media. You have been licensed one copy of this document for personal use only. Any other reproduction or redistribution is strictly prohibited. All rights reserved.

113. D: Air pollution would not be a direct result of clear-cutting forests. It would result in increased atmospheric CO_2, however, as well as localized climate change. Transpiration from trees in the tropical rain forest contributes largely to cloud formation and rain, so rainfall decreases because of clear-cutting, resulting in desertification.

114. B: When sulfur dioxide and nitrogen dioxide mix with water and other substances in the atmosphere, they produce sulfuric acid and nitric acid. These acids kill plants and animals when they reach the surface of the earth.

115. E: Genetic engineering is a general term to describe altering DNA sequences through adding or removing pieces of DNA from a native sequence. Restriction enzymes perform this "clipping" function.

Copyright © Mometrix Media. You have been licensed one copy of this document for personal use only. Any other reproduction or redistribution is strictly prohibited. All rights reserved.

Image Credits

Licensed Under CC BY 4.0 (creativecommons.org/licenses/by/4.0/)

Mitosis: "Mitosis Stages" by Wikimedia user Ali Zifan
(https://commons.wikimedia.org/wiki/File:Mitosis_Stages.svg)

Pineal and Pituitary Glands: "Pineal and Pituitary Glands" by Wikimedia user Cancer Researcher UK Uploader
(https://commons.wikimedia.org/wiki/File:Diagram_showing_the_pineal_and_pituitary_glands_CRUK_468.svg)

Meiosis: "Meiosis Overview New" by Wikimedia user Rdbickel
(https://commons.wikimedia.org/wiki/File:Meiosis_Overview_new.svg)

Cell Cycle Checkpoints: "Cell Cycle with Cyclins and Checkpoints" by OpenStax CNX user CNX Anatomy and Physiology (https://cnx.org/contents/FPtK1zmh@8.25:fEI3C8Ot@10/Preface)

Compact and Spongy Bone: "605 Compact Bone" by OpenStax CNX user CNX OpenStax
(https://cnx.org/contents/FPtK1zmh@8.25:fEI3C8Ot@10/Preface)

Sickle Cell Anemia: "Sickle Cell Anemia" by Wikimedia user BruceBlaus
(https://en.wikipedia.org/wiki/File:Sickle_Cell_Anemia.png)

Homology: "Homology Vertebrates-en" by Волков Владислав Петрович
(https://commons.wikimedia.org/wiki/File:Homology_vertebrates-en.svg)

Neuron Structures: "Neuron Hand-tuned" by Quasar Jarosz at English Wikipedia
(https://commons.wikimedia.org/wiki/File:Neuron_Hand-tuned.svg)

DNA Replication: "DNA Replication" by OpenStax CNX user CNX Anatomy and Physiology
(https://cnx.org/contents/FPtK1zmh@8.25:fEI3C8Ot@10/Preface)

Energy Pyramid: "Ecological Pyramid" by Wikimedia user Swiggity.Swag.YOLO.Bro
(https://commons.wikimedia.org/wiki/File:Ecological_Pyramid.svg)

Licensed Under CC BY-SA 3.0 (creativecommons.org/licenses/by-sa/3.0/deed.en)

Chloroplast Structure: "Chloroplast Structure" by Wikimedia Commons user Kelvinsong
(https://en.wikipedia.org/wiki/File:Chloroplast_structure.svg)

Golgi Apparatus: "Golgi Apparatus (Borderless Version)" by Wikimedia Commons user Kelvinsong
(https://commons.wikimedia.org/wiki/File:Golgi_apparatus_(borderless_version)-en.svg)

Cell Cycle: "Cell Cycle Simple" by Wikimedia user Simon Caulton
(https://commons.wikimedia.org/wiki/File:Cell_cycle_simple.png)

ATP: "Structure of Adenosine Triphosphate (ATP)" by OpenStax CNX user OpenStax
(https://cnx.org/contents/FPtK1zmh@6.27:zMTtFGyH@4/Introduction)

Leaves: "Leaf Tissue Structure" by Wikimedia user Zephyris
(https://commons.wikimedia.org/wiki/File:Leaf_Tissue_Structure.svg)

Copyright © Mometrix Media. You have been licensed one copy of this document for personal use only. Any other reproduction or redistribution is strictly prohibited. All rights reserved.

Alternation of Generations: "Sporic Meiosis" by Wikipedia user Menchi
(https://commons.wikimedia.org/wiki/File:Sporic_meiosis.svg)

Nitrogen Cycle: "Nitrogen Cycle" by Wikimedia user Nojhan
(https://commons.wikimedia.org/wiki/File:Nitrogen_Cycle.svg)

Copyright © Mometrix Media. You have been licensed one copy of this document for personal use only. Any other reproduction or redistribution is strictly prohibited. All rights reserved.

Thank You

We at Mometrix would like to extend our heartfelt thanks to you, our friend and patron, for allowing us to play a part in your journey. It is a privilege to serve people from all walks of life who are unified in their commitment to building the best future they can for themselves.

The preparation you devote to these important testing milestones may be the most valuable educational opportunity you have for making a real difference in your life. We encourage you to put your heart into it—that feeling of succeeding, overcoming, and yes, conquering will be well worth the hours you've invested.

We want to hear your story, your struggles and your successes, and if you see any opportunities for us to improve our materials so we can help others even more effectively in the future, please share that with us as well. **The team at Mometrix would be absolutely thrilled to hear from you!** So please, send us an email (support@mometrix.com) and let's stay in touch.

If you'd like some additional help, check out these other resources we offer for your exam:

http://MometrixFlashcards.com/ILTS

Copyright © Mometrix Media. You have been licensed one copy of this document for personal use only. Any other reproduction or redistribution is strictly prohibited. All rights reserved.